Inside Mahler's Second Symphony

Inside Mahler's Second Symphony

A Listener's Guide

LAWRENCE F. BERNSTEIN

OXFORD
UNIVERSITY PRESS

OXFORD
UNIVERSITY PRESS

Oxford University Press is a department of the University of Oxford. It furthers
the University's objective of excellence in research, scholarship, and education
by publishing worldwide. Oxford is a registered trade mark of Oxford University
Press in the UK and certain other countries.

Published in the United States of America by Oxford University Press
198 Madison Avenue, New York, NY 10016, United States of America.

CIP data is on file at the Library of Congress
ISBN 978–0–19–757564–2 (pbk.)
ISBN 978–0–19–757563–5 (hbk.)

DOI: 10.1093/oso/9780197575635.001.0001

1 3 5 7 9 8 6 4 2

Hardback printed by Bridgeport National Bindery, Inc., United States of America
Paperback printed by LSC Communications, United States of America

For Harriet,
who listens to music as she
attends to everything:
with Verstand, *compassion,*
sensitivity, and love

Contents

APPENDICES

List of Figures and Tables

Figures

Tables

List of Music Examples

List of Audio Examples

The recording of Mahler's Second Symphony that provides the central core of the exemplification in this book is that of Bruno Walter and the New York Philharmonic made in February 1958. (See the introduction to this performance in the section below entitled "The Recording.") The audio examples listed here are limited to those that contain music other than that drawn from this performance. All the others come from the Bruno Walter recording, which is reused with permission of Sony Music Entertainment.

Preface

P.1 Excerpt from the first version of the closing theme from the last movement of W. A. Mozart's Piano Quartet in G Minor, K. 478. Emanuel Ax (piano), Isaac Stern (violin), Jaime Laredo (viola), Yo-Yo Ma (violoncello). Sony Classical CD

P.2 Excerpt from the second version of the closing theme from the last movement of W. A. Mozart's Piano Quartet in G Minor, K. 478. Emanuel Ax (piano), Isaac Stern (violin), Jaime Laredo (viola), Yo-Yo Ma (violoncello). Sony Classical CD

Chapters

1.1 Excerpt from Mahler's Piano Quartet in A Minor, first movement. *Domus.* Susan Tomes (piano), Krysia Osostowicz (violin), Timothy Boulton (viola), Richard Lester (violoncello). EMI Classics CD

1.2 Excerpt from the third part of Mahler's *Das klagende Lied.* City of Birmingham Symphony Orchestra and Chorus conducted by Sir Simon Rattle. EMI Classics CD

1.3 Excerpt from the third part of Mahler's *Das klagende Lied.* City of Birmingham Symphony Orchestra and Chorus conducted by Sir Simon Rattle. EMI Classics CD

2.6 A dotted rhythm, reflecting its conventional notation

2.7 A dotted rhythm, reflecting Mahler's meticulous notation

Appendices

Glossary

Acknowledgments

No one forgets their first encounter with the music of Gustav Mahler. Mine took place on January 24, 1954, when I was a sophomore in high school. There, the relatively few students who were partial to symphonic music tended to bond closely. I was one of four such enthusiasts who generally spent Sunday afternoons driving around aimlessly in a family car that was available to us. In fact, those excursions were not entirely without purpose because we always listened, as we cruised about, to the weekly Sunday broadcasts of the New York Philharmonic. On this Sunday, we were to hear a concert conducted by Bruno Walter. All of us knew the name of that famous conductor. The program included Mahler's First Symphony. In 1954, the Mahler renaissance was still at an early stage, and Gustav Mahler was not yet a familiar name to us. It did not take long, however, before we needed to pull over to the curb to listen—spellbound—to this extraordinary work. Notwithstanding the power and beauty of the symphony, in my adolescent naïveté, I had no sense at all then of what it meant to have heard a Mahler symphony for the first time interpreted by his devoted follower and long-time amanuensis. Perhaps it is not too late, even after sixty-seven years have passed, to acknowledge what a privilege it was to have been introduced to Mahler's music in this way.

In 1997, I reached what was, for me, another Mahler milestone. Sir Simon Rattle conducted the Philadelphia Orchestra in the Mahler Second. It was not the first live performance of that symphony I had heard, but there was something very special about this extraordinary performance. I found myself moved to tears at three different moments and discovered months later, in discussions with friends who attended the same concert, that they had been similarly transported at the same junctures in the symphony. This experience filled me with wonder about the musical mechanisms that can lead to emotional reactions of this magnitude. That, in turn, prompted me to offer an undergraduate course on the Mahler Second at the University of Pennsylvania and ultimately sent me down the path that led to this book. My debt to Sir Simon is formidable, indeed.

I taught the course on the Mahler Second four times to a variety of students, ranging from undergraduates (music majors and general liberal arts students) to retirees in the University's program for senior associates. My indebtedness to these students is substantial. Their enthusiasm for Mahler's music amplified my own, and, over the years, I learned much from them about how best to share insights into this composer's music.

My colleagues at the University of Pennsylvania included several who were steeped in the music of Mahler: Eugene Narmour, the late James Primosch, Jay Reise, and Richard Wernick. Over the years, they shared their insights freely and enthusiastically, which provided me with equal measures of pleasure and wisdom.

I am grateful to the School of Arts and Sciences at the University of Pennsylvania and to its Associate Dean for Arts and Letters, Jeffrey Kallberg, for allowing me to use research funds to help defray the costs of both audio and visual exemplification in this book. Professor Kallberg's own wide-ranging knowledge of Mahler and his music has been a source of inspiration for me.

Peter Schöne, the acclaimed German baritone, is the force behind the Schubert Lieder Project, a website devoted to assembling performances of all the Schubert songs (sung by Mr. Schöne accompanied by an array of excellent pianists). The site also includes scores, texts, and facsimiles of early editions, along with bibliographical and historical data (www.schubertlied.de). Mr. Schöne graciously allowed me to use his performances of two Schubert songs to exemplify my discussion of form in the Lieder repertory (Chapter 5). I am deeply grateful for his generosity in doing so.

Our bibliography lists a number of important studies of Mahler's symphonies and of the Second Symphony in particular. Two of these were especially helpful to me as my own sense of the work emerged: Constantin Floros's *Gustav Mahler: The Symphonies* (first published in German in 1985 and translated into English in 1993), and Stephen E. Hefling's "Zweite Symphonie" in the collection of essays, *Gustav Mahler: Interpretationen seiner Werke* (2011).

I am grateful to the American Musicological Society for a publication subvention. AMS subventions are drawn from the society's general fund, which is supported, in part, by the National Endowment for the Humanities and the Andrew W. Mellon Foundation.

For the staff at Oxford University Press and its production affiliate Newgen Publishing, the process of helping to turn ideas into books is a labor of love. I benefited from the passion they bring to bear on this effort at every turn. As

Acquisitions Editor, Norman Hirschy read my first proposal and recognized in it a significant flaw. The revisions I made on the strength of his brief, but very astute, criticism greatly improved the scope and content of the project. He went on to help in myriad ways as the proposal began to take shape. I am particularly grateful for the seriousness with which he engaged my concerns about the design of the book. His sense of the relationship between the appearance of a book and its power to communicate rests on the foundation of his own impeccable taste. Emma Clements could serve as any author's paragon of the perfect Production Editor. I profited greatly from her exhaustive knowledge of every aspect of book production. Every one of my numerous questions was addressed fully, promptly, and adeptly. It is her responsibility, in addition, to ride herd on authors in the name of keeping the publication on schedule. She carries this out with such graciousness, however, that I found myself altogether eager to meet those deadlines. The role of copy-editor fell to Tim Rutherford-Johnson. His keen sensitivity to language improved the flow of my prose at numerous junctures, and I am deeply grateful to him for the many improvements he brought about.

It was my great good fortune that Morten Solvik, the distinguished Mahler expert, agreed to read my manuscript. He did so in a year filled with the chaos wrought by the COVID-19 pandemic and despite his manifold responsibilities as Director of the Vienna Center of the Institute of European Studies. Dr. Solvik's carefully wrought critique of my book was of inestimable value to me. He rescued me from several blunders (of the sort that can readily occur when a Renaissance scholar-turned-Mahler enthusiast attempts to address the complexities of Mahler's music). And he pointed me in good directions that had not occurred to me. My work was greatly improved by his meticulous labor. In a few instances, I succumbed to my more stubborn impulses and opted not to follow his advice. For this, of course, I assume responsibility.

I am also deeply grateful to the anonymous readers who evaluated my manuscript for Oxford University Press. They undertook the charge most seriously, and their hard work brought forth a number of recommendations that led to improvements.

Of all the people who supported me in writing this book, no one did so more abundantly and more constantly than my wife, Harriet. Her response to my Mahler fixation was one of bounteous generosity. She allowed it to assume a portion of my attention well beyond what might be deemed reasonable. She read and listened, advocated and argued, and shored up my spirits at moments of self-doubt—many of them. Mahler's music became a central component of Harriet's consciousness, despite her lack of formal training in music. At performances we shared, I took delight, for example, when a faint raising of her eyebrow could silently communicate to me her displeasure with the length of a *Luftpause*, while a mere hint of a smile crossing her lips seemed to say so clearly "Those saccharine gestures of Viennese sentimentality could not have been played better." Harriet got so good at understanding Mahler that it could sometimes feel threatening, as when I might present to her a new and cherished idea, only to witness its collapse in the wake of issues she pointed out to me, always with crystalline clarity. This book owes much to such contributions by Harriet. The combination of strength, insight, competence, patience, devotion, and love that motivated her in all of this is but a microcosm of what she has brought to my life for more than fifty-six years. I lovingly dedicate this book to her.

Preface

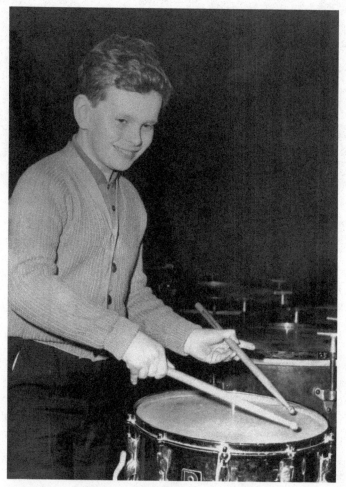

Fig. P.1 An eleven-year-old percussionist in Liverpool

In the mid-1960s, the eleven-year-old percussionist depicted here heard a performance of Mahler's Second Symphony by the Royal Liverpool Philharmonic under the baton of George Hurst. By his own account (related a half century later), the young musician decided at that very moment he had to be an orchestral conductor.

Fig. P.2 The same musician some years later
PA Images / Alamy Stock Photo

The features of the youthful snare-drum player in the Merseyside Youth Orchestra near Liverpool may be recognized by some concertgoers as those of Sir Simon Rattle, arguably among the greatest interpreters of Mahler's music of our time. At the heart of this story is the extraordinary magnetism of the Mahler Second. With the force of an epiphany, it engulfed the young Simon Rattle, capturing him in an unyielding grasp, the power of which never diminished over the course of his career. As he wrote in 2010 about that fateful first hearing of the symphony: "My mind and senses had clearly been incredibly stimulated; it was as if I had been pleasurably flayed. My incurable virus—the wanting-to-conduct-Mahler virus—started there and then. It's because of that evening that I'm a conductor."[1]

Only six years after his revelatory first hearing of the symphony, Rattle—then a student at the Royal Academy of Music—organized and conducted a performance of the work at the conservatory. His recording of the

---

[1] Simon Rattle, "How Mahler Made Me a Maestro," *The Times*, November 29, 2010, https://www.thetimes.co.uk/article/simon-rattle-how-mahler-made-me-a-maestro-36c7jllxxvx.

symphony with the City of Birmingham Symphony Orchestra in 1987 helped to catapult both the conductor and his regional orchestra on to the center stage of European concert life. Then, fittingly, after eighteen years at the helm of the CBSO, and just before he took over as conductor of the Berlin Philharmonic, Rattle's final concert with the CBSO in 1998 consisted in a stunning performance of the Mahler Second.

Sir Simon was not alone in his susceptibility to the mesmerizing allure of this symphony. The story of the economist Gilbert Kaplan and how he literally gave over his life to the Mahler Second defies the imagination. Kaplan founded and managed *Institutional Investor*, a successful magazine for pension fund and asset managers. In 1965, he accompanied a friend to a rehearsal of the Mahler Second in Carnegie Hall; Leopold Stokowski led the American Symphony. The experience was to change Kaplan's life. That night, haunted by the music he had heard, he could not sleep. He bought a ticket for the performance the next day, during which he was brought to tears.[2] In Kaplan's own words: "Zeus threw the bolt of lightning. I walked out of that hall a different person."[3] Like the young Simon Rattle, Kaplan was overcome in the wake of this concert by a burning need to conduct. His path, however, differed from Rattle's in that he did not pursue a career as a conductor. He yearned to conduct just one work, the Mahler Second, believing fervently that only by conducting it could he come to understand the extraordinary power it held over him. In 1981, he took intense conducting lessons from Charles Bornstein, a graduate of the conducting program at the Julliard School, and he even managed to secure a two-hour lesson with Georg Solti, then music director of the Chicago Symphony Orchestra. A year later, Kaplan rented Avery Fisher Hall (now called David Geffen Hall) at Lincoln Center in New York, hired the American Symphony and the Westminster Symphonic Choir, and, on September 9, 1982, led a performance of the Mahler Second before an invited audience. It was the first of many performances he was to conduct of this symphony with more than fifty orchestras—many of them major ensembles—around the world.[4]

[2] "Desperately Seeking Mahler," *The Economist*, November 27, 2008, https://www.economist.com/books-and-arts/2008/11/27/desperately-seeking-mahler.

[3] Emily Langer, "Gilbert Kaplan, Millionaire Businessman and Self-taught Maestro of Mahler, Dies at 74," *The Washington Post*, January 4, 2016, https://www.washingtonpost.com/entertainment/music/gilbert-kaplan-millionaire-businessman-and-self-taught-maestro-of-mahler-dies-at-74/2016/01/04/53ec1f9c-b2f6-11e5-9388-466021d971de_story.html.

[4] Margalit Fox, "Gilbert E. Kaplan, Publisher and Improbable Conductor, Dies at 74," *The New York Times*, January 6, 2016, https://www.nytimes.com/2016/01/07/arts/music/gilbert-e-kaplan-publisher-and-improbable-conductor-dies-at-74.html.

What I mean to bring out with these two anecdotes is the extraordinary capacity of this Mahler symphony to take hold of a listener and dramatically change his or her life. This often takes place (less dramatically, to be sure) among many of us who are so deeply devoted to this work that it is hard to imagine life without it. Our passion for it manifests itself in various ways: in the great distances we travel to hear yet another performance of it; in the multiple recordings of it we own; in the number of times we are moved to tears (like Gilbert Kaplan) by various musical events in this symphony; or in the delight that accompanies the frequent new discoveries we make about a work we thought we knew well.

What enables this symphony to exert so potent a hold on us? The pursuit of answers to questions like this one lies at the heart of this book. That quest needs to be undertaken, however, with appropriate diffidence. First, it needs to be acknowledged that, because words can never take the place of music, they will inevitably fall short of fully explaining the mysterious forces that contribute to the power of this work. Second, countless listeners have engaged this symphony successfully without benefit of any effort to explain it. They love the work intensely and feel its power profoundly. Why intrude on a process that seems to be working so well?

Although any attempt to demystify *all* the forces that enable a work of music to move us deeply is doomed to failure, that realization need not discourage us altogether from engaging the music with the aim of explaining as much as we can. Sometimes, we can elucidate a lot, even if we cannot unravel all the mysteries. The progress we make, however incomplete, may bring us closer to an understanding of how a great piece of music works and—more importantly—of how it works its magic upon us.

Similarly, as we suggested, legions of serious listeners who are devoted to Mahler's Second respond to it intensely, but viscerally—that is, without ever feeling the need to explore the work from various perspectives— music-theoretical, historical, or autobiographical—all of which relate to the genesis and nature of this symphony intensely. The decision to pursue or not pursue the symphony from such perspectives must be theirs, and either decision is defensible. I strongly believe, however, that a firmer intellectual grasp of this symphony can only lead to an appreciable enhancement of the extent and depth to which it is appreciated and loved. For example, we shall see that this symphony is motivated, at every turn, by a powerful spiritual agenda that explores deeply some of the most challenging questions about the meaning of life and death. The ways in which Mahler works these questions into the music and uses the rhetoric of his music to posit, explore, and resolve them lies at the heart of how we understand this composition.

Mahler's Second is a paradoxically dichotomous composition; it is, at once, a work of crowning transparency and of great complexity. The transparency arises largely from the striking, even exaggerated, boldness of its conception. Its climactic events are either stunningly massive or exquisitely understated. Either way, they are eminently conspicuous. Its contrasts are drawn vividly. Its orchestral sonorities frequently call attention to themselves for their brilliant originality and matchless beauty. And the work is filled with moments of high drama. All of this provides the listener with an abundance of material that is presented with consummate clarity. Such material is often so striking—so self-evident—that it barely requires comment. In this sense, it is hardly surprising that many listeners react so strongly to vast stretches of this work without benefit of engaging it from an analytical perspective.

This is only half the story, however, for in other ways the symphony is quite complex and, therefore, less immediately accessible. In composing it, Mahler was driven by several agendas that inevitably complicate significantly how this symphony falls upon the listener's ears. I call attention to four of these. First, as an avowed modernist, Mahler aimed at creating what he considered the "New Symphony." A work of this type needed to introduce change to be "new," but it also had to subscribe to some traditional elements in order to present itself convincingly as a "symphony." In composing a work like this one, therefore, Mahler was constantly attempting to strike a balance between tradition and change. The first movement of the Second Symphony, for example, is based on the same formal design as is the opening movement of Beethoven's Fifth. That design, however, surfaces as much in the ways in which Mahler rejects or transforms it as in how he adheres to it. A pervasive collision between old and new forces like this one can give rise to confusion, especially for listeners who tend to be more familiar with the time-honored procedures.

A second source of complexity in the Second Symphony arises from the nature of its extra-musical agenda. Mahler's idea of extra-musical content in symphonic music—what was often called a *program*—went beyond the mere deployment of an underlying literary narrative like those that guided Franz Liszt in his tone poems. In symphonies like the First and Second,

Mahler introduces a protagonist, meant to represent himself in some ways. The extra-musical content of the symphonies, however, does not simply mirror specific events in Mahler's life. Rather, it takes on a philosophical cast, attempting to portray his hero's existential struggle (i.e., his own struggle) with questions about the meaning of life. These questions lie at the very heart of Mahler's intended meaning in the Second Symphony, but the linking of abstruse philosophical issues to specific musical content can be very challenging and greatly in need of explanation.

A third source of complexity in the Second Symphony arises from Mahler's universal outlook on the symphonic genre. In a meeting with the great Finnish composer Jan Sibelius in the fall of 1907, Mahler characterized this approach in a statement that is often cited as his symphonic credo: "The symphony must be like the world. It must be all-embracing."[5] This statement reverberates with many implications for the kind of symphony Mahler wished to compose, especially for the broad and highly diversified scope of its content. Mahler favored the lifting of numerous barriers to music that might be considered inappropriate content for a symphony. As we have seen, his symphonies embraced complex philosophical issues. He was equally ready to introduce into them poetry, preexistent songs (with or without the words), and music from plebian sources not generally found in more traditional symphonies. Among these, one might encounter rustic dances, folk tunes, or military music. The introduction of such stylistic outliers was made with specific purposes in mind—purposes that demand explanation. And Mahler's symphonies abound with musical quotations from widely varying sources like Gregorian chant, his own music, Wagner's operas, and Liszt's tone poems. These quotations are often so deftly embedded into the music that the listener who does not recognize them will not know that they are, in fact, external quotations. Lost on such listeners, too, might be the important symbolic significance often attached to intertextual allusions like these. That level of meaning becomes explicit only if the sources of the quotations and the context in which they originally appeared are known.

A fourth contributor to the complexity of the Mahler Second is its length: nearly an hour and a half in performance. That is approximately a third longer than Beethoven's Ninth Symphony and three times as long as Beethoven's Fifth. An expanse of music of this duration was without precedent in symphonic music at the time Mahler's Second was composed. The sheer

---

[5] Henry-Louis de La Grange, *Gustav Mahler, Volume 3, Vienna: Triumph and Disillusion* (Oxford: Oxford University Press, 1999), 753.

length of the work is not, in and of itself, problematical. What challenges both the composer and the listener in a work this long are matters of pacing and proportion. We are trained by acculturation to expect symphonic movements to adhere (very roughly) to certain conventional temporal dimensions. When the temporal compass of a work is expanded way beyond these customary limits, the conventional relationship between form and the expanse of real time is apt to become skewed, which requires the composer's intervention and ingenuity. Mahler struggled valiantly and most successfully with this problem in the Second Symphony, but the matter is, understandably, one of significant complexity and subtlety, and it cries out for explanation.

What we know about the premiere of the Second Symphony also has something to tell us about how to gain an understanding of the composition. Mahler directed the first complete performance of the Second Symphony with the Berlin Philharmonic on December 13, 1895. It was a great success with the audience, which included many students and musicians from the Berlin Conservatory to whom free tickets had been distributed (the general sales having been meager). According to an account attributed to Mahler's sister Justine, who attended the performance, grown men wept openly, and strangers embraced each other at some of the more breathtaking moments. At the end, the ovation was sustained and exuberant.[6] Among our objectives will be to offer some speculation about which moments would have stimulated such powerful emotional reactions, and to attempt an explanation of what forces in the music brought them about.

The critics who reviewed the premiere, however—almost every one of them—took a dim view of the symphony. Generally, they excoriated it for anything that was even mildly unorthodox. This reaction was, in part, ideologically inspired. Music critics in Berlin, Hamburg, and Vienna adopted a conservative stance with respect to new music. They tended to keep the musical avant-garde in their crosshairs and often vilified the music of modernist composers.

One Berlin critic, Oskar Eichberg, reacted favorably to the Second Symphony in his review for the *Berliner Börsen-Courier*, but he advised the listeners that its great novelty demanded of them "a certain preparation."[7] There is much to be learned, I believe, from this suggestion. What Eichberg seems to have intended with this phrase is that the unusual and innovative characteristics of this modernist work would be more readily appreciated

---

[6] Henry-Louis de La Grange, *Gustav Mahler: The Arduous Road to Vienna (1860–1897)*, completed, rev., and ed. by Sybille Werner (Turnhout: Brepols, 2020), 644.

[7] Henry-Louis de La Grange, *Mahler, Volume 1* (Garden City, NY: Doubleday, 1973), 347.

by a listener who had been alerted in advance to their presence—a listener, in short, who, from the outset, *expected* the work to depart from traditional norms. Eichberg made a most prescient observation with this suggestion. A half-century before music theorists well-versed in Gestalt psychology began to explain the seminal role expectation plays in our understanding of music, Eichberg exhibited a precocious glimmer of insight into the concept.[8]

The role of expectation in perceiving music is based on the use by composers of musical patterns to enable the listener to predict specific musical events. Those predictions are then either realized or not. Routine fulfilment of an expectation generally produces a milder emotional reaction than an expectation planted in the listener's consciousness that goes unrealized. This approach to understanding music plays a central role in how I attempt to explain the Mahler Second, and some preliminary remarks on how it works are in order here. As an example of this process, listen to a brief excerpt from the last movement of Wolfgang Mozart's Piano Quartet, K. 478. The example is a mere seven seconds long, and it serves as the end of a closing passage—meant to bring a strong sense of finality to the music. What is the most striking feature of this example {⊙ Audio Ex. P.1}?[9]

In searching for the "most striking feature of this example," did you settle on the last note? Would you agree with a characterization of the final sonority as "a surprise, perhaps even something of a shock"? What is it about the passage that encourages us to react to its ending with a feeling of shock, deception, or surprise? Is it, perhaps, that we didn't *expect* it to end that way? If so, how *did* we expect it to end? Might the ending provided in the next example have been more in accord with our expectations {⊙ Audio Ex. P.2}?

Acknowledging that the ending in the first example is unexpected (and, thus, aberrant) and that the ending of the second example is expected (and, thus, normative), leads to a more central question: how do we know this? A listener with some background in music theory might respond that a passage designed to achieve a sense of closure almost always ends with the sonority we call the tonic. The second example does, whereas the first ends with something called a deceptive close, one deployed frequently and known specifically as "flat-6." But the listener with no training in music theory will also know—and with no less conviction—that the first example sounds "wrong," and the second one "right."

---

[8] A pioneering study on the use of expectation theory to explain music is Leonard B. Meyer, *Emotion and Meaning in Music* (Chicago: University of Chicago Press, 1956).

[9] For instructions on how to gain access to the audio examples, see the section below entitled "How to Use this Book."

They know it not from theoretical formulations and concepts. Rather, they know it from experience, from listening. They have heard enough examples of closing passages to have embedded in their consciousness an *expectation* that they will close as the second example did.

You may also wish to ask another question about this pair of examples: which of the two do we find more bracing, more gripping, more noteworthy? Surely, it is the first, aberrant version that triggers the deeper emotional reaction. Our sense of deprivation at the withholding of a musical event we have been primed to expect easily outweighs in emotional intensity what we feel when everything simply turns out just as we expected it to. On hearing the conventional close, one may react by thinking "That's right, but so what?" The aberrant version is more apt to prompt something like "Oh my God, what's happening?" A metaphor drawn from newspaper headlines is apt: the conventional close calls to mind DOG BITES MAN, while the deceptive solution resembles the more newsworthy MAN BITES DOG![10]

There is great power inherent in the systematic exploitation of musical expectation. It sets up highly effective lines of communication between composer and listener, and we shall rely on this concept heavily in our encounter with Mahler's Second Symphony. It will help us understand what makes certain musical events seem right and others surprising. It will shed light on how we know that a climactic moment is needed or about to happen. And it will explain the effect upon us when Mahler sews musical enigmas into the fabric of his symphony and keeps us waiting for their resolution for over an hour.

Most importantly, the concept of musical expectation should offer encouragement to the untrained listener who may never have heard this symphony, and who finds somewhat daunting references we have made to form and pacing, orchestration and modernism, program music and musical quotations. "Is all of this within reach in the absence of training in music theory?" they may ask. I would answer affirmatively, because many aspects of the Mahler Second—indeed, of music in general—are already as much a part of every listener's musical consciousness as is the "knowledge" that one of the two points of closure in the Mozart example is normative, and the other aberrant. What is needed is the gentle movement of that knowledge to a more prominent tier in the listener's consciousness. That is also a primary objective of this guide.

---

[10] We shall return to this pair of musical examples in our discussion of sonata form (Appendix 1), where they will be addressed at a greater level of detail.

The Recording

Selecting the recording of Mahler's Second Symphony to use as the performance for this guide proved to be a rewarding but daunting task. As one of the composer's most popular symphonies, the Second has been recorded many times. Vincent Mouret's definitive discography of Mahler's music lists 185 recorded performances of the complete symphony made between 1924 and 2018, along with twenty-one recordings of individual movements and five arrangements of the symphony.[1] This *embarrass de richesses* rests upon a heady statistic, but it hardly simplifies the task of selecting one recording as the primary focus of this listener's guide.

The plethora of recorded performances of the Second Symphony reflects a very wide range of approaches and assets, which inevitably requires some prioritization in choosing among the various strengths they offer. One might aim, for example, to present the symphony in a manner that approached how it might have been performed at the time of its composition. That would be possible (although with significant limitations) because Oskar Fried, who was close to Mahler, and who conducted the extraordinarily successful performance of the Second Symphony in Berlin in December 1905, recorded the work with the orchestra of the Berlin State Opera in 1924. The opportunities for projecting a sense of historical "authenticity" by relying on this recording are tempting, but the drawbacks inherent in using it are formidable. It is an acoustical recording, made, that is, before the advent of electronic microphones. As a result, not all the musical forces performing could be located close enough to the recording horn to be faithfully captured. The double basses, for example, were too large to crowd around the horn. Fried decided, therefore, to double many of the bass parts with a tuba because that instrument is small enough to gain proximity to the recording horn. Thus, the extraordinary opportunity to gain a sense of historical authenticity in

---

[1] Mouret's discography may be consulted on the website of the Mahler Foundation. Its listings for the Second Symphony appear at: https://mahlerfoundation.org/mahler/discography/symphony-no-2/. A serious discussion of a smaller selection of recorded performances of the Second Symphony is provided in "The Mahler Symphonies: A Synoptic Survey by the Late Tony Duggan (1954–2012)": http://www.musicweb-international.com/Mahler/Mahler2.htm.

this recording comes, owing to the limitations of the technology, at the expense of other distortions in the soundscape. Moreover, modern listeners are used to a standard of precision in orchestral ensemble playing that was far from the norm in 1924.

We might opt, on the other hand, to privilege fidelity of sound and precise orchestral playing as we select our recording. We could turn to Claudio Abbado's studio recording of the symphony made with the Chicago Symphony in 1976. It offers stunning sound in the context of a highly disciplined performance led by a conductor who specialized in the Mahler Second, having recorded it five times. Abbado, however, is not the only conductor known for having had a special relationship with the Mahler Second, and others demand consideration, too. In the Preface, for example, we traced the prominent role the symphony played throughout Simon Rattle's musical life; he recorded it three times. Leonard Bernstein's relationship to Mahler is legendary. He identified intimately with Mahler as conductor, composer, and as a Jew, and he did more, perhaps, than any other musician to bring about the Mahler renaissance of the 1950s and 1960s. Seven performances of the Mahler Second were recorded under Bernstein's baton, in many of which he captured matchlessly a sense of the underlying dramatic flair of the work.

The Second Symphony also figured prominently in Otto Klemperer's repertoire. Not only did he record it eight times, but his connections to the work go back to the performance of it in Berlin in December 1905—the one conducted by Oskar Fried. At that concert, the twenty-year-old Klemperer conducted the offstage-band in the last movement of the symphony, which makes him an obvious contender for the choice before us.[2]

Yet another conductor had uniquely close ties to Mahler and his music: Bruno Walter, who recorded the Second Symphony five times. Born in 1876 to Jewish parents named Schlesinger, Walter met Mahler for the first time in September 1894, just before his eighteenth birthday. Walter had been hired as a *répétiteur* (a coach and accompanist) by Bernhard Pollini, the director of the Hamburg State Theater, where Mahler had been serving as chief conductor since 1891. The young musician had read the scathing reviews of the Weimar performance of Mahler's First Symphony, which only left him all the more eager to meet the composer of a work that seemed to him so boldly innovative from what he had read in those reviews. The meeting went very well, and Mahler gave the young coach various opportunities to

[2] For further discussion of Klemperer's role in this performance, see below, p. 181.

demonstrate the intensity and quality of his musicianship. Mahler became a mentor to Bruno Walter, and the two musicians worked closely together, with the younger man soon advancing to the role of choral director and then to what Walter characterized as that of a "real" conductor of a number of operas Mahler entrusted to him.

This professional relationship—deeply valued by both musicians—continued for two years until Walter moved on to Breslau, where he assumed the directorship of the municipal opera on Mahler's recommendation. The close personal relationship between these two musicians did not end with Walter's departure for Breslau. More and more, Mahler felt at liberty to discuss with Walter his innermost struggles with the compositional process, as in the discussions they held about the Third Symphony during a visit at Steinbach am Attersee (site of Mahler's summer residence) in July 1896. Their close collaboration was to resume in the autumn of 1901, when Mahler appointed Walter as his assistant at the Vienna Court Opera, a position he held until the end of Mahler's tenure as music director there in 1907.[3] A sense of the deep friendship that bound these two musicians together resonates strongly from a photograph of them strolling through the streets of Prague in 1908 (Fig. R.1).

One may assess further the closeness of their relationship in several ways. Walter was present at Mahler's deathbed on May 18, 1911. And he led the posthumous premiere of *Das Lied von der Erde* in Munich on November 20, 1911, and of the Ninth Symphony in Vienna on June 26, 1912. It is Walter's special relationship with the Second Symphony, however, that weighed most heavily on our decision regarding the choice of recording for this guide. Walter was present at the premiere of the Second Symphony in Berlin on December 13, 1895. He wrote of the occasion that "the impression of the magnitude and originality of the work, of the power of Mahler's nature, was so profound that the ascent of the composer can justly be dated from that day."[4] The assignment to arrange the Second Symphony for piano four hands fell to Bruno Walter. And, at the memorial concert in Munich on November 20, 1911, at which Walter conducted the premiere of *Das Lied von der Erde*, he also included on the program a performance of the Second Symphony. It would be hard to find any contemporary figure who was closer to the Second

---

[3] On the relationship between Mahler and Bruno Walter, see Bruno Walter, *Gustav Mahler*, trans. James Galston (London: Kegan Paul, Trench, Trubner, 1937); and Henry-Louis de La Grange, *Gustav Mahler: The Arduous Road to Vienna (1860–1897)*, completed, rev., and ed. by Sybille Werner (Turnhout: Brepols, 2020), 581–591.

[4] Walter, *Gustav Mahler*, 19–20.

Fig. R.1. Mahler strolling in the streets of Prague with Bruno Walter (1908)

Photograph in the Médiathèque musicale Mahler, Paris. The man in the background is the Russian-born American pianist and conductor, Ossip Gabrilowitsch

Symphony than Bruno Walter, and we have, therefore, opted to link to this guide his recording of the work with the New York Philharmonic (Sony Classical SM2K 64 447).

That recording was made in Carnegie Hall on February 17, 18, and 21, 1958. Soloists Maureen Forrester (contralto) and Emilia Cundari (soprano) joined the Westminster Choir (John Finley Williamson, chorus master) and the New York Philharmonic.[5] Forrester's rendition of "Urlicht" (the fourth movement) has attained a legendary stature. The sound quality of the original recording offers a fine example of the technology available in

---

[5] The recording was made on the stage of Carnegie Hall, but at a recording session, not a live concert. The origins of the recording lie in a performance of the Second Symphony presented a year earlier in Carnegie Hall on February 17, 1957, with the same performing forces except for the part of the soprano soloist, which was sung by Maria Stader. A live recording of that concert appeared on the Music & Arts label.

the late 1950s. It was remastered later using High Definition 20-bit Sound. Presenting this music in our guide necessarily required compression of the music into MP3 files.

It would be ludicrous to claim that this recorded performance reflects all of Mahler's intentions. Even conductors who strive to be scrupulously faithful to the composer's wishes—and Walter generally adheres to this approach—must inevitably wrestle with a daunting challenge: their allegiance to the composer's intentions may sometimes come into conflict with their own powerful musical instincts as they assume the role of a recreative artist. Indeed, we shall cite some instances in which Walter overrides what are clearly Mahler's intentions. Notwithstanding these occurrences, Walter's is a fine performance of the Second Symphony and one that offers a unique potential for reflecting musical decisions that had to have been formed under the spell of his close relationship with Mahler.

How to Use this Book

The central emphasis of this guide will be on a direct encounter with the music of the Second Symphony. We shall study the entire work in detail. Its commentary is exemplified by a network of audio files—manageably short musical excerpts—that are linked directly to the text of the commentary. Such examples are meant to provide an opportunity for each reader to gain genuine ownership of the music by listening to them repeatedly until they are successful in illuminating the commentary convincingly. The number of *repetitions* needed will vary for each reader, but multiple iterations of the examples is meant to be the norm. This guide is not a book that can profitably be read from start to finish in one continuous pass. It is intended, rather, as a means of gaining, at every reader's personal pace, a state of immersion in the intricacies, form, and beauty of this extraordinary (and very long) symphony. That can come about, I suggest, only gradually—by listening to the various musical excerpts again and again. This road to mastery of the music demands patience, which, I hope will be richly rewarded by the ways in which it facilitates understanding.

The focus on short musical segments has distinct pedagogical advantages, but it does not come without risks. Obviously, a symphony is not a patch quilt of artificially detached segments. It is meant to proceed uninterrupted in a manner that preserves its continuity, pacing, and the interdependence of the smaller parts. To avoid the danger that a focus on smaller units of music may lead to an impression of the symphony as a series of fragments, an uninterrupted audio file of each movement, along with an abbreviated commentary, is provided in Appendix 4. Readers are urged to experience the music in this uninterrupted manner at the end of the discussion of each movement. The placement of these complete performances in an Appendix is aimed to achieve a tidy presentation and to facilitate listening to even larger swaths of the symphony than a single movement. It is not meant to minimize, in any way, the importance of listening to complete movements at the end of each chapter.

Specific musical events within the audio files are located by references to the time stamps embedded in them that are displayed as you listen to each file. These are measurements of the elapsed time in minutes and seconds of a given segment of music. They always appear in our text in boldface (e.g., **03:17**). Note that in our text, the time stamps begin at zero in each of the audio files that exemplify the discussion. As a result, they differ from the numbers provided in the uninterrupted audio files (in Appendix 4), which offer a single, continuous series of time stamps for each movement (or for each of the three parts into which the last movement has been divided).

The audio files are identified in callouts in the text that appear between curly brackets (e.g., {⊙ Audio Ex. 3.1}). Both the print and electronic versions of this book offer access to its audio examples by way of an internet browser. If you are reading the print version of this book, you will turn to the accompanying website to access the audio files. If you have chosen the electronic version of the book, clicking directly on the callout for a particular audio file will send you automatically to that example as it appears on the website. In either case, an internet browser will take you to the selected audio file. Your choice of browser can affect the display of time stamps. At the time of this writing, most of the major browsers will display the time stamps exactly as they appear in the text of the book. One browser, however—Mozilla Firefox—introduces a one-second discrepancy from the time stamps as are they are recorded in the book, which can be disconcerting. Readers who use Firefox as their default browser should select another browser to gain access to the audio examples in this book.

The fluidity of the internet must also be borne in mind. Over the years, browsers can change in ways that may affect the display of the time stamps. The accompanying website, under *Browsers and Timestamps*, provides more detailed suggestions about which browsers to use or to avoid. It will be updated as needed in the unlikely event that changes made by a particular browser should ramify adversely for the display of our time stamps.

The first three movements of the Second Symphony are related to standard formal templates, the forms we call sonata form, alternating variation form, and scherzo and trio, respectively. Guides to each of these structural designs are provided in Appendices 1–3. These guides should be assimilated carefully before attempting the discussion of the movements of the Mahler Second that rely on one or another of these structural designs.

Although the emphasis in this book is on *listening* to Mahler's Second Symphony by way of the numerous audio files provided, some readers may wish to consult a score of the symphony, and a link is provided here to an online edition on the platform of the International Music Score Library Project

(IMSLP.org). It is the first edition of the orchestral score, published in 1897 by Friedrich Hoffmeister in Leipzig: http://ks4.imslp.info/files/imglnks/usimg/e/e2/IMSLP415748-PMLP49406-GMahler_Symphony_No.2_fe_UE_reprint_RSL1.pdf. This edition is also reprinted by Dover Publications, Inc., Mineola, NY.

Universal Edition Vienna published a score of the Mahler Second in 1910, reprinting it in 1971 with many corrections. The corrected edition is also available online from the International Music Score Library Project (IMSLP.org), but it is not in the public domain in the United States: http://imslp.eu/files/imglnks/euimg/e/ec/IMSLP211806-PMLP49406-Symphony_No.2_-_Resurrection.pdf.

Currently, the definitive edition of the Mahler Second is that of the International Gustav Mahler Society. It is edited by Renate Stark-Voit and Gilbert Kaplan and was published by Universal Edition and the Kaplan Foundation in 2010.

Readers who wish to correlate musical events described in this book with the score may do so easily by consulting the sections devoted to complete performances of each movement (in Appendix 4). Each musical event listed there is provided with a reference to its precise location in the score.

Technical vocabulary is used freely in the commentaries. Terms like *arpeggio, chromaticism, diminution, dissonance, Ländler, Luftpause,* and *on the bridge* will be clear for some readers and in need of explanation for others. The Glossary offers succinct definitions of many such terms, often along with discrete musical examples. If you are uncertain about the meaning of a technical term, look it up in the Glossary. You are apt to find a definition there.

About the Companion Website

To gain access to the website that accompanies this book, go to:

www.oup.com/us/insidemahlerssecondsymphony

It contains all of the audio files and figures—the latter in full color when relevant. Audio examples are marked in the text in this manner: {▶ Audio Ex. 3.1}. Updated information about browsers will also appear on the website.

PART I
PRELIMINARIES

1

Setting the Stage for the Second Symphony

A Young Conductor Comes to Leipzig • Mahler's Youth and Musical Education •
The Music of Mahler's Student Years • Vienna •
The First Symphony • On to the Second Symphony • *Todtenfeier*

A Young Conductor Comes to Leipzig

We enter the life of Gustav Mahler at the beginning of 1888. As the city of
Leipzig ushered in the new year, a rising star among the principal musicians
there had little time to celebrate. Gustav Mahler had just turned twenty-six
when he set out for Leipzig at the end of July 1886. He came to assume the
post of second conductor of the Leipzig opera in the opulent new hall it oc-
cupied in 1867, the *Neues Stadttheater* (Fig. 1.1). The appointment at Leipzig
was not Mahler's first major conducting position. It came in the wake of similar positions in Prague and Kassel.

The pace of Mahler's activities in his newest post at Leipzig was dizzying.
His share of the conducting during his two years in Leipzig amounted to an
astonishing 219 performances of forty-eight different operas.[1] Beyond the
onerous demands of rehearsing and conducting a great number of operas
was yet another source of considerable tension: the conflicting claims on
Mahler's time and energy of his responsibilities as a conductor, on the one
hand, and his burning need to compose, on the other. This conflict was to
plague him throughout his life. He often characterized himself as "a summer
composer," referring to the few months when the opera was closed—the only
time when he could devote himself adequately to composition.

Thus, as the new year of 1888 began in Leipzig, Mahler struggled to carry
out his grueling responsibilities as conductor, while laboring as much as

---

[1] Knud Martner, *Mahler's Concerts* (New York: Overlook Press, 2010), 366–371.

Inside Mahler's Second Symphony:. Lawrence F. Bernstein, Oxford University Press. © Oxford University Press 2022.
DOI: 10.1093/oso/9780197575635.003.0001

Fig. 1.1. A view of the *Neues Stadttheater* in Leipzig designed by Karl Ferdinand Langhans
Color photochrom. Washington, DC, Library of Congress, Print no. 6851

he could on a critically important project, the work we know as his First Symphony. (Mahler had composed several symphonies earlier, during his student years, but these do not survive.) On March 9, Wilhelm I, Emperor of Germany and King of Prussia, died, and musical performances throughout Germany were suspended for a ten-day period of mourning. Mahler capitalized on the additional time for composing this brief respite afforded him and made substantial progress on the First Symphony. By the middle of the month, he was able to write to his friend Friedrich (Fritz) Löhr, "Well! My work is finished. . . . [I]t came gushing out of me like a mountain torrent."[2] We shall turn presently to this important work, which, as the direct precursor to the Second Symphony, provides vital—sometimes intimate—insights into what motivated Mahler to compose his next symphony. First, however, it behooves us to explore briefly some other important sources of influence on Mahler: his upbringing and both his musical and liberal education.

[2] Knud Martner, ed., *Selected Letters of Gustav Mahler: The Original Edition Selected by Alma Mahler,* trans. Eithne Wilkins, Ernst Kaiser, and Bill Hopkins (London: Farrar, Straus, Giroux, 1979), no. 64.

Mahler's Youth and Musical Education

Mahler was born on July 7, 1860 in the town of Kalischt (then in Bohemia, but now a part of the Czech Republic and known as Kaliště). He lived in the modest house in which he was born for the first three months of his life (Fig. 1.2). Gustav's parents were Bernhard Mahler and Marie Hermann Mahler, Jews of the lower middle class. His father was a distiller and purveyor of liquors; his mother, the daughter of a soap maker. A few months after Gustav's birth, the family moved to Iglau, a small town in Western Moravia (now part of the Czech Republic and known as Jihlava). It was only twenty-five miles from Kalischt. There Bernhard Mahler set up his distillery and tavern in the same building in which the family lived.

Gustav was the second child of fourteen born to Bernhard and Marie, but only seven survived infancy, among whom Gustav was the oldest. Notwithstanding how common this high mortality rate was in Central Europe, the death of so many siblings weighed heavily on Gustav, who lost

Fig. 1.2. The Mahler home in Kalischt from a postcard in the Wien Museum
© Wien Museum. Reproduced with permission

many of his brothers while he was himself still a child: Karl (1865), Rudolf (1866), Arnold and Friedrich (1871), and Ernst, with whom he was closest (1875).[3] Bernhard was a resourceful businessman, and his distillery and tavern prospered. He was highly impetuous by nature, however, and prone to abusive outbursts, aimed principally at his wife. The home environment in which Gustav grew up was not a happy one.

Despite his quick-tempered manner and bouts of abuse, Bernhard Mahler was deeply committed to the education of his children, and he provided an ample library for the household. He was equally sensitive to the earliest signs of Gustav's musical talent. These surfaced in his ability to play melodies by ear on the accordion he was given at the age of three. Bernhard took note of this mark of musical talent and set out with his son for Ledeč, home of Gustav's maternal grandparents, to try out their piano; it was dispatched by ox cart to the Mahler home in Iglau the next day. Piano lessons were soon provided by several local musicians. Mahler would have been four or five years old at the time.

The young Mahler must have heard a good deal of music in Iglau, for the town's musical resources included an orchestra and a theater that from time to time mounted fully staged operas. A central figure in this milieu was Heinrich Fischer, a next-door neighbor of the Mahlers and the father of Theodor, Gustav's closest boyhood friend. Fischer conducted the town's male choir, served as Kapellmeister of the town theater, and led the choir at the central Catholic church, the Jakobskirche (the Church of Saint James the Greater). He gave Mahler lessons in music theory and, just as importantly, allowed him to join the choir at the Jakobskirche, where he was exposed to a wide repertory of sacred music, including works of Mozart and Beethoven, among others.[4]

We lack many of the details of how Mahler grew in his musicianship at this time, but by his early teens he was routinely giving piano recitals in Iglau,[5] and he soon turned towards composition, first with a song on a text by Gotthold Lessing he wrote for his father, then, at the age of fourteen, with an attempt at an opera, *Herzog Ernst von Schwaben*, a work the young Mahler

[3] Peter Franklin, *The Life of Mahler* (Cambridge: Cambridge University Press, 1997), 22.

[4] Franklin, *The Life of Mahler*, 20.

[5] An article in *Der Vermittler,* the local newspaper in Iglau (October 16, 1870) reports on a concert on October 13 before a large audience by a nine-year-old boy named Maler [*sic*], describing it as his first public performance. Kurt Blaukopf with contributions by Zoltan Roman, *Mahler: A Documentary Study,* trans. Paul Baker et al. (London: Thames and Hudson, 1976), 150.

may have intended to memorialize his beloved brother Ernst, who died that year. Unfortunately, neither of these compositions survives.

Portions of the projected opera seem to have come to the attention of Gustav Schwarz, the manager of an estate in the town of Ronow where Mahler visited to help assess the value of some musical manuscripts that were discovered there. Schwarz recognized the magnitude of the young Mahler's talent and traveled to Iglau to convince a skeptical Bernhard Mahler that the conservatory in Vienna would be the appropriate venue in which to further Gustav's musical education. Schwarz succeeded in this mission, and, in September 1875, Mahler enrolled in the Conservatory of Music in Vienna.[6] Only five years before Mahler's matriculation there, the conservatory had moved into the headquarters of the Society of the Friends of Music (*Gesellschaft der Musikfreunde*), newly designed by the Danish architect, Theophil Hansen (Fig. 1.3). It also housed the *Musikverein*, the main concert hall of Vienna.

When he matriculated at the Vienna Conservatory, Mahler entered the bailiwick of one antagonist in a fiercely intense culture war that divided European composers of the day. On one side were the conservatives who looked to Johannes Brahms as their champion and to the critic and aesthetician Eduard Hanslick as their defender. Their aim was to preserve continuity with the traditions inherent in the music of Beethoven, which meant perpetuating the traditional musical forms that governed the shape of his music. It also meant exercising restraint in the handling of the harmonic language—the vocabulary of chords used and the ways in which they relate to one another. The objective was to assure the clarity of tonality, the system that distributes importance among the tones of the scale hierarchically, privileging one tone among all others (the tonic), along with the harmony based upon it, as the ultimate embodiment of stability and repose in music.[7]

This conservative position was, in part, defensive, aimed at staving off the onslaught of the avant-garde, or, as it was sometimes called, the New German School. The heroes of this group included Richard Wagner, Franz Liszt, and the French composer Hector Berlioz. Anton Bruckner, who taught at the Vienna Conservatory, also incorporated some features of the musical agenda

---

[6] Franklin, *The Life of Mahler*, 23. Schwarz's commitment to the young Mahler was obviously deep. After the decision to attend the conservatory in Vienna was made, Schwarz accompanied Mahler on his journey there. Blaukopf, *Mahler*, 151.

[7] We elaborate further on these concepts in our discussion of sonata form in Appendix 1.

Fig. 1.3. The Conservatory of Music in Vienna, housed in the *Society of the Friends of Music* (*Gesellschaft der Musikfreunde*)
Reproduced under the Creative Commons Attribution-ShareAlike License (Austria)

of the New German School in his music. Members of the avant-garde, to a greater or lesser degree, aimed to shake the foundations of the Beethoven tradition. They did so by attacking the hegemony of the traditional forms, often substituting a more continuous music governed by an external literary narrative or program; by complicating the harmonic palette to a degree that threatened tonal clarity; and by creating works that aimed at monumental proportions. The Conservatory of Music in Vienna was a bastion of musical conservatism. Mahler entered the conservatory as a piano student of Julius Epstein, but, by 1877, he had shifted his concentration to composition, studying under Franz Krenn, who was known primarily for his sacred music.[8]

---

[8] Frank Walker, the biographer of Hugo Wolf (a fellow student of Mahler at the Conservatory) characterizes Krenn as a "dry-as-dust, monosyllabic pedant, known to everyone as 'Old Krenn'... for he gave the impression of never having been young at all." Frank Walker, *Hugo Wolf: A Biography*, 2nd ed. (London: J. M. Dent, 1968), 41.

The Music of Mahler's Student Years

Mahler composed a number of works during his years at the Conservatory: movements for about five chamber works, fragments for a pair of songs, and several symphonies.[9] Unfortunately, only a few of these pieces survive: the song fragments and the first movement (and the beginning of a scherzo) of the Piano Quartet in A Minor, which was probably composed in 1877.[10]

In composing a piano quartet while still a student at the Vienna Conservatory, Mahler turned to a genre with an enduring Viennese tradition that included compositions by Mozart, Beethoven, and a good number of other primarily Viennese composers. It was the piano quartets by Johannes Brahms, however, that are most apt to have made a direct impression on Mahler. Brahms composed three piano quartets, one of which (Op. 60) had its premiere in Vienna on November 18, 1875, which coincided with the onset of Mahler's studies at the conservatory.

Upon listening to an excerpt from Mahler's Piano Quartet movement {▶ Audio Ex. 1.1}, what strikes the ear most vividly are the sobriety and restraint that govern many aspects of this music. It seems largely couched in a style that is evocative of such masters as Schubert, Schumann, and Brahms. Clarity prevails in much of the movement—in the consistency of its somber atmosphere, for example, and in the transparency of its thematic material. Much, but not all, of the harmonic writing is relatively bland and conventional. A longer sampling of the piece would reveal an underlying reliance on many of the features of the structural design known as sonata form.[11]

Another work that seems to have its origins in Mahler's years at the Vienna Conservatory, but which was composed shortly after he completed his studies there, cries out for comparison with the Piano Quartet movement. In May 1876, several drama students at the Vienna Conservatory put on a reading of a dramatic ballad, *Das klagende Lied* (*The Sorrowful Song*), by the German poet Martin Greif (the pseudonym for Friedrich Hermann Frey).[12]

---

[9] Donald Mitchell, *Gustav Mahler: The Early Years* (Woodbridge: Boydell Press, 2003), 116–120.

[10] Jeremy Barham, Review of *Gustav Mahler: Sämtliche Werke. Supplement, III: Klavierquartett, I. Satz, Music & Letters*, 80 (1999): 164.

[11] For additional discussion of sonata form, see Appendix 1.

[12] Henry-Louis de La Grange, *Gustav Mahler: The Arduous Road to Vienna (1860–1897)*, completed, rev., and ed. by Sybille Werner (Turnhout: Brepols, 2020), 110.

Greif's dramatic ballad was based upon a well-known fairy tale that appeared in major anthologies of this genre, *Grimms' Fairy Tales* and Ludwig Bechstein's *Neues deutsches Märchenbuch* (*The New Book of German Fairy Tales*), for example. It was a grizzly tale of sibling rivalry, courtly intrigue, fratricide, deception, and calamity. The queen offers her hand in marriage to whoever secures for her a unique flower. One of two brothers finds the prize but is slain by his brother, who steals the flower and takes it to the queen. A travelling minstrel comes upon the murdered brother's remains and fashions a flute from one of his bones. The flute, of its own accord, relates the tale of fratricide.

Mahler composed the music for this work to his own libretto between 1878 and 1880. His setting is a work of monumental proportions, lasting (in its first version) over an hour and calling for massive performing forces: a huge orchestra, an offstage band, six vocal soloists, and a large mixed chorus. *Das klagende Lied* resists any attempt at assigning it to a specific genre. For lack of a better term, it is often classified as a cantata or a cantata-like composition, but Mahler adopted the ballad style of the fairy tale in his libretto, and the work achieves significant levels of dramatic potency even without the staging and character portrayal that are among the central dramatic assets of opera. In its rejection of any traditional generic type, *Das klagende Lied* reveals a boldly experimental attitude on the young Mahler's part. The same might be said of Mahler's approach to standard formal structures: generally, he avoids them in this work, substituting for the recognizable patterns of the standard forms long, continuous passages that reflect the theatricality of the libretto and the trajectory of the narrative.

The harmonic language Mahler deploys in *Das klagende Lied* often goes well beyond both the vocabulary and syntax of the conservative harmony we observed in the A Minor Piano Quartet movement. After the revelation of the fratricide in the third part of *Das klagende Lied*, for example, we hear a much more expansive and complex range of harmonic sonorities than is present anywhere in the piano quartet, and the movement among these chords is far less predictable, less routine, than in the quartet movement {▶ Audio Ex. 1.2}. We would describe the harmony of this passage as *chromatic*; that of the piano quartet as *diatonic*. Diatonic harmony relies on a vocabulary of seven tones based on the major and minor scales. Chromatic harmony widens the vocabulary to include all twelve of the available tones. It is richer and more colorful than diatonic harmony, and it has the capacity of being eminently more complex.

The sizeable offstage band not only expands the orchestral resources of the work[13] but also functions in an extraordinarily novel way. These instruments enter in what was to have been a celebration at the royal court of the wedding of the queen to the brother who won the queen's hand by killing his brother and stealing the flower. The festivities are interrupted, however, when the fratricide is revealed, and catastrophe ensues. Celebratory music appropriate for the wedding is played by the main orchestra, while the offstage instruments play crude military motifs, evocative of an entirely different and very harsh reality. Sometimes, during the course of the "scene," the two kinds of music alternate; sometimes, they are combined. The juxtaposition is powerful dramatically. It embodies the simultaneous portrayal of two temporal spheres: the celebration of the present and the immutable truth that imposes itself from the past. The two musical elements clash gratingly, whether they appear simultaneously or, as in the example provided here, in alternation {▶ Audio Ex. 1.3}.

Where did Mahler learn to write this kind of music, which contrasts so vividly with the sound of the A Minor Piano Quartet? The sources of influence on *Das klagende Lied* lead us outside the walls of the Vienna Conservatory and into a very different musical world, that of the avant-garde. Indeed, the essential musical features that distinguish *Das klagende Lied* from the A Minor Piano Quartet are some of the central hallmarks of the avant-garde style: chromatic harmony, continuous form based on a literary narrative, and a striving for monumentalism, both of duration and performing forces. Tracing where Mahler learned this style takes us into the wide-ranging musical and intellectual life of the city of Vienna.

Vienna

His third year at the conservatory brought Mahler the prerogative of matriculating at the University of Vienna as well. There he studied Art History, Early German Literature, and History of Philosophy. In some of these classes and, more importantly, within literary societies in which he participated, Mahler gained knowledge of epic medieval German poetry like the *Niebelung's Ring*,

---

[13] Mahler was to become particularly fond of having instruments play offstage. He was not, however, the first to do so. To mention two early examples, Hector Berlioz placed a number of instruments offstage in *Les Troyens* (1856–58), and Beethoven used offstage trumpets in *Fidelio* and in the *Leonore* Overture (both works Mahler conducted).

and of the philosophical writings of Arthur Schopenhauer, among others. These studies contributed to Mahler's skill as a poet and librettist. And they enhanced his propensity to plumb deeply into serious existential issues.

One of the most seminal influences on Mahler's intense struggle to understand the meaning of life was his long friendship with a fellow student at Vienna, Siegfried Lipiner. Mahler and Lipiner were members together of the Reading Society of German Students in Vienna, founded by Victor Adler and Engelbert Pernerstorfer in 1872, just a few years before Mahler's arrival in Vienna. They maintained strong and enduring personal and intellectual bonds for many years (until Mahler's marriage in 1902 to Alma Schindler, who could not abide Lipiner). Lipiner was a talented writer and dramatist whose celebrated poem, *Prometheus Unbound*, was published in Leipzig in 1876. In it, he probed the theme of salvation through suffering and annihilation, along the lines of the treatment of this idea in Nietzsche's *Birth of Tragedy*.[14] Lipiner became an early follower of Nietzsche, disseminating his views to other members of the reading circles at Vienna, Mahler among them. In addition to *Prometheus Unbound*, Lipiner dealt with the themes of suffering, self-overcoming, and death as necessary preludes to eternal life in a lecture he gave to the Reading Society on January 19, 1878: *On the Elements of a Renewal of Religious Ideas in the Present*. Lipiner was, thus, a conduit for Nietzsche's philosophical outlook well before it had become more directly accessible in Vienna.[15]

Richard Wagner became the hero of the young intellectuals in Mahler's circle in Vienna. He kindled in them enthusiasm for the romantic spirit inherent in ages past, and they developed a deep admiration for Wagner's ability to capture that spirit in German music of the highest quality.[16] In 1872, the Viennese Academic Wagner Society was founded, and Mahler

[14] Stephen E. Hefling, "Mahler's 'Todtenfeier' and the Problem of Program Music," *19th Century Music*, 12 (1988): 28–29.

[15] Lipiner's lecture was published in Vienna in 1878. For a modern edition and English translation of this text, see Siegfried Lipiner, "Über die Elemente einer Erneuerung religiöser Ideen in der Gegenwart / On the Elements of Renewal of Religious Ideas in the Present," ed. and trans. Stephen E. Hefling, in *Mahler im Kontext / Contextualizing Mahler*, ed. Erich Wolfgang Partsch and Morten Solvik (Vienna: Böhlau Verlag, 2011), 115–151. For a penetrating study of this lecture and its importance for Mahler, see Stephen E. Hefling, "Siegfried Lipiner's *On the Elements of a Renewal of Religious Ideas in the Present*," in *Mahler im Kontext / Contextualizing Mahler*, 91–114.

Engelbert Pernerstorfer, founder of the reading circle of which both Mahler and Lipiner were members, wrote Lipiner's obituary in 1912 and described him therein as "the finest intellect" he had ever encountered. Blaukopf, *Mahler*, 156–157.

[16] Morten Solvik, "The Literary and Philosophical Worlds of Gustav Mahler," in *The Cambridge Companion to Mahler*, ed. Jeremy Barham (Cambridge: Cambridge University Press, 2007), 23–24.

became a member soon after his matriculation at the University of Vienna. He remained involved in the Society until his resignation in 1879 (apparently in opposition to the rising levels of German nationalism and anti-Semitism that began to enter its activities).[17]

It was not Wagner's writings about music and philosophy that made the deepest impact on Mahler, however. It was, of course, his music. During Mahler's first year at the conservatory, Wagner was in Vienna to supervise performances of *Tannhäuser* and *Lohengrin*. Productions of *Die Walküre* and *Siegfried* were mounted at the Vienna Court Opera in 1878, and the entire *Ring* cycle was produced there in the following year.[18]

There was yet another means by which Mahler absorbed the impact of the avant-garde style. Among the principal composers who were influenced by this approach, as we have noted, was Anton Bruckner. Although Bruckner taught at the Vienna Conservatory, he taught harmony and counterpoint, not composition. This is not surprising, given that he was thought to have been too much under the spell of the avant-garde to have been made a member of the composition faculty at the doggedly conservative school of music. Indeed, his Third Symphony—a work that shares features with the music of Wagner and Liszt and that was dedicated to Wagner—was openly derided by some members of the faculty at the conservatory. Bruckner assigned the task of arranging the symphony for piano four hands to Mahler and his fellow student Rudolf Krzyzanowski. There are few better ways to achieve an intimate grasp of a work of orchestral music than the challenge of reducing a complex orchestral score to a piano arrangement. Mahler must have absorbed a great deal of Bruckner's approach to symphonic writing as he worked on his share of this assignment: the first three movements.

Returning now to our comparison of the A Minor Piano Quartet movement to *Das klagende Lied*, it seems that the two works are reflective of altogether different enterprises. The quartet was part of Mahler's training in the fundamentals of his craft, made, apparently, to satisfy the requirements of an institution that privileged a conservative approach to musical composition. *Das klagende Lied*, on the other hand, shows the young composer's turning to the music of the avant-garde as he attempted, *on his own*, to find his voice as a composer. He tells us as much in a letter he wrote to the German critic

[17] Jens Malte Fischer, *Mahler*, trans. Stewart Spencer (New Haven, CT: Yale University Press, 2011), 63–64.
[18] Alfred Orel, "Richard Wagner in Vienna," *The Musical Quarterly*, 19 (1933): 36–37.

and composer Max Marschalk in December 1896, in which he describes *Das klagende Lied* as "the first work in which I really came into my own as 'Mahler.'"[19] Having both honed his craft and found his compositional voice, Mahler was ready to embark on what was a signature venture for any young composer, a symphony. And that brings us full circle to the hectic months in Leipzig in early 1888 that brought forth the First Symphony.

The First Symphony

As Mahler rushed to complete the First Symphony in early 1888, the stakes for him were very high. Of all genres, the symphony held a privileged place as a token of success for an aspiring composer. Mahler had achieved notable success as a conductor, but he still had not fully established his credentials as a composer of note. A public success with a symphony was a proven path to this prize, and this helps us to understand the fervor and the seriousness with which Mahler worked on his First Symphony.

As he envisioned this work, Mahler did not merely aim at producing a symphony from a traditional mold. Some of the same adventurous instincts that informed the composition of *Das klagende Lied* guided many of the artistic decisions that went into the First Symphony. Indeed, an agenda that was to become increasingly important to Mahler emerged at this time: Mahler strove to redefine the genre of symphony, to create what he called the New Symphony. The First Symphony embodied many attributes that resulted from these efforts:

- Like many works by composers of the New German School, Mahler's First aimed at achieving monumentality with respect to both the size of the orchestra and the length of the symphony.
- Mahler blurred the borders that traditionally separated the musical genres by incorporating instrumental versions of two of his earlier songs (from the *Songs of a Wayfarer*) in the First Symphony.
- The choice of these two songs served an important purpose. They were originally composed in 1885 as an expression of Mahler's bitterness and despair over the end of a love affair he had with Johanna Richter,

---

[19] Martner, ed., *Selected Letters of Gustav Mahler*, no. 189.

a soprano in the Royal Opera of Kassel. Three years later, as he worked on the First Symphony, Mahler had recovered from his dejection over the break-up with Richter, but he was now in a greater state of misery from the failure of another relationship, with Marion von Weber, that ended in the late spring of 1888 (although a voluminous correspondence continued between the two lovers even after Mahler assumed the directorship of the Royal Budapest Opera in the fall of 1888). This loss was to cause Mahler years of pain.[20] Incorporating these songs in the First Symphony was part of a broader plan—one that carves out a place for a protagonist (in many ways suggestive of Mahler himself) in the symphony. The work reflects various aspects of his personal suffering, including the effects upon him of lost love and the pain he felt from life-long feelings of alienation. Of critical importance in the First Symphony, thus, is the presence therein of music that reflects the composer's deepest personal feelings.

- Mahler embraced a universal outlook toward the symphony that extends both to musical materials that may be drawn into the symphonic fabric and to other sources that may have exerted an influence on it. In the First Symphony, he quotes the two *Wayfarer* songs mentioned above, the opening motto of his 1880 song "Maitanz im Grünen," a distorted version of the folk song "Bruder Martin" (also known as "Frère Jacques"), and a motive associated with the inferno from Franz Liszt's *Dante Symphony*. He acknowledges as important sources of influence on the First Symphony an allegorical woodcut by the Austrian painter Moritz von Schwind and the spirit that informed the grotesquely ironic prints of the distinguished French artist, Jacques Callot.[21]

- At its premiere in 1889, Mahler described the First Symphony as a "Symphonic Poem," a term (*symphonische Dichtung*) Franz Liszt had

[20] Morten Solvik and Stephen E. Hefling, "Natalie Bauer-Lechner on Mahler and Women: A Newly Discovered Document," *The Musical Quarterly*, 97 (2014): 24–30.

[21] There is no reason to believe that, in describing the grotesqueries in the third movement of the First Symphony as having been conceived "in the manner of Callot," Mahler had ever actually seen any of the prints of the great French master of irony. The suggestion for this characterization appears to have been made to Mahler by the Hamburg music critic Ferdinand Pfohl, who called to Mahler's attention E. T. A. Hoffmann's use of the same trope to describe the fanciful curiosities in his acclaimed collection of fantastic stories, *Fanatasiestücke in Callots Manier* (the literary effort that established Hoffmann's reputation). Pfohl claims to have purchased a copy of this book for Mahler. Ferdinand Pfohl, *Gustav Mahler: Eindrücke und Erinnerungen aus den Hamburger Jahren*, ed. Knud Martner (Hamburg: Verlag der Musikalienhandlung Karl Dieter Wagner, 1973), 17, cited in Blaukopf, *Mahler*, 195.

coined in the 1840s to designate an orchestral work that combined a symphonic approach with the musical expression of an external referential component like a poem, story, or painting. For the next performance in 1893, Mahler provided a program to inform the listeners more specifically about the extramusical content of the work. Eventually, however, Mahler withdrew the program, attributing this decision to serious doubts about the efficacy of the program itself and especially about the advisability of offering it to the listening public, which he felt was prone to being misled by it.

- Mahler's ambivalence about providing a program for his symphonies arose from complex causes. The program he issued for the second performance of the First Symphony was assailed by the critics, and he may have felt that averting a similar reaction to subsequent performances was reason enough to abandon the program. More substantial matters concerned him about his program, however. Unlike symphonic programs that were rooted in a sequence of narrative events, Mahler's programs dealt with philosophical issues. A central philosophical pillar of the First Symphony, for example, is the theme of the redemption of the hero through annihilation that Mahler absorbed from reading the works of Siegfried Lipiner (as we observed in our discussion of Mahler's studies at the University of Vienna). In the symphony, the protagonist's levels of suffering enable him to triumph through death. A complex philosophical argument like this one hardly lends itself to concise presentation in a printed program for the audience.

Mahler, as we have seen, completed the First Symphony in mid-March 1888, but the premiere did not take place until November 1889. It was poorly received by critics and the public alike. What is of greatest interest to us here is the extraordinary alacrity with which Mahler moved on to the Second Symphony. On August 8, a mere five months after finishing the First Symphony, he appears to have completed a preliminary draft of the first movement of what would be his next symphony. The fair copy of the orchestral score was finished about a month later (on September 10).[22]

---

[22] Edward R. Reilly, "*Todtenfeier* and the Second Symphony," in *The Mahler Companion*, ed. Donald Mitchell and Andrew Nicholson (Oxford: Oxford University Press, 1999), 86; and Donald Mitchell, *Gustav Mahler: The Wunderhorn Years. Chronicles and Commentaries* (Woodbridge: Boydell Press, 2005), 161.

On to the Second Symphony

The forces that motivated Mahler to plunge directly into work on the Second Symphony immediately upon completing the First were very strong. Both his need to capitalize on free time in the summer months and the impulse to ride the crest of creative momentum must have seemed irresistible to Mahler. There were other compelling incentives, however. The two works share a common bond—at once powerful and intimate. As we have suggested, the First Symphony presents a heroic protagonist and expresses, in musical terms, his emotional struggles with the pain of lost love, rejection, and alienation. In the important letter mentioned above that Mahler wrote to the Berlin music critic Max Marschalk in 1896 (some three months after the premiere of the Second Symphony), he identifies the same protagonist as the hero of his Second Symphony, projecting an important continuity of meaning between the two works:

> I called the first movement [of my new symphony] "Todtenfeier." It may interest you to know that it is the hero of my D major symphony [i.e., the First Symphony] who is being borne to his grave, his life being reflected, as in a clear mirror, from a point of vantage
> . . . . What it comes to, then, is that my Second Symphony grows directly out of the First![23]

That Mahler saw the Second Symphony as a sequel, in some ways, to the First helps us to understand the sense of urgency he felt about continuing work on the new symphony. Moreover, Mahler appears to identify the hero of both symphonies as himself. In 1893, he told his close friend and life-long confidante Natalie Bauer-Lechner that "My [first] two symphonies contain the inner aspect of my whole life; I have written into them in my own blood everything that I have experienced and endured."[24] Thus, the Second

---

[23] Martner, ed., *Selected Letters of Gustav Mahler*, no.158.

[24] Natalie Bauer-Lechner, *Recollections of Gustav Mahler*, ed. Peter Franklin, trans. Dika Newlin (New York: Faber & Faber, 2013), 30, 231. Bauer-Lechner's name will surface in these pages so often that a few words about her are in order here. Mahler first knew her from when they were students together in Vienna. By her account, they were intimate, but their romantic relationship never took on the constancy she desired. Mahler respected her musical judgments, cherished her confidence, and shared widely with her many details of his compositional processes and philosophical outlook. She kept meticulous notes on their conversations, and a great deal of this valuable record was published shortly after her death in 1921. Given the closeness of her relationship with Mahler, care must be exercised in evaluating the accuracy of Bauer-Lechner's reports. Nonetheless, our knowledge of Mahler's life and the circumstances surrounding his composition depends heavily on this record,

Symphony is inextricably intertwined with the First at the most intimate level of the composer's deepest feelings about his own identity. Small wonder, then, that Mahler attached such importance to moving on to the Second Symphony.

Todtenfeier

As we continue to set the stage for Mahler's Second Symphony, one more issue needs to be pursued: the title he was to give to the first movement— *Todtenfeier* (which he also mentions in the 1896 letter to Max Marschalk). The idea for this title may have entered Mahler's consciousness as early as a year before he began work on the Second Symphony. Mahler's letter to Max Marschalk shows that the first movement projects a funereal image: the bearing of a hero to his grave. That image is thoroughly consistent with the somber nature of the music. Not surprisingly, the movement has been characterized as a funeral march, a generic type that occurs in other Mahler symphonies. Mahler identifies them variously: *Todtenmarsch* or *Trauermarsch*, for example. *Todtenfeier*, however, does not mean funeral march. We need to know what it does mean and what Mahler's source for this singular term was.

As we have seen, the concept of redemption through suffering and death, which lies at the heart of the First Symphony, is a concept Mahler learned from Siegfried Lipiner. Lipiner's influence on Mahler was no less significant as the plans for the Second Symphony began to unfold. In 1887, the Leipzig publishing firm of Breitkopf & Härtel brought out the second volume of Lipiner's translation into German of the works of Adam Mickiewicz, the leading Romantic poet of Poland in the early nineteenth century (Fig. 1.4). His major works included an epic, four-part poem, *Dziady*, which appeared beginning in 1823. *Dziady* is really a poetic drama, meant for the stage, and it came to be known as one of the seminal works of European Romanticism.

The title page of Lipiner's edition of Mickiewicz's poetry (reproduced in Fig. 1.4) shows that the German title Lipiner used in his edition for Mickiewicz's *Dziady*, is *Todtenfeier*, which might best be translated as "mourning rite." Given Mahler's close friendship with Lipiner and his presence in Leipzig in 1887, where Lipiner's translation was published in the same year, there can

---

which we know was the product of a deep and selfless devotion to Mahler. For further discussion of Bauer-Lechner, see Solvik and Hefling, "Natalie Bauer-Lechner on Mahler and Women: A Newly Discovered Document."

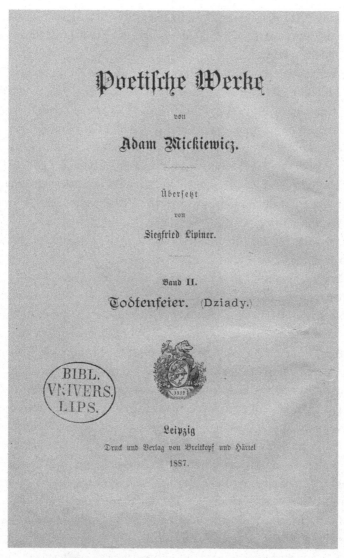

Fig. 1.4. Siegfried Lipiner's translation of the poetic works of Adam Mickiewicz: The title page of Volume 2, from a copy in the Biblioteca Albertina, Universitätsbibliothek Leipzig, Lit.slav.38-x: 2

be little doubt but that this work came to Mahler's attention. Certainly, this must be the source of the title Mahler was to assign to the first movement of the Second Symphony.

Mickiewicz's poetic drama centers on a folk festival, Forefather's Eve, that was celebrated in the Baltic region around the same time of year as the Roman Catholic All Souls' Day. Similarities link the two celebrations. Both address ancestral souls in purgatory, either to offer them nourishment (in the Baltic festival) or pray for their redemption (in the Catholic observance).[25] If these aspects of the Baltic observance do indeed lie behind Mahler's choice of the title *Todtenfeier* for this movement, it would seem clear that his use of the term was not meant to signify a funeral march per se, but refers, rather, to some sort of mourning ritual.

Exactly what lies behind Mahler's choice of this title is something we need to examine as we study the first movement of the Second Symphony. It will be helpful, therefore, to have, in advance of our encounter with the first movement, a sense of the content of Mickiewicz's poem that seems relevant to Mahler's music. In a seminal study of *Todtenfeier* and its relationship to Mahler's concept of "program music," Stephen Hefling formulates a compelling argument for a significant relationship between Mickiewicz's poem and the first movement of Mahler's symphony. What follows on this subject, both here and in the next two chapters, is drawn largely from Hefling's study.[26]

The fourth section of *Dziady* includes what has come to be known as the "Gustav poem," after its protagonist, whose circumstances appear related to events in Mickiewicz's life. The poet had fallen in love with Maria Wereszcak, who was already engaged. Her subsequent marriage left Mickiewicz utterly distraught. This theme becomes a central thread of the Gustav poem. The protagonist loves Maria, who rejects him for another man. He takes his own life and is transformed into a wandering soul, condemned to remain in this state until Maria dies and becomes an angel.

The Gustav poem is divided into three hours—of love, despair, and warning—each marked off by the chiming of a clock:

- In the first hour, the hapless wandering soul returns to the home of a priest he knew years before and sings three laments on lost love, of which the last mentions suicide. He draws a dagger, apparently to reenact the

---

[25] Hefling, "Mahler's 'Todtenfeier' and the Problem of Program Music," 29.
[26] Hefling, "Mahler's 'Todtenfeier' and the Problem of Program Music."

original suicide but does not use it yet. Instead, he strives for optimism, recalling thoughts of heroic deeds and inspiration he had drawn from poetry. Here Mickiewicz gives lines to Gustav drawn from some optimistic sections of his own earlier work, *Ode to Youth.*

- In the second hour, Gustav's despair and rage grow as he recalls his beloved's wedding to another man. He stabs himself in reenactment of his suicide but does not die of his wounds immediately.

- In the third hour, the dying Gustav sets out to offer warning. He mentions the spirits who live after death and asks the priest why he is not celebrating Forefather's Eve (*Todtenfeier*). The clock strikes midnight, and Gustav disappears.

In the next two chapters, as we explore the first movement of the Second Symphony, we shall learn about the extent and nature of the impact Mickiewicz's poem had on it. Having gained a basic understanding of the content of that poem, along with an appreciation of Mahler's agenda for a New Symphony, the stage for our broad encounter with Mahler's Second Symphony has now been adequately set, and we proceed in the next chapter to the beginning of our consideration of its first movement.

PART II
THE FIVE MOVEMENTS

2

The First Movement: Its Opening and a Two-Part Exposition

The Opening: "A Dreadfully Serious Voice" Articulates Existential Concerns •
Echoes of Beethoven •
Exposition (Part One): The Impact of Traditional Sonata Form •
Exposition (Part Two): Intensification, Experimentation, and Quotation

Before reading this chapter, you should avail yourself of the introduction to sonata form in Appendix 1.

The Opening: "A Dreadfully Serious Voice" Articulates Existential Concerns

Beginnings are important. The initial moments of a composition can offer us all kinds of valuable information. An early sense of orientation can be ours, as we identify the tonic of the piece or take note of signature melodic material we may expect (and want) to hear again. We can gain an immediate impression of the emotional tone of the work.

The first movement of Mahler's Second Symphony relies on sonata form, but the template is stretched and altered extensively. In the sketches for the symphony, Mahler identifies (with German terminology) the principal components of sonata form.[1] The primary theme does not appear until nearly a minute into the movement. Everything before it, therefore, must be considered the Opening (the various components of which we designate with the letter O and a series of numbers). Opening material is not necessarily of less consequence than the primary theme that follows. In fact, within this brief

---

[1] Stephen E. Hefling, "Mahler's 'Todtenfeier' and the Problem of Program Music," *19th Century Music*, 12 (1988): 35 (Table 1).

Inside Mahler's Second Symphony:. Lawrence F. Bernstein, Oxford University Press. © Oxford University Press 2022. DOI: 10.1093/oso/9780197575635.003.0002

section, Mahler reveals a great deal about the movement—indeed, about the entire symphony.

Listen carefully to the entire Opening section of this movement {▶ Audio Ex. 2.1}. It offers six musical motives, first presented here together in a continuous, preliminary outline of the passage.

Abbreviations for the Formal Functions in Sonata Form:
O = Opening   P = Primary Material   T = Transition
S = Secondary Material   K = Closing Material

Outline

00:00	O1	Tremolando
00:04	O2	Turning-note figure
00:10	O3	Anticipatory ascending scale, leading immediately into . . .
00:11	O4	A swift disjunct descent in uneven rhythm
00:14	O5	Interval of the perfect fourth in uneven rhythm
00:18	O6	Triplets
00:20		Permutations and repetitions of the preceding motives

Discussion

Now let's examine how these motives work individually. We shall try to discover what each motive contributes to the aggregate impression of the Opening. Later, Mahler will bring back many of these motives separately, so it is useful to identify and label them individually. The Opening is less than a minute long, but it prepares us for this symphony in important ways.

O1 {▶ Audio Ex. 2.2} The first gesture is forceful. It is just the note *G*, played in octaves by the violins and violas. But it is played tremolando, an effect produced by swiftly drawing the bow back and forth across the string sharply and rapidly. It sounds agitated. What is the effect of beginning a work in an agitated manner? It lends an unsettled, ominous quality to the opening of the symphony. Mahler had used the same device to achieve an identical effect in the opening of the second part of *Das klagende Lied*—in the section of that early work in which the grisly fratricide that lies at the center of the story is discovered. (You may refer to the brief discussion of *Das klagende Lied* in Chapter 1.)

O2 {▶ Audio Ex. 2.3} Next, we hear another bold gesture, a turning-note figure, played very loudly in the lower strings while the tremolando continues in the violins and violas. Mahler annotates the score, indicating with the German word *wild* that this passage should be played fiercely. The motive is strikingly brief; it lobs its five sharply etched notes angrily in our direction and is then abruptly cut off, shifting our attention back to the continuing tremolando. A moment later, the terse turning-note figure is sequenced at a higher pitch level.

O3 {▶ Audio Ex. 2.4} Our focus returns to the violoncellos and basses, which play a brief ascending scale that quickly spans an entire octave from C to c. Mahler directs that the already rapid ascent must accelerate as it tears upward. It catapults us into the motive that follows.

O4 {▶ Audio Ex. 2.5} This curt motive seems to be an antipode of the preceding propulsive scale. It spans the same octave, but in swift *descent*, and, in place of the smooth motion of a scale, it leaps over notes in wide, disjunct intervals. Its rhythm is uneven—jagged, one might say. Mahler fusses over this rhythm. Usually, it would be notated like this:

But Mahler inserts space in the form of brief silence (a rest) between the incipient long note and the short one that follows it:

He discussed his approach to the notation of rhythmic figures like this one with Bauer-Lechner in January 1896:

In order that there should not be the slightest inaccuracy in rhythm, I have racked my brains to notate it as precisely as possible. Thus, I avoid indicating the shortness of notes, or the space between them, by dots or other staccato marks. Instead, everything is spelled out in detail by means of note values and rests.[2]

In this motive, Mahler's idiosyncratic notation produces a strikingly different sound than what results from the conventional notation. Here is a realization of the conventional notation of our motive {⏵ Audio Ex. 2.6}. Compare it to what results from the execution of Mahler's novel notation {⏵ Audio Ex. 2.7}. The instant of silence Mahler introduces after the first note adds a vivid quality to the rhythmic profile, which leads, in turn, to a sense of edginess that will contribute to the high-strung, biting effect of this motive.

O5 {⏵ Audio Ex. 2.8} Mahler now focuses on the interval of a perfect fourth, an interval he often introduces as an important melodic building block.

O6 {⏵ Audio Ex. 2.9} The last piece of motivic material in the Opening appears now: a figure that is distinguished by its triplet rhythm.

In the rest of the Opening {⏵ Audio Ex. 2.10}, we hear various permutations and combinations of the motives already presented.

We used a variety of terms to characterize the minute-long opening of this movement: *agitated, angry, biting, edgy, fierce, high-strung,* and *jagged.* Such musical qualities would seem to be appropriate vehicles for the reflection of earnest, intense, and weighty sentiments. This is no surprise, given what we know of Mahler's expressive objectives for this movement. For a performance of the symphony in Dresden in 1901, Mahler provided an explanatory guide to the symphony. It characterizes the first movement with these words:

> We stand by the coffin of a well-loved person. His life, struggles, passions and aspirations once more, for the last time, pass before our mind's eye.—And now in this moment of gravity and of emotion which convulses our deepest being, when we lay aside like a covering everything that perplexes us and drags us down, our heart is gripped by a dreadfully serious voice which always passes us by in the deafening bustle of daily life: What now? What is this life—and this death? Do we have an existence beyond it? Is all this only a confused dream, or do life and this death have a meaning?—And we must answer this question if we are to live on.[3]

---

[2] Natalie Bauer-Lechner, *Recollections of Gustav Mahler,* ed. Peter Franklin, trans. Dika Newlin (New York: Faber & Faber, 2013), 45–46.

[3] Donald Mitchell, *Gustav Mahler: The Wunderhorn Years. Chronicles and Commentaries* (Woodbridge: Boydell Press, 2005), 183.

The fervently intense qualities we detected in the music of the Opening seem aimed at capturing the emotional intensity that "dreadfully serious voice" unleashes.

To some listeners, the Opening may seem longer than the mere fifty-three seconds devoted to it in our performance. (To take the measure of this, you should listen again to the entire Opening, played uninterrupted {(▶) Audio Ex. 2.1}.) Sir Donald Tovey once focused on the relationship between time and content in music and concluded that the listener's perception of the time scale is less a product of actual length than of the density of the material ensconced within a given expanse of time.[4] This concept resonates aptly with the opening of Mahler's Second Symphony. Its scant fifty-three seconds *do* seem longer than they really are because they are chock-full of so many motives that are flung at us in rapid-fire succession. It is the compression of this rich and diverse motivic array that provides the opening moments of this symphony with a strong sense of *gravitas*. It offers us the promise of a movement that will go on to contain substantial musical material.

Bruno Walter's interpretation of this passage adds much to the auspicious manner in which the symphony begins. He adheres strictly to Mahler's characteristically extensive and exacting instructions for the dynamic level and articulation of virtually every note in the Opening. This bestows upon each motive a sharply etched character that brings out its individuality, a quality that is enhanced all the more by the precision of the playing and the pervasive intensity Walter demands. The uniqueness of each motive is, thus, enhanced, which adds to the sense that a great deal is transpiring in this relatively short passage.

Gravitas is only part of the promise projected by this Opening. Each of its six motives is vivid, expressive, and memorable. Yet, they fit together well and are immediately subjected to transformation and permutation. This signals the need for a canvas broad enough to accommodate material richness of this magnitude and further transformation of it. In this way, the Opening portends a work of commanding proportions. Once again, Sir Donald Tovey captures the kind of initiation we experience in the opening of the Second Symphony: "It is a privilege of the greatest works of art that they can, if they will, reveal something gigantic in their scale, their range, and their proportions at the very first glimpse or moment."[5]

---

[4] Donald Francis Tovey, *Essays in Musical Analysis* (London: Oxford University Press, 1935), 2:5.
[5] Tovey, *Essays in Musical Analysis*, 2:3.

Interestingly, neither of the preceding quotations from Tovey, both of which seemed such fitting characterizations of the opening of the Mahler Second, were specifically concerned with that symphony. Tovey was writing about the Ninth Symphony of Beethoven. That is the symphony that gave rise to an existential crisis for symphonists of the next generation. The specter of Beethoven towered imposingly over any composer who attempted a symphony after the Ninth. Those composers struggled with the seemingly irreconcilable objectives of carrying on the Beethoven tradition while still maintaining their individuality. Mark Evan Bonds describes the paradox elegantly, suggesting that all of Beethoven's successors among symphonists had to confront Beethoven, by mirroring his achievements while simultaneously striving to overcome them.[6] Mahler was hardly impervious to these challenges, and the ways in which he reacted to them require some comment before we continue with our discussion of the first movement.

Echoes of Beethoven

The depth of Mahler's commitment to the ideals of the avant-garde never brought about any diminishment in the level of his adulation for Beethoven, who maintained a privileged place among many composers of the avant-garde. Thus, for Mahler, *both* Beethoven and Wagner were his idols, as he once related to Bauer-Lechner:

> Those who are born after such great spirits as Beethoven and Wagner, the epigones, have no easy task. For the harvest is already gathered in, and there remain only a few solitary ears of corn to glean.[7]

Mahler's ability to transcend unconditional allegiance to one or the other of the two competing camps that divided composers into conservatives and modernists served him well as he formulated the language and style of the New Symphony he strove to develop.

Mahler knew Beethoven's Ninth Symphony intimately. On February 13, 1886, the work was the centerpiece of a concert at the State Theater in Prague commemorating the third anniversary of Wagner's death. Although the

---

[6] Mark Evan Bonds, *After Beethoven: Imperatives of Originality in the Symphony* (Cambridge, MA: Harvard University Press, 1996), 1–3.
[7] Bauer-Lechner, *Recollections of Gustav Mahler*, 38.

Fig. 2.1. Mahler conducting Beethoven's Ninth Symphony in the Palais des Fêtes in Strassburg (1905)
Lebrecht Music & Arts / Alamy Stock Photo

Ninth Symphony was conducted by Karl Muck at that concert, it was Mahler who rehearsed the orchestra in it daily and who directed it in the reprise of the concert a few days later.[8] He went on to conduct the work at least ten times over the years, including at a concert in Strassburg in 1905, shown here in a somewhat deteriorated archival photo (Fig. 2.1).[9]

It stands to reason that, as Mahler began working on a symphony that he envisioned attaining monumental proportions, he would have turned to the *locus classicus* among earlier symphonies that aimed to a achieve similar scope, Beethoven's Ninth.[10] Thus, it comes as no surprise that the opening

---

[8] In an unsigned review of the concert in the edition of *Bohemia* for February 23, 1886, the reviewer pointed out as evidence of the depth of his mastery of the scores that Mahler had conducted both the Ninth Symphony and a long extract from *Parsifal* from memory. Kurt Blaukopf with contributions by Zoltan Roman, *Mahler: A Documentary Study*, trans. Paul Baker et al. (London: Thames and Hudson, 1976), 175.

[9] Knud Martner, *Mahler's Concerts* (New York: Overlook Press, 2010), 51, 318.

[10] As he planned a symphony with obvious similarities to Beethoven's Ninth, most notably its ending with a choral finale, Mahler did so with a measure of trepidation. In a letter to Arthur Seidl dated February 17, 1897, he reported: "I had long contemplated bringing in the choir in the last movement, and only the fear that it would be taken as a formal imitation of Beethoven made me hesitate again and again." Knud Martner, ed., *Selected Letters of Gustav Mahler: The Original Edition Selected by Alma Mahler*, trans. Eithne Wilkins, Ernst Kaiser, and Bill Hopkins (New York: Farrar, Straus, Giroux, 1979), no. 205.

of the Mahler Second closely resembles the start of Beethoven's Ninth. The sense of monumental reach and substantial content it projects arises largely from its close emulation of the opening of the Ninth Symphony, along the lines described by Tovey. There are other resemblances, too.

Listen to the openings of the Ninth Symphony and the Mahler Second, and note the following keen resemblances between them {▶ Audio Ex. 2.11} (Beethoven) and {▶ Audio Ex. 2.1} (Mahler):

- The use of the minor mode
- Rapid repeated notes in the strings resembling a tremolo at the beginning
- Incipient motives using the intervals of the fourth and fifth
- Unusually sharp rhythmic profiling of very brief motives
- Emphasis on uneven rhythms
- A restless, edgy, agitated, and anticipatory feeling

In both symphonies, the openings project breadth of scope, serious purpose, and an incipient sense of a struggle that lies ahead. We shall be mindful throughout this guide of the role Beethoven played as a provider of prototypes for Mahler, while searching, at the same time, for evidence of how Mahler's New Symphony escaped the powerful hold of the Beethoven archetype.

Exposition (Part One): The Impact of Traditional Sonata Form

This section of the movement offers several components of a traditional sonata-form exposition. We shall hear it first in its entirety and then discuss its individual components in detail.

Outline {▶ Audio Ex. 2.12}

00:00	P.1	Primary theme, Pt. 1, along with much material from the Opening
00:11	P.2	Primary theme, Pt. 2, along with much material from the Opening
00:15		Permutations of the foregoing material

01:01	Pk	Closing of the primary material
01:22	T	Transition begins
01:31		Modulation
01:38	S	Secondary theme (Gentle, lyrical song [*Gesang*])
02:05		Shift to E♭ Minor
02:22		Abrupt end to the first part of the exposition

Discussion

P.1 {▶ Audio Ex. 2.13} The primary theme enters arrestingly to mark the beginning of the exposition per se. The theme is divided into two parts, of which this is the first. Mahler lends prominence to this theme with the pungent and reedy sound of the instruments that play it: two oboes and English horn, to be joined in the second part of the theme by two clarinets. This orchestration is sufficiently singular to render the primary theme conspicuous and memorable despite the totally familiar thematic milieu into which it is lodged, which consists in motives from the Opening: the jagged rhythm, turning-note figure, and upward scalar run.

P.2 {▶ Audio Ex. 2.14} The second part of the primary theme enters (00:00–00:10). Unlike the first part, it is not new. Rather, it is comprised of familiar material from the Opening: the triplet figure and the jagged descent. Two other motives from the Opening—the perfect fourth and the triplets—continue to accompany the short-lived second part of the primary theme. The two parts of the primary theme will be treated separately later in the movement. Beginning at 00:11, the various motives are subjected to a variety of changes and permutations. Eventually, the primary theme cedes its fleeting moment in the sun to the ubiquitous presence of the unyieldingly sober material from the Opening.

Pk {▶ Audio Ex. 2.15} The orchestration expands, the music grows louder, and the section culminates in a forceful closing gesture for the primary theme, based largely on the jagged rhythms that were ubiquitous throughout the Opening. In shaping this exposition, Mahler seems to be rationalizing conflicting aims: he wants to lend due prominence to the primary theme, but he also seems unwilling to relinquish the heavy-duty emotional component of the Opening. He succeeds in attaining both objectives.

T {▶ Audio Ex. 2.16} After the imposing close of the primary section, Mahler reverts to the distinctive woodwind choir he linked to the primary theme and expands it to include two flutes, three oboes, and two clarinets. The wind melody seems new, even if its orchestration resembles that of the primary theme, and even though a familiar triplet figure circles below in the violoncellos and basses. Almost immediately (at **00:09**), a swift modulation slips us unexpectedly into a new and surprisingly remote key, E Major. This very brief passage must be the transition. Modulation, after all, is the central burden of transitions. Beyond the change of key, however, nothing in this passage resembles the traditional conventions of a transition. Missing is the abstract and a-melodic quality often found in transitions. Mahler seems in a hurry to get on with the secondary material. He adds a touch of drama here: the oboes and clarinets are required to play with the bells raised—that is, with the instruments pointed directly out at the audience. This enhances somewhat for the audience the penetrating quality of the woodwind sound, but, more importantly, it adds a dramatic visual effect to the performance, in which the physical act of raising the bells reinforces the importance of the orchestration of this passage.

S {▶ Audio Ex. 2.17} The exposition, until this point, has been saturated with the terrifying music from the beginning of the movement. Secondary themes often contrast vividly with primary material, and this one does starkly. Here, however, the contrast is uncommonly sharp. The violins play an expansive and eminently lyrical melody, replete with the hesitations and sighing gestures that epitomize many Romantic melodies. It is rendered even more soothing by the warm environs of E Major, an unusual choice of key. (In a sonata form that begins in C Minor, E♭ Major would be the traditional secondary key.) The extent to which this melody differs from everything we have heard thus far is so great that we hardly notice the discreet presence of the triplet figure (**O6**) from the Opening rotating quietly in the violoncellos and basses below. We might wonder if this eminently calming melody introduces its high level of serenity not simply in fulfillment of its role as a secondary theme, but, rather, to suggest that a satisfying resolution to the grim existential questions posed by this movement may ultimately be found.

It is also possible that Mahler's emphasis on the lyrical qualities of this melody is meant as a reference to Mickiewicz's *Todtenfeier* (*Dziady*), the poem from which Mahler took the name for this movement (see the discussion at the end of Chapter 1). The centerpiece of the Gustav poem in that epic poetic drama resides in the protagonist's singing. As Stephen Hefling points out, Gustav laments, but he also sings of the joy of love. The extraordinary emphasis Mahler attaches to the secondary theme may have been meant to reflect the centrality of song in the Gustav narrative, for the melody Mahler emphasizes here serves in its unbridled lyricism as a veritable archetype of song.[11]

Quintessentially Romantic in character as it may be, this theme is also short-lived. The key begins to shift (at **00:27**), and the melody loses some of its cogency, settling unexpectedly in the distinctly cooler clime of E♭ Minor. (We shall discover in Chapter 3 that E♭ Minor—a key that is used very rarely—will take on a special significance for this movement.) In a conventional exposition, this would be the place for closing material, but Mahler offers none. Instead, this section of the movement ends suddenly *in medias res* (at **00:45**).

Listening to an uninterrupted performance of the first part of the exposition would be beneficial now {⏵ Audio Ex. 2.12}.

Exposition (Part Two): Intensification, Experimentation, and Quotation

Here, Mahler strikes a more experimental pose with respect to his handling of sonata form. We begin with an overview of the section.

Outline {⏵ Audio Ex. 2.18}

00:00	O1, O2, O3, O4, O6	Motives from the Opening in rapid succession in the tonic
00:13	P.1	Primary theme, Pt. 1, intensified
00:26	T	Swift modulation to A♭ Major
00:31	New S: Victory theme	"Victory theme" from the First Symphony as an abbreviated, new secondary theme
00:45		Sudden return to the tonic (C Minor)
01:11	Pk	Intensification, then waning, using the gesture that closed the primary theme
01:28	K	Quiet closing section

[11] In his sketches for this movement, Mahler labels this theme *Gesang*, German for "song," which might allude to the centrality of song in Mickiewicz's *Todtenfeier*. On the other hand, *Gesang* is also an abbreviation for various technical terms in German for secondary theme: *Gesangsatz*, *Gesangsgruppe*, or *Gesangsperiode*. Hefling, "Mahler's 'Todtenfeier' and the Problem of Program Music," 34 and n. 36.

Discussion

O Motives {▶ Audio Ex. 2.19} Right after the abrupt ending of the previous section, Mahler leaps back to the opening gestures of the movement. He returns to the tremolando—in the tonic key of C Minor. This is followed by other motives of the Opening: the turning-note figure, ascending scale, jagged descent, and the triplets. Returning to this material in the tonic key seems to signal a standard convention of sonata form: the repeat of the exposition. The motives behave differently here than they did at the beginning of the movement, however, and they appear so swiftly and so compactly as to engender an impulsive character. The rapid pace of the motivic array, moreover, gives the impression that the music is careening toward a goal.

P.1 {▶ Audio Ex. 2.20} That goal is attained quickly when the first part of the primary theme returns. Its uncommon woodwind sonority is unmistakable, but the sense of haste that accompanied the compressed return of motives from the Opening persists here, too. The theme appears in diminution—at twice the speed at which it was originally played. We hear only the opening motive of the primary theme, and then it is subjected to further diminution and rapid-fire repetition (**00:04**), all of which generates tension.

Why does Mahler make these changes to the primary theme? Perhaps it is because they are part of a musical allusion added here to make a symbolic statement. The hurried, intensified version of **P.1** bears a close resemblance to an earlier work by Mahler: the third of the four *Songs of a Wayfarer*. Compare the altered version of **P.1** we just heard ({▶ Audio Ex. 2.20} and Music Ex. 2.1) to the opening of "Ich hab' ein glühend Messer" ("I have a glowing knife in my breast"), a harrowingly painful song, in which the protagonist expresses the agony of lost love in suicidal terms ({▶ Audio Ex. 2.21} and Music Ex. 2.2).[12] The repeated groups of three ascending notes in both excerpts spell out the same dissonant harmony. Thus, the intensification of **P.1** appears to contain a deliberate reference to the song. This allusion seems

Music Ex. 2.1. The intensified version of the primary theme in Part 2 of the exposition

---

[12] Hefling, "Mahler's 'Todtenfeier' and the Problem of Program Music," 33–34.

Music Ex. 2.2. The opening of "Ich hab' ein glühend Messer"

linked to Mickiewicz's *Todtenfeier*—specifically to the protagonist Gustav's suicide by stabbing.[13]

T {▶ Audio Ex. 2.22} The intensified version of **P.1** and the reverberations of "Ich hab' ein glühend Messer" combined with it barely register with the listener when Mahler continues the frenetic pace of this section of the symphony with a swift transition that modulates to A♭ Major—another unusual choice of key. Inserting a transition here, however, does follow the mandates of a traditional sonata exposition. Thus, some features of this section of the symphony fit the mold of the repeat of the exposition, but others introduce change in the manner of a development.

S: Victory theme {▶ Audio Ex. 2.23} As soon as the new key is established, Mahler provides what seems to be a brief attempt at a secondary theme, different from the one we heard earlier. It seems celebratory at first, adding, then, a series of gestures reminiscent of triumphant martial music. The melody is based on one from the last movement of Mahler's First Symphony. Compare the jubilant melody we just heard (in Audio Ex. 2.23) to a seminally important theme from the First Symphony {▶ Audio Ex. 2.24}. It is the very prominent opening three notes that the two themes have in common. The music from the First Symphony upon which Mahler draws here appears at what is probably the most decisive moment in that work, the appearance of the "Victory theme" that signifies the hero's triumph over anguish, alienation, and death.

At this juncture in our symphony, the reference is surely meant to suggest a reminiscence of the earlier life of the hero the First and Second Symphonies have in common. In a work that begins, as the Second Symphony does by Mahler's own account, with a depiction of the hero's burial, the reference to the First Symphony takes us back to a triumphant moment in his life. This conspicuous, if brief, allusion may also be linked to Mickiewicz's *Todtenfeier*. It seems to run parallel to a literary device Mickiewicz uses to

---

[13] Hefling, "Mahler's 'Todtenfeier' and the Problem of Program Music," 33–34.

enable his protagonist, Gustav, to reflect on his own youth. He accomplishes this by having him sing optimistic verses drawn from one of Mickiewicz's own earlier works, the *Ode to Youth*.[14]

Return to the tonic {⊙ Audio Ex. 2.25} Suddenly, we are thrust back into the principal key of the movement, C Minor. This is most unusual because traditional sonata forms generally withhold a prominent return to the tonic until the most decisive moment of the movement, the recapitulation. We may take Mahler's decision to return to the tonic here as another marker of his experimental perspective on sonata form.

Two motives are combined in this section from its very beginning: the trumpet blares out an ascending melody based on the rhythm of the A♭ Major theme we just heard, while the upper strings play the sweeping descending lines in jagged rhythms that were used in the opening exposition to close the primary material (**Pk**).

Pk {⊙ Audio Ex. 2.26} The music intensifies, expanding on the reference to **Pk** in the previous section. Here, the scale in jagged rhythms of which **Pk** is comprised is played ascending and descending simultaneously. The intensification soon reverses itself, and the passage ends quietly.

K {⊙ Audio Ex. 2.27} The second part of the exposition ends with a rather restrained closing passage, precisely the component of a traditional sonata exposition that was missing in the first part of the exposition. The violoncellos and basses (along with two harps) continuously intone and repeat a slow, descending chromatic line (Music Ex. 2.3). With the appearance of distinct closing material, the status of this section of the symphony as a sonata exposition—albeit a significantly altered one—takes on additional force.

The pervasive descending line in the lower strings calls to mind another important melody from the First Symphony: a darkly portentous and ominous passage with which the introduction to the first movement ends (Music Ex. 2.4 and {⊙ Audio Ex. 2.28}). The two melodies are not identical—the theme from the First Symphony ascends sequentially, while the closing theme from our movement offers a straight descent—but they still have a lot in common. They share the same grim character, identical rhythm, chromatic melodic writing, and scoring for lower string instruments.

The order in which Mahler presents two prominent allusions to the First Symphony in our movement seems important. The glumly portentous

---

[14] Hefling, "Mahler's 'Todtenfeier' and the Problem of Program Music," 36.

Music Ex. 2.3. The closing theme

Music Ex. 2.4. The end of the opening section of Mahler's First Symphony

motive from the beginning of the First Symphony recurs frequently within the struggles of its last movement. Whatever strides the hero makes at over-coming Fate, it is this motive, to rely on the words of Bauer-Lechner, that wrests the music "from brief glimpses of light" and tosses it into "the darkest depths of despair."[15] Only later—at the end of the work—does the hero achieve victory over Fate with the triumphant Victory motive. Thus, the First Symphony first presents the grim and augural motive near the beginning of the first movement, reuses it frequently in the last movement, and ends the finale with the Victory theme.

In our passage from the Second Symphony, however, the order in which the allusions to these two motives appear is reversed. The Victory theme precedes the ominous descending line. Despair follows triumph, suggesting, perhaps, that important questions that may have seemed resolved for our hero (Mahler?)—and for us—in the First Symphony were not really answered at all. Perhaps this offers another reason Mahler brought back the trium-phant theme from the First Symphony: to negate its positive significance by following it with the grim closing theme. Undoing this aspect of the closure presented in the First Symphony may be a necessary means of justifying the composition of its sequel. Mahler may also have attempted to underscore the lack of progress in the hero's existential journey this order projects with his unusual choice of key for the ending of the exposition. As we have seen, con-trary to normative practice in sonata form, it closes in C Minor: the same key with which the movement began. Normally, the tonal design in a sonata ex-position begins in the tonic and ends somewhere else. By ending this section back in C Minor, Mahler seems to hint that, for all the emotional intensity of the music in this movement so far, we have really gone nowhere.

[15] Bauer-Lechner, *Recollections of Gustav Mahler*, 31.

Music Ex. 2.5. The inferno motive from Franz Liszt's *Dante Symphony*

In addition, Mahler may have intended a touch of symbolism in the morose closing theme. Recall its downward motion, chromatic writing, and regular alternation of quarter notes and triplets from Music Ex.2.3, above. Then consider the following passage (Music Ex. 2.5 and {▶ Audio Ex. 2.29}).

The two themes are similar. Both offer chromatic descent in a mixture of quarter notes and triplets. The second of the two melodies is the Inferno motive from Franz Liszt's *Dante Symphony*. It plays a prominent part in the last movement of Mahler's First Symphony, in which the program describes a journey from inferno to paradise. The allusion to this motive here recalls the first section of Dante's *Divine Comedy*, notably, its vivid portrayal of the suffering of sinners in the nine concentric circles of hell. Thus, it hints at some of the existential concerns Mahler will go on to raise in subsequent movements of the Second Symphony: life and death, judgment and punishment, forgiveness and immortality.

If you listen very closely to the end of the closing passage {▶ Audio Ex. 2.30}, you may hear in the background the almost imperceptible shimmering sound of ten soft strokes on the tam-tam. (They appear clustered together at the beginning of the passage, then more intermittently thereafter. They are not easy to detect in this recording.) This unusual sonority helps to demarcate the end of the exposition. The tam-tam is rarely used as a means of structural demarcation, but it is used in this way not only at this juncture, but at two other important divisions of the movement (as we shall see in Chapter 3). This unusual orchestral sonority may also be related to Mickiewicz's poem. It is probably meant to represent the chiming clock in the Gustav poem that similarly delineates the three "hours" into which its dramatic action is divided (as we reported in Chapter 1).[16]

How does the music we have heard thus far relate to the concept of sonata form? Clearly, Mahler stretches the concept of the sonata exposition considerably. In lieu of the traditional repeated exposition, Mahler seems to offer two expositional sections, neither of them conventional. The first lacks a closing section, and the second, which does provide a closing section, moves

---

[16] Hefling, "Mahler's 'Todtenfeier' and the Problem of Program Music," 32.

into the realm of developmental procedures and uses a quotation from the First Symphony to hint at a secondary theme different from the one we heard earlier. And the tonal design of both sections is highly unusual. Nonetheless, taken together, the two sections cohere to produce an overriding sense of symphonic exposition, notwithstanding the significant structural anomalies they contain. These anomalies are a part of Mahler's efforts at developing a New Symphony free of the constraints inherent in strict adherence to a formal template.

We are ready now for deeper development, which we shall explore in the next chapter. First, however, it would be helpful to listen again to the second part of the exposition uninterrupted {▶ Audio Ex. 2.18}.

3

The First Movement: Development and Recapitulation

Development (Part One): Traditional Development
and a Pre-occupation with a Gentle Theme •
The Connection between Parts One and Two of the Development:
The Rhetoric of Antithesis •
Musical Keys and the Emotions •
Development (Part Two): Explosion, an Enigmatic Motive,
and a Parade of Quotations •
Recapitulation: Conventional Return and an Ominous Synopsis •
Mahler Suspends Work on the Second Symphony

Development (Part One): Traditional Development and a Preoccupation with a Gentle Theme

Think back to our archetypal example of sonata form—the diminutive Haydn symphony movement you heard in Appendix 1. As you do, recall the nature and purpose of the development section described there. It generates uncertainty and tension in the service of creating a need for a return to the more stable and predictable music of the recapitulation. The sample development achieved these objectives by altering material from the exposition, tearing from it the comfort we associate with familiar material in its original guise, and subjecting it to rapid changes of texture and of key. With that in mind, listen to the beginning of the development of our movement.

S {⏵ Audio Ex. 3.1} Mahler begins the development by restating the opening of the gentle secondary theme from the first exposition. That theme, when we first heard it, seemed so serene and mellifluous that we felt it necessary to explain those qualities as something beyond the routine level of contrast that distinguishes primary from secondary themes. We sought to attribute the lyrical qualities of this theme to an attempt to express in music a portent of a possible solution to the intimidating existential questions Mahler

Inside Mahler's Second Symphony:. Lawrence F. Bernstein, Oxford University Press. © Oxford University Press 2022.
DOI: 10.1093/oso/9780197575635.003.0003

raises in this movement. Or perhaps the flowing secondary theme is meant to provide a link to the emphasis on song in Adam Mickiewicz's *Todtenfeier*.

Now that theme returns as the opening of the development. Rather than altering it in ways that render it tense or unstable, as we might expect in a symphonic development, Mahler preserves the very essence of the melody. It comes across as a paradigm of simplicity and quiet elegance. Moreover, it appears in C Major. C is the tonic of the movement, a choice that seems the very antithesis of the journey to far-flung keys that often commences at the beginning of the development. None of this resonates in ways we associate with a symphonic development. Instead, Mahler seems to demonstrate a fixation on the gentle qualities of this theme, probably for the same reasons we advanced earlier for the extent of its sense of repose: that it anticipates a satisfying solution to the central existential problems of this symphony, or that it is meant to reflect the centrality of song in Adam Mickiewicz's epic poem.

Changes of key {▶ Audio Ex. 3.2} Mahler has not altogether forgotten that this is a development section, however, and, toward the end of the lyrical secondary theme he begins changing keys, as is common in developments. He touches on A Minor (**00:08**) and F Major (**00:12**) as waystations on the road to E Major (**00:24**). The "warm" key of E Major was used prominently earlier in the movement. It is the tonality in which the secondary theme originally appeared, and it seems linked to the sense of quietude we associated with that theme when we first heard it.

N1 {▶ Audio Ex. 3.3} E Major also brings with it a new theme played by the English horn. Adding a new theme in a symphonic development section became almost obligatory after Beethoven introduced one—with dramatic flair—in the first movement of his third symphony, the "Eroica." The new theme unfolds, and Mahler expands upon it gently, while a lengthy pedal on the tonic is sustained throughout the passage, reinforcing its stability. This passage flows as placidly as did the melody with which the development began.

Mahler headed this theme *Meeresstille* ("becalmed seas") in his sketches for the movement. The peaceful aquatic image that seems to be projected by this word may not be as idyllic as it first appears. "Meeresstille" could refer to Goethe's well-known poem of that name, in which stillness, in the form of a lack of wind, poses a mortal threat to the sailor:

Todesstille fürchterlich!	Dreadful silence of death!
In der ungeheuren Weite	In the immense expanse
Reget keine Welle sich.	No wave is moving.[1]

[1] Constantin Floros, *Gustav Mahler: The Symphonies*, trans. Vernon and Jutta Wicker (Portland, OR: Amadeus Press, 1993), 59.

Mahler, who deeply admired Goethe—he could declaim wide swaths of *Faust* from memory—must have been aware of Goethe's poem.[2] If Mahler's annotation to this theme is viewed from the perspective of Goethe's poem, the serene new theme in the English horn may be an ironic reference to death, which plays so central a role in this movement. The tranquility of this new theme may also be associated with a different use of the word *"Meeresstille,"* one Mahler certainly must have known. Among his favorite books was Schopenhauer's *Die Welt als Wille und Vorstellung* (*The World as Will and Representation*). For Schopenhauer, the will is the powerful force to which humankind is shackled; it condemns us to pursue life in a state of blindness, unless the force of the will can be overcome. Achieving that brings about a dissolution of the self. Schopenhauer describes the tranquility he attributes to this state as a quality of "peace that is higher than all reason, . . . an ocean-like calmness [*Meeresstille*] of the spirit."[3]

The theme contains melodic material from *Die Walküre*, the second opera in Wagner's *Ring of the Niebelungs*, specifically, the Magic Fire Music from the third act {▶ Audio Ex. 3.4}.[4] Mahler's new theme and the Magic Fire Music are not identical, but they are very close. Both begin with an expansive upward leap, followed by a descent that pauses on the note one step lower than the apex; then they continue the descent in a mixture of steps and leaps. Mahler highlights this theme by giving it to the English horn, an instrument whose highly distinctive timbre often serves Mahler as a means of providing special emphasis.

At this moment in *Die Walküre*, Brünnhilde, a demigoddess and daughter of Wotan, one of the principal gods in Norse mythology, has defied her father's will, and Wotan is about to mete out his punishment. This music accompanies the kindling of the wall of flames that will protect Brünnhilde as Wotan abrogates her godly immortality and condemns her to eternal sleep unless a hero courageous enough to brave the fire awakens her. Why

---

[2] On Mahler's admiration for Goethe, see Jens Malte Fischer, *Gustav Mahler*, trans. Stewart Spencer (New Haven, CT: Yale University Press, 2011), 133.

[3] Morten Solvik, "The Literary and Philosophical Worlds of Gustav Mahler," in Jeremy Barham, ed., *The Cambridge Companion to Mahler* (Cambridge: Cambridge University Press, 2007), 33.

[4] The resemblance of the English horn theme (N1) to the Magic Fire Music is pointed out by Rudolf Stephan in *Gustav Mahler: II. Symphonie c-moll*, Meisterwerke der Musik, 21 (Munich: Wilhelm Fink Verlag, 1979), 46. Early in his tenure as second conductor in Leipzig, Mahler had demanded that he conduct a share of the performances of Wagner's *Ring* cycle, a perquisite that would normally go to the first conductor, Arthur Nikisch. In February 1887, Nikisch was seriously ill, and Mahler took over responsibility for conducting the entire cycle. Thus, the excerpt from *Die Walküre* he quoted in the first movement of the Second Symphony a year later would have been at his fingertips.

has Mahler introduced Brünnhilde into the narrative of this movement? The allusions to eternal sleep and immortality are clearly related to the existential questions Mahler raises in this movement, but the significance of the relationship has not yet been made explicit. Moreover, as we shall discover, this is not Brünnhilde's only appearance in this movement. When she returns (in about seven minutes), the important symbolic significance of the references to the *Ring* cycle will become clearer. Whatever the association of the term *Meeresstille* with Mahler's new theme may connote, and whatever its relationship to the Magic Fire Music means, the development section, thus far, remains almost completely devoid of tension.

Modal change {▶ Audio Ex. 3.5} The first hint at departure from the persistent tranquility of this development section comes with a switch to the minor mode (from E Major to E Minor, **00:06**). Mahler is fond of using a change to the minor mode to signal a new direction or, sometimes, that trouble is brewing. In the third movement of the First Symphony, for example, the melody of *Frère Jacques* (known in the German-speaking world as *Bruder Martin*) appears in the minor mode instead of its original major key, and the modal change introduces a level of distortion that is part of Mahler's attempt to project the topic of alienation symbolically. The key of E Minor in the movement at hand will go on to host a variety of developmental techniques as this section of the movement finally begins to generate tension.

Mixture of motives {▶ Audio Ex. 3.6} At last, Mahler gradually begins to introduce higher levels of complexity and tension in a manner that befits a traditional symphonic development. They arise principally from the combination of different themes that were presented earlier. At the outset of this passage, the higher strings play a smooth, somewhat meandering line. If you listen closely to the violoncellos and basses, however, you will hear them playing the edgy, jagged rhythms that were prominent in one of the early motives from the Opening (**O4**) and in the closing tag for the primary theme (**Pk**). In this new context, in which these familiar rhythms are combined with something new, it is natural for us to struggle somewhat to identify the source of this rhythmic figure. "I think I recognize it, but I can't recall from where," we are likely to wonder. Just a bit later (at **00:08**), the turning-note figure from the Opening (**O2**) enters in the violoncellos and basses—briefly and in a hushed manner. Its addition to the complement of motives only adds to the listener's burden of identifying all this material. Then (at **00:13**), Mahler superposes on these continuing muted quotations from the Opening another new theme (N2) in the English horn and bass clarinet. The listener who is already straining to identify vaguely familiar material in this passage might well wonder if and where he has heard N2 before, even though it is, in fact, entirely new. In this way, the combination of new material with several motives from the Opening presented simultaneously gives rise to a significant measure of confusion. We might characterize this as "good confusion," meant to bring about in its wake the tension we associate with development in the context of sonata form.

You should not regard as a setback an inability to identify or even recognize all the motives enumerated here. Rather, the complexity of the combination of motives Mahler has brought about seems intentionally designed to strain the listener's cognitive grasp of the material in this section. This may seem troublesome for the listener at first, but discomfiture of this sort is apt to be precisely the reaction the composer intends. It is highly characteristic of the ethos of symphonic development.

Motivic intensity {⊙ Audio Ex. 3.7} The motivic references continue to multiply (**00:00**). As the English horn and bass clarinet proceed with their new melody (**N2**), the French horns quietly introduce a motive resembling the opening of the primary theme, **P.1**, over continuing jagged rhythms in the strings. This grows to a forceful moment (**00:19**) when the rhythm of **P.1** combines with the triplet rhythm of **O6**. The field of motives then expands greatly. **P.2** reappears (**00:30**), blared out by six French horns, quickly followed by fragments of other motives from the Opening: the jagged descent (**O4**) and the rapid ascending scale (**O3**). Suddenly (at **00:39**), the trumpets and French horns sound a vivid reference to the Victory theme from the First Symphony that was quoted in the second part of the exposition. At last, the development section appears to be free of the constraints on generating tension that was brought on by its incipient concentration on the placidly lyrical secondary theme.

Climax {⊙ Audio Ex. 3.8} Mahler reaches for even higher levels of intensity in this passage, beginning it with the simultaneous presentation of three motives: the rhythm of **P.1** (in the French horns), the jagged descent of **Pk** (in the woodwinds), and the closing material (**K**) from the end of the exposition (in the trombones and lower strings). At **00:19**, triplets (**O6**) are added to the mix. The same combination of motives is repeated (beginning at **00:26**), but in a more commanding orchestration. Following all these strands simultaneously makes serious demands on the listener. Once again, the objective here seems more to be engendering the struggle to recognize and identify the content of this passage than achieving success in that effort. The passage grows louder and its harmonies increasingly harsh, which leads to an explosive crest at **00:44**. The force of this moment is so great that it brings about a pressing need for abatement. Tension begins to wane (**00:52**), and a quick modulation to F Major is accomplished (at **01:04**).

S {⊙ Audio Ex. 3.9} With the arrival of F Major, Mahler brings back the gentle secondary theme yet again. Its lyrical qualities are preserved, and its assignment to a solo flute lends an aura of bucolic translucence. Once more, its reappearance coincides with the suspension of intense developmental techniques. We suggested earlier that we might view this theme as a hopeful portent in a milieu of existential despair; that seems even more appropriate now. It may also be linked, as we pointed out earlier, to the concept of song that figured so prominently in Mickiewicz's poem. The secondary theme begins in F Major, wends its way (at **00:17**) into C Major, as it is taken over by a solo violin, and settles finally into B Major (at **00:33**). Changes of key like these often occur in development sections, but their developmental force is outweighed here by the extent to which the gentle stability of the secondary theme shines through. The music then gradually dissolves into some hushed pastoral motifs before fading away into silence, which brings us to the end of the first part of the development. Once more, the unusual use of the tam-tam at a major subdivision of the form (**01:04**) reminds us of the chiming of the clock that marks off the three hours of Mickiewicz's poem.

In the early portions of this movement, the relationship of the music to Mahler's existential concerns seemed transparent. It is easy to detect in the Opening and the Expositions the austere musical affect that seems appropriate to a sobering confrontation with the meaning of life. Our characterization of the Development so far, however, is suggestive of a different musical rhetoric—one more concerned with themes and motives, modulations and tension, than with life and death. Except for the veiled possible references to the Mickiewicz poem, the technical apparatus upon which we drew to explain the development—at least thus far—seems of little relevance to the musical expression of the powerful emotions that defined the earlier sections of this movement.

At first blush, the stark unevenness of this dichotomy, which emphasizes extramusical topics, on the one hand, and concentrates on abstract musical form, on the other, seems so lopsided that it might be suggestive of an aesthetic flaw. But it really is not. To begin, the emphasis on form in one part of a movement and on extra-musical content in another is hardly a mark of an internal contradiction. Indeed, the partition of this movement into two arenas—one that projects extra-musical concepts and emotion, and another that is largely concerned with music in the abstract, say, with sonata form—is a natural outgrowth of Mahler's agenda for this work. He intends the composition to reflect a struggle in the pursuit of existential meaning. Significantly, however, he originally headed this movement *Sinfonie in C moll* ("Symphony in C Minor"), and the lofty status of the symphony in the pantheon of musical genres was not to be taken lightly. It implies the presence of a range of technical conventions and procedures. Thus, a symphony that embraces an extra-musical agenda will demonstrate from time to time what might be called dual loyalties. Sometimes, it will lavish its musical resources on its extra-musical content; sometimes, it will simply behave like a symphony. Our discussion, therefore, will reflect an awareness of these two approaches.

The Connection between Parts One and Two of the Development: The Rhetoric of Antithesis

The preceding section (Part One of the Development) ends in a most unusual way. Its concluding tranquil motives gradually dissolve as the texture thins and the dynamic level grows softer. Thus, the first section of the development goes out with a whimper. If the aim of a development section is to generate tension, the impassivity of this passage—like that of some others we have cited—seems antithetical to that objective. The purpose served by the disintegrating fade-out that concludes the first part of the development may be better understood when the passage is juxtaposed to what follows. Here {⊙ Audio Ex. 3.10} is the end of Part One (**00:00**) and the beginning of Part Two (**00:33**) of the development.

Mahler invokes here the rhetoric of antithesis, and he does so with a vengeance. The first part of the development dwindles away to nothing to augment the contrast between the two sections and to intensify the massive shock that accompanies the beginning of the new section. Out of nowhere, the opening material of the movement returns at a high dynamic level, its intensity redoubled by explosive bursts from the percussion instruments. The magnitude of the contrast is compelling, and it seems "bigger than life" in ways not often encountered in symphonic music. The intensity of the contrast inherent in what we have called "the rhetoric of antithesis" seems powerfully dramatic, which should not surprise us, perhaps, considering how much of

Mahler's life was devoted to the performance of opera and how readily he might have been able to adapt its conventions to orchestral music.

This passage, too, fades away rather soon after its stormy onset. The deep tam-tam and bass drum trill softly and continuously, while the music retreats into a soft, descending chromatic scale, played tremolando by the strings and rendered somewhat spectral in its effect by Mahler's direction that it be played *am Steg*, meaning "on the bridge," a mode of performance on string instruments that produces an eerily thin, nasal sound.

The violent shock with which this section of the development begins plays an important role: after the preoccupation with the structural conventions of sonata form that permeated the preceding section of the development, we are now emphatically thrust back into the maelstrom of existential angst. It is the emotionally laden opening material of the movement that returns here, and its compellingly forceful reappearance rekindles our awareness of the central extra-musical problem of this symphony.

The issues of sharp contrast and forceful return to the symphony's extra-musical agenda are important, but another dimension of this brief but powerful passage needs to be considered: the emotions it arouses. I find this passage utterly terrifying. No matter how well I know that it is coming, I am somehow able to shield myself from that knowledge, and I succumb every time to a profound sense of surprise, shock, and fear, as I bear witness to this alarmingly explosive and bone-chilling music.[5] This quality is enhanced, in part, by Mahler's orchestration. The turning-note motive (O2) at the very beginning of the symphony was played by the violoncellos and basses, and that was forceful enough. Here, it seems overpowering, played by all the strings. The loud entrance of the low tam-tam right after the sequence of the turning-note motive adds a raucous, snarling quality to the sonority, compounded by the relentless rolling of two timpani. Then, the descending fourth motive in jagged rhythm (O5) makes an arresting appearance. At the opening of the symphony it was played by the bassoons, contrabassoon, and lower strings. Here, it is played by the timpani—not often used as a melodic instrument—and this uncommon choice adds a surreal quality to the passage.

---

[5] In a pioneering study, Leonard B. Meyer struggles with the conundrum of how we react to a piece of music that embodies an important surprise when we know the piece well and, on a subsequent hearing, can readily predict the arrival of the surprise. He argues that, in such circumstances, we make recourse to aesthetic illusions of our own fashioning to keep viable a sense of the unexpected. Such illusions are not unlike the mental game we play that enables a drama to seem real even when we know it is make believe. See "On Rehearing Music," *Journal of the American Musicological Society*, 14 (1961): 256–267.

Another feature of this blistering return of the opening material warrants consideration: it is in E♭ Minor, a key used very rarely and that is very remote from B Major, the tonality of the preceding music. The juxtaposition of the two keys is jarring, and the move to E♭ Minor is achieved suddenly, without a graded, systematic process of modulation. Moreover, the infrequency with which this key appears in the musical literature is so striking that Mahler's choice to use it demands further attention.

Musical Keys and the Emotions

Some theorists and aestheticians of the eighteenth and nineteenth centuries believed that individual keys convey discrete emotional content. The German poet and composer Christian Schubart, for example, associated C Major with innocence, D Major with triumph, and F Minor with depression and misery. On the affective significance of E♭ Minor, Schubart had this to say:

> [E♭ Minor expresses] feelings of the anxiety of the soul's deepest distress, of brooding despair, of blackest depression, of the most gloomy condition of the soul. Every fear, every hesitation of the shuddering heart, breathes out of horrible E♭ Minor. If ghosts could speak, their speech would approximate this key.[6]

Had Mahler believed in the inherent emotional properties of various keys, he is not apt to have sought guidance on this phenomenon from a writer like Schubart. More likely, he would have turned to the music he knew and respected to gain a sense of the emotional content inherent in one key or another. The relatively few known examples of music in E♭ Minor are revealing with respect to the emotions they seem aimed to project.

Franz Schubert's song on a poem by Matthias Claudius, "Am grabe Anselmos," D. 504 (1816), for example, gives voice in a graveside lament to the inconsolable sentiments of its mourning protagonist. The fourth movement of Robert Schumann's Third Symphony (1850) is cast in a funereal style, projected, in part, by a choir of four trombones (instruments widely used in funeral processions). "Ich hab in Traum geweinet" from the same composer's

---

[6] Rita Steblin, *A History of Key Characteristics in the Eighteenth and Early Nineteenth Centuries*, 2nd ed. (Rochester, NY: University of Rochester Press, 2002), 117.

song cycle, *Dichterliebe*, offers the poignantly anguished image of the speaker weeping within his own dream as he mourns the disaffection, abandonment, and death of his lover.[7]

Of all the works to rely on E♭ Minor for its capacity to express a complex of dark emotions, the most prominent is probably Beethoven's *Christus am Ölberge* (*Christ on the Mount of Olives*), Op. 85. This early oratorio (1803) vividly portrays the emotional turbulence of Christ in the garden of Gethsemane on the eve of the crucifixion. It focuses on death, grief, fear, suffering, and martyrdom, moving on finally to redemption and eternal life. The oratorio opens with a bleak, somber, and highly dramatic introduction that centers on E♭ Minor {ⓞ Audio Ex. 3.11}. The spiritual message underlying Beethoven's oratorio thus dovetails neatly with Mahler's existential agenda for the Second Symphony. Moreover, some of the issues taken up in the oratorio lie close to an important aspect of Mahler's persona. Indeed, when he was at work on the Third Symphony, Mahler identified closely and *even personally* with the figure of Christ on the Mount of Olives. In a discussion of his work on the Third Symphony with Bauer-Lechner, Mahler empathized with Christ's having to imbibe the cup of sorrow and with the dreadful fear Mahler was certain he must have felt, even after having done so willingly. He saw a parallel to his own feelings on composing the first movement of the Third Symphony, fearing he would not live to experience the acceptance of the work.[8] He characterizes himself, in this sense, as a martyr to his own creation, a life view that resonates consonantly with the family story of the youthful Mahler's response to a relative who wondered what he wanted to be when he grew up; "a martyr," was the young boy's reply.[9]

Mahler is not known to have conducted Beethoven's *Christ on the Mount of Olives*, but an anecdote about his early years in Iglau links him to the oratorio. Theodor Fischer, Mahler's childhood friend from Iglau, recalled that his father conducted the choir in the church of St. Jakob, in which both he

---

[7] I am grateful to Robert Moreen for calling Schumann's use of this key to my attention. Too late to have been a source of influence on Mahler's use of E♭ Minor but a striking example of the use of this key to denote morose sentiments is the sixth and last movement of Johannes Brahms's *Klavierstücke*, Op. 118, composed in 1893 and dedicated to Clara Schumann. This most somber intermezzo in E♭ Minor reflects on death through its series of references to the *Dies irae*, the Gregorian chant used in the Roman Catholic Requiem Mass. We shall focus on Mahler's use of the *Dies irae* in the Second Symphony later in this chapter.

[8] Natalie Bauer-Lechner, *Recollections of Gustav Mahler*, ed. Peter Franklin, trans. Dika Newlin (New York: Faber & Faber, 2013), 62.

[9] Peter Franklin, *The Life of Mahler* (Cambridge: Cambridge University Press, 1997), 23.

and Mahler sang. Among the works they heard (or, perhaps, even sang) there was *Christ on the Mount of Olives*.[10]

This terrifying moment in the Second Symphony is not the only instance in which Mahler uses E♭ Minor to portray somber or mournful sentiments. At the end of the funeral march from the First Symphony, when Mahler wants to intensify the musical representations of alienation and its attendant pain, he does so by transposing music that was originally in D Minor into E♭ Minor. The same tonal progression can be found in the third of the *Wayfarer* songs, "Ich hab' ein glühend Messer," in which the suicidal speaker bemoans a lost love and the haunting presence of her ubiquitous image.

Development (Part Two): Explosion, an Enigmatic Motive, and a Parade of Quotations

We retrace our steps a bit now and return to the beginning of the second part of the development to initiate our discussion of this section of the symphony.

Explosion {▶ Audio Ex. 3.12} A violent opening abruptly reintroduces the existential agenda of the symphony. In immediate and rapid succession, several of the important motives from the opening of the movement reappear here, but with a fierce, snarling tone: the turning-note figure (O2 at **00:00**), the ascending scale (O3 at **00:07**), and the jagged descent (O4 at **00:08**). This intensely combustible moment promptly recedes in an eerie-sounding tremolando reminiscent of O1 (beginning at **00:09**) that fades away to inaudibility, after the jagged descent is echoed by the timpani (at **00:12**). Fading away to nothingness (as we have learned from previous examples) may often be read as Mahler's signal that something of significance is about to follow.

Enigmatic motive {▶ Audio Ex. 3.13} The important musical event that was augured by the dissolution into inaudibility of the explosive passage is

---

[10] Norman Lebrecht, *Mahler Remembered* (London: Faber & Faber, 1987), 15 and n. 1; and Kurt Blaukopf with contributions by Zoltan Roman, *Mahler: A Documentary Study* (London: Thames and Hudson, 1976), 148–149. Fischer's account of Mahler's childhood experiences was offered in remarks made in Iglau in 1931 in commemoration of the twentieth anniversary of Mahler's death. They were published in Theodor Fischer, "Aus Gustav Mahlers Jugendzeit," *Deutsche Heimat*, 7 (1931): 264–268. The original typescript of Fischer's remarks may be found at the Muzeum Vysočiny Jihlava in Book Collection Iglaviensia, inv. n. 975. It differs from the published account in various ways, and it makes no mention of the Beethoven oratorio, as is also true of Blaukopf's account. The reference to *Christ on the Mount of Olives* is on p. 265 of the article in *Deutsche Heimat*. See also Henry-Louis de La Grange, *Gustav Mahler: The Arduous Road to Vienna (1860–1897)*, completed, rev., and ed. by Sybille Werner (Turnhout: Brepols, 2020), 45. I am grateful to Ludmila Moržolová, Manager of the Muzeum Vysočiny in Jihlava, for providing me with a copy of Fischer's typescript.

not provided immediately. First (**00:00**), the jagged rhythms of the Opening (**O4**) and of **Pk** resume, hesitantly and very quietly, in the lower strings. To this are added passing references to the turning-note figure—also from the Opening—(beginning at **00:11**). After that (at **00:15**), however, we hear something at once mysterious and auspicious; it would appear to be the musical event we have been led to anticipate. An English horn enters, and, against the continuing jagged rhythms in the strings, it offers the barest of gestures: a simple minor second. The two notes of which this interval is comprised seem inconsequential melodically, but the sonority of the English horn is so pungent and arresting that it endows the sparse melodic material with a striking presence. Despite this commanding entrance, however, the English horn motive remains vexingly inscrutable, for the bare-boned minor second seems too meager melodically to warrant the degree of prominence its sonority bestows on it. We find ourselves in the throes of an intensely enigmatic moment, one that demands resolution. That will come, but not for a long time. In the meantime, the listener needs to keep this mystery in mind.

Quotations-1 {▶ Audio Ex. 3.14} The jagged motive continues quietly and relentlessly in the strings. Another familiar thematic element is added to it: **P.2**, first played by the flute (**00:00**), while the trumpet and trombone play **N2**. Some developmental alteration ensues. Together, these motives provide an ongoing backdrop, against which will be juxtaposed a parade of musical quotations, drawn from far-flung external sources. At **00:26**, the French horns present the first four notes of the *Dies irae*, the fourteenth-century Gregorian chant that describes the Day of Judgment, and which is sung as a part of the Requiem Mass, the Roman Catholic rite for the dead (Music Ex. 3.1). The chant fragment and its new continuation are played—in true developmental fashion—in combination with the jagged rhythmic motive and the second half of the primary theme.

Quotations-2 {▶ Audio Ex. 3.15} The second half of the primary theme (**P.2**) continues to serve as the glutenous agent that holds together the fabric of these musical quotations. It is restated emphatically at the beginning of

Music Ex. 3.1. The beginning of the *Dies irae*

Di-es i-rae, di-es il-la sol-vet   tae - clum   in   fa-vil-la te - ste   Da-vid   cum sy-bil - la.

Fig. 3.1. Siegfried awakens Brünnhilde, from a painting by Otto Donner von Richter, engraved by Richard Bong
Niday Picture Library / Alamy Stock Photo

this passage. At **00:10**, another quotation enters: the opening of the "Victory theme" from the last movement of the First Symphony. (Mahler had already quoted this earlier in this movement, in Part 2 of the exposition and in the first part of the development.)

Back-to-back with the "Victory theme," another quotation appears, ever so briefly. This is the moment when Brünnhilde puts in a second appearance in this movement. At this point, we hear music from the last scene of Richard Wagner's *Siegfried*, the third of the operas in *The Ring of the Niebelungs*. In this scene, Brünnhilde is awakened from her sleep by Siegfried, who penetrates the ring of fire that surrounds her (Fig. 3.1). She sings about immortality—about the eternal life she once had as a demigoddess and which she had forfeited, and about a new kind of immortality that derives from her love for Siegfried. Her revealing words are "Ewig war ich; ewig bin ich." ("I was immortal; I am immortal").[11] Mahler quotes (at **00:20**) the first five notes of this music, a musical figure that was known in the context of Wagner's *Siegfried* as the immortality motive.

---

[11] Mahler conducted *Siegfried* in Leipzig in 1886, replacing the ailing Arthur Nikisch.

Significant meaning and exquisite symmetry emerge from the juxtaposition of Brünnhilde's two cameo appearances in this movement, some seven minutes apart. In the first one, the allusion to the Magic Fire Music reminds us of Brünnhilde's loss of immortality and the possibility that her repose may be the sleep of death. In her second appearance, she awakens from a potentially eternal sleep and proclaims that, through love, she has gained a new kind of immortality. The shift from eternal sleep to a different kind of immortality, gained through love, has obvious relevance in a symphony that contemplates how life can be meaningful even if it inevitably leads to death. The reference to *Siegfried* has scarcely made its presence felt when (at **00:25**) the *Dies irae* fragment returns.

A dramatic moment {⏵ Audio Ex. 3.16A} Right after the last repetition of the *Dies irae* (**00:05**), the music slows down and broadens grandly (**00:10**), suggesting that it is about to close. Instead, Mahler calls (at **00:13**) for one of his favorite and most dramatic devices, a *Luftpause*, literally, a "break of air" (sometimes, he calls this device a *caesura*). This is a brief moment of silence that interrupts the primordial, regular pulse that controls the flow of music through time (what we call meter). That silence may be very short, but the drama that can result from it is powerful. Our need for a regular metrical pulse is so great that this miniscule cessation in the ubiquitous regularity of the meter might almost be taken (with a little hyperbole) to be the musical equivalent of a transient cardiac arrest! Listen to Audio Ex. 3.16A and concentrate on the *Luftpause* (*caesura*) that Mahler calls for at **00:13**.

You would not be amiss if you were to register difficulty in identifying the presence of this *Luftpause*. "I heard nothing in the music suggestive of a cardiac arrest here," you might justifiably protest. In fact, Bruno Walter fails to observe the *Luftpause*. Compare his reading of the passage to that of Leonard Bernstein in a recording with the New York Philharmonic {⏵ Audio Ex. 3.16B}. The *Luftpause* in this rendition (at **00:10**) creates a momentary sense of suspended animation within the meter, which results in a fleeting burst of high drama.

Clearly, Bruno Walter overrides Mahler's intentions here. Why? One can only speculate about what informed his decision, but that process can be illuminating. Several possible reasons come to mind. One is purely practical. The execution of *Luftpausen* in performance can be treacherous. All it takes to create a disaster is for one orchestral musician to remain so instinctively wedded to the meter that he or she adheres to it and plays through the *Luftpause*, filling the intended momentary silence with one lonely (and clearly errant) bit of sound. It happens! Not infrequently, therefore, conductors avoid Mahler's *Luftpausen* in live performance.

Walter's rendition of this *Luftpause*, however, was made in a recording session, not in a live performance. He would have had an opportunity to correct a mishap. We must pursue other reasons for his choice. His decision to take a pass on this *Luftpause* may have arisen from a broad aesthetic that plays an important part in his conducting style. Although he generally adheres meticulously to the composer's intentions, he also tends to frame his interpretations within an approach that privileges restraint and sobriety. The predilection for high drama inherent in such gestures as Mahler's *Luftpausen* may, in this context, have seemed somewhat "over the top" to Walter, more melodramatic than dramatic, and in need, therefore, of mitigation or suppression.[12]

Walter was not alone in his concern about Mahler's penchant for the *Luftpause* (*caesura*). The Hamburg music critic, composer, and friend of Mahler, Ferdinand Pfohl criticized Mahler for adding caesuras to the music of other composers when he conducted, citing as an example the well-known C Major Waltz in Johann Strauss the Younger's *Die Fledermaus*. In Pfohl's view, the pauses Mahler introduced had the effect of impeding the graceful flow of the melody. Pfohl goes on to quote Hans Richter, the celebrated Wagnerian conductor and Mahler's predecessor as director of the Vienna Court Opera. Richter, he suggests, perceived in Mahler's addition of such pauses the origin of what ultimately came to be known as Mahler's "caesuramania" (*Caesurenwahns*).[13] The dramatic force of the *Luftpause* Mahler intended here goes on to unleash a paroxysm of developmental tension in the next section.

End of development {▶ Audio Ex. 3.17} The call to continue struggling with Mahler's existential agenda returns again suddenly, and this time it rages furiously. Many prominent motives from the Opening and the Exposition reappear—the tremolando (O1), the swift descent in jagged rhythm (O4), the perfect fourth (O5), the triplets (O6), and the second half of the primary theme (P.2)—but they are often significantly modified from their original form. In addition, many of these motives in their altered form are presented

[12] Walter's aversion to this *Luftpause* appears to have been an ingrained fixture of his interpretation of the Second Symphony. He omits it in his recordings of the work in 1942 with the New York Philharmonic and in 1948 with the Vienna Philharmonic.

[13] Ferdinand Pfohl, *Gustav Mahler: Eindrücke und Erinnerungen aus der Hamburger Jahren*, ed. Knud Martner (Hamburg: Verlag der Musikalienhandlung Karl Dieter Wagner, 1973), 48. See also La Grange, *Gustav Mahler: The Arduous Road to Vienna*, 589 and nn. 87 and 88; and 596 and n. 134.

simultaneously. The combination of substantial transformation of the motives with their concurrent presentation creates a high level of instability. The piercing tension inherent in this passage is enhanced greatly by the brute force of its emotional content. This music projects intense pain. It does so by various means: its melodic lines, which leap about in a wildly disjunctive manner; its fiercely percussive rhythm; its booming, hyperactive orchestration; and, most important of all, its intensely dissonant harmony.

At this moment, the dual loyalties to which we alluded earlier—to symphonic conventions *and* to the extra-musical program—coalesce compellingly. The emotions that underlie Mahler's concern about the meaning of life leap to the surface, but they do so in the context of a masterful example of symphonic development. The developmental intensity is so powerful, as it often is when the development section nears its end, that it engenders a particularly potent need for the resolution that most often comes with the recapitulation.

Before that moment of resolution arrives, the music broadens (beginning at **00:18**), becoming heavy and ponderous. The texture grows simpler as the competing motives give way to increasing rhythmic uniformity, which permits some thematic material, like the triplet rhythm of O6, to be more readily discerned. A mighty excerpt from the primary theme (**P.2**) blares forth clearly in the trumpets and trombones (at **00:26**), followed by an emphatic return of the jagged rhythm (at **00:50**), and even more simplification of texture (at **00:58**). Notwithstanding the clarity of texture and our enhanced capacity to identify familiar thematic material, the music continues to sustain a high level of ferocity by way of its rhythmic intensity and sharply dissonant harmonies.

Finally, Mahler introduces a series of dissonances that are so excruciatingly harsh as to seem painful (at **01:10**). For the intensity of its harmonic asperity, there are few equivalents to this passage anywhere in the music of Mahler's day. The nature and extent of these unusually caustic dissonances seem somewhat baffling, given that the intensity of the passage in which they appear is already more than adequate to create an urgent need for resolution. The need for the recapitulation would be just as forceful without the series of acrid dissonances. When we can bear the burning sting of the dissonances no longer, at the very end of the passage a resolution takes place. We find ourselves back in C Minor, which sets the stage for the recapitulation that follows immediately. Although technically still part of the development, the dissonant passage is so remarkably prominent that it successfully competes with the recapitulation that follows for the listener's sense of which moment is the most privileged. (Normally, of course, as we have seen, the recapitulation is the most powerful musical event in a sonata form.)

An anecdote about the premiere of the Second Symphony illustrates just how successful this passage can be in commandeering the spotlight. The performance was attended by Wilhelm Kienzl, an Austrian composer who was a member of Richard Wagner's inner circle. He shared a box with two eminent musicians, the composer Richard Strauss (who sat to Kienzl's left) and the conductor Karl Muck (who sat to his right). As the dissonances were performed, Kienzl's companions reacted simultaneously. Strauss exclaimed enthusiastically that "there are no limits to the power of musical expression," while Muck grimaced in disgust, allowing a single word to escape his lips: "Hideous!" (*scheusslich*).[14] One can hold this passage in esteem or loathe it, but it cannot escape one's attention. It serves as a cardinal example of Mahler's extraordinary skill at endowing a passage with a most arresting sense of presence.

This passage offers a fearsome musical moment, whose frightful properties may be related to the Mickiewicz poem. The unusually caustic quality of these dissonances would seem altogether appropriate as a means of reflecting the irony, pain, and raw horror inherent in Gustav's reenactment of his suicide. Indeed, as Hefling points out, a musical relationship links the dissonant passage to the opening of Mahler's "Ich hab' ein glühend Messer," the last of the *Wayfarer Songs* that expresses the agony of lost love in suicidal terms ("I have a glowing knife in my breast"). The dissonances are introduced by an ascending triplet in the trumpet and trombone that, along with the first note to which they lead, outlines a dissonant harmony:

At the beginning of "Ich hab' ein glühend Messer," the same harmony is spelled out in a very similar rhythmic configuration:

<hr />

[14] Wilhelm Kienzl, *Meine Lebenswanderung: Erlebtes und Erschautes* (Stuttgart: Engelhorns, 1926), 143; cited in Stephen E. Hefling, "Zweite Symphonie," in Peter Revers and Oliver Korte, eds., *Gustav Mahler: Interpretationen seiner Werke* (Laaber: Laaber-Verlag, 2011), 1:222. A full English translation of Kienzl's account of this episode appears in Blaukopf, *Mahler*, 201.

Mahler seems to be referring to the text of his song to attach a suicidal topos to the dissonant passage, one that reinforces the relationship to the content of Mickiewicz's poem.[15] Stephen Hefling's case for linking this and other musical events in this movement to Mickiewicz's epic poetic drama seems very compelling. He identifies a series of anomalous musical events that are unusual enough to require explanation, which he convincingly finds in their linkage to events within Mickiewicz's narrative.

Would the average listener be aware of Mahler's reliance on the Mickiewicz poem? Surely not, because the literary source is too recondite to expect listeners to know of it. Then why did Mahler work so assiduously at coupling various musical oddities of this movement with specific literary themes in Mickiewicz's *Todtenfeier*? Reading that poem must have caused Mahler biting pain, for it contains elements that would have called to mind extremely disconsolate circumstances in the composer's life. The protagonist of the poem shares Mahler's given name. Like the Gustav of *Dziady*, Mahler had been seriously in love with a married woman, Marion von Weber, who would remain beyond his reach. Her given name happens to be a diminutive of Maria, the woman Gustav (the protagonist of the poem) loved and who rejected him for another man. Mahler's affair with Marion von Weber began in the same year Lipiner's translation of *Dziady* was published—a year before Mahler composed *Todtenfeier*. All these connections to events in Mahler's life are coincidental, of course, but they must have resonated powerfully with him, and he was distraught for years over the end of his affair with Marion von Weber.[16]

Thus, the musical reflections of events in Mickiewicz's poem in the first movement of the Mahler Second may be taken to be reverberations of some of Mahler's innermost feelings—about lost love and an ebbing confidence in the meaning of life. The musical allusions to *Dziady* may be too personal and cryptic to be identified by the listener, but the feelings that underlie them must have been so overpowering that Mahler could

[15] Stephen E. Hefling, "Mahler's 'Todtenfeier' and the Problem of Program Music," *19th Century Music*, 12 (1988): 34. The musical examples provided here simplify Hefling's examples to focus on the spelling out of the dissonance melodically.

[16] Morten Solvik and Stephen E. Hefling, "Natalie Bauer-Lechner on Mahler and Women: A Newly Discovered Document," *The Musical Quarterly*, 97 (2014): 24–28.

scarcely resist incorporating them in this movement. More importantly, the theme of Mickiewicz's poem centers on ideas that go to the heart of Mahler's agenda for the Second Symphony. The protagonist of Gustav's poem, after all, confronts death and contemplates life after death. If the principal existential question Mahler entertains in the Second Symphony centers on the meaning of life if it ultimately must lead to death, then what more powerful way is there to emblemize this question than with the topos of suicide?[17]

Recapitulation: Conventional Return and an Ominous Synopsis

The recapitulation seems, at least initially, to draw us back to purely musical concerns. Our pressing need for resolution of the high level of tension we experienced toward the end of the development is adroitly served by the recapitulation. The tonic key of C Minor returns for a faithful but telescoped reprise of the principal thematic material with which the movement began, along with one of the new themes first aired in the development {▶ Audio Ex. 3.18}.

Opening motives

Tremolando (O1)	00:00
Turning-note figure (O2)	00:03
Ascending scale (O3)	00:05
Jagged descent (O4)	00:06
Perfect fourth (O5)	00:09
Primary theme	
P.1	00:16
P.2	00:19
Triplets (O6)	00:25
Permutation of motives	00:27
Pk	01:11

---

[17] A very different approach to the relationship between Mickiewicz's *Dziady* (*Todtenfeier*) and what became the first movement of the Second Symphony may be read in Carolyn Abbate, *Unsung Voices: Opera and Musical Narrative in the Nineteenth Century* (Princeton, NJ: Princeton University Press, 1991), ch. 4, esp. 139–155.

T   01:24 Modulation to E Major (not remaining in C, as we would expect in a conventional sonata recapitulation).

S   01:39 The ubiquitous lyrical secondary theme returns—in its original key of E Major. (Normally, in the recapitulation, the modulation to a new key is disengaged, and the secondary material appears in the tonic.) Mahler's preoccupation with this gentle, lyrical melody continues.

N1   02:07 The theme Mahler called *Meeresstille* from Part One of the development, reappears and is presented in its entirety. It, too, is in E Major.

Modal inflection   03:17 The mode begins to shift back and forth from major to minor, and the section approaches an eerie close when the first violins play a very quiet tremolando on E♮ (at **03:25**). Then it shifts back to E♭, signaling an impending return to C Minor, as it fades almost to inaudibility. More than once, we observed that when Mahler's music seems poised on the verge of disappearing, the apparent dissolution is really a means of alerting us to the importance of what follows.

Closing synopsis   {▶ Audio Ex. 3.19} What comes next at this point in the recapitulation seems natural enough; it is the closing material, **K**, which fleshes out the traditional shape of an exposition or recapitulation: P–T–S–K. Why should Mahler want to lend special emphasis to this routine closing material by preceding it with one of his sections of near total disintegration? The importance Mahler attaches to this theme has little to do with its place in sonata form; rather, it is its role in Mahler's existential agenda that comes to the fore here.

This is the theme that is related, as we have seen, both to the enigmatically ominous introductory material in the First Symphony and to the Inferno motive from Liszt's *Dante Symphony*. Mahler assigns it a special role here by using it to introduce a synopsis of the diverse musical material that opened the movement. Earlier, we characterized this music as *agitated, angry, biting, edgy, fierce, high-strung,* and *jagged*. And we linked those musical qualities to a particularly overt expression of Mahler's extra-musical agenda: our encounter with the "dreadfully serious voice" that forces upon us confrontation with fundamental existential questions. Mahler gives pronounced emphasis to this music here, and to the extra-musical issues underlying it. Thus, the movement begins and ends with the same intense and introspective material.

These concluding moments of the first movement comprise more than a compendium of familiar musical motives; the thematic elements are woven into a complex musical texture, an elaborate web, in which many of the familiar musical elements are fragmented and presented simultaneously

{(▶) Audio Ex. 3.20}. Among these, we encounter the second half of the primary theme, the jagged rhythm, the descending fourth, the cascading upward scale, the turning-note figure, and the triplets. The intensity that results from both the fragmentation and simultaneous presentation of these motives endows this music with a greater sense of severity and emotional anxiety than the same musical figures projected at the beginning of the movement. As a result, the central existential question addressed in this movement takes on greater acuity as the movement draws to an end. Note also, at the start of this passage, eleven soft strokes on the tam-tam (reminiscent yet again of the chimes that marked off each hour in Mickiewicz's poem).

This closing section has a distinct shape: that of an arch. It begins softly and slowly, but its dynamic level, rhythmic complexity, and level of dissonance expand gradually, swelling more rapidly at **00:47**, and reaching a climax at **01:19**. Thereafter, nearly every aspect of the music recedes quickly, allowing the unusual sound of six soft strokes on the tam-tam, to reverberate again, beginning at **01:50**. (They appear at the same time as the descending-fourth motive is played in triplet rhythm by the timpani, and the sound of the tam-tam, therefore, is difficult to discern.) The music begins to recede even more at **02:12**. Suddenly, the orchestra enters forcefully once more with this line at **02:43** (Music Ex. 3.2).

Music Ex. 3.2. The concluding gesture of the first movement

Mahler gives the last word in the first movement to this simple, descending chromatic scale. The line exhibits a distinct similarity to the Inferno motive from Franz Liszt's *Dante Symphony* (Music Ex. 3.3). Thus, at the very end of the movement, the listener must confront a musical allusion to a particularly grim premise about the nature of death, the trials of the inferno. It transports us back yet again to the fearsome existential issues with which the movement began.

Music Ex. 3.3. The inferno motive from Franz Liszt's *Dante Symphony*

Mahler Suspends Work on the Second Symphony

Mahler worked fervently to complete this movement right after finishing the First Symphony, and he did so in relatively short order (six months). In this light, it seems puzzling that he stopped working on the Second Symphony after finishing the first movement, resuming the effort only five years later. At some point during this interval, he removed the words "Symphonie in C Moll" ("Symphony in C Minor") from the first page of the autograph and added the title *Todtenfeier*, which suggests that he redefined the movement as a free-standing composition. He left intact, however, the reference in the title to "1. Satz" ("first movement"). Mahler seems to have been undecided regarding whether the work would remain as the one-movement *Todtenfeier*, turn out to be a multi-movement symphony, or become a multi-movement tone poem. The need to find a way of resolving this uncertainty may have contributed to Mahler's temporary shelving of this major work.

Other matters of a practical and personal nature must have played a role in precipitating the long hiatus, including Mahler's mourning the death of his parents. His father died on February 17, 1889, and his mother on October 11 of the same year. His sister Leopoldine also died in 1889.[18] Still other distractions included the profound disappointment Mahler experienced over the poor reception accorded the First Symphony and the heavy demands on his time as director of the opera in Budapest.[19] And Bauer-Lechner attributes his difficulty in composing during these years to the depression he suffered after his relationship with Marion von Weber broke off.[20]

Another factor surely contributed to Mahler's long break in working on the symphony. It involves an incident rich in drama that took place late in that year. Mahler appears to have related it to his friend the Czech composer Josef Bohuslav Förster, who published an account of it. According to this narrative, Mahler approached Hans von Bülow (Fig. 3.2) to gain his impressions of the *Todtenfeier* movement.

Von Bülow was then the conductor of the Philharmonic Concerts in Hamburg and a seminal figure in the emergence of orchestral conducting as a discrete discipline. He was universally revered and just as widely feared. When Mahler and von Bülow met over this matter, Mahler assumed that

---

[18] Michael Kennedy, *Mahler* (Oxford: Oxford University Press, 1990), 34.

[19] Edward R. Reilly, "*Todtenfeier* and the Second Symphony," in Donald Mitchell and Andrew Nicholson, eds., *The Mahler Companion* (Oxford: Oxford University Press, 1999), 86.

[20] Solvik and Hefling, "Natalie Bauer-Lechner on Mahler and Women," 30.

Fig. 3.2. Hans von Bülow (1830–1894), a postcard published by Breitkopf & Härtel in Leipzig between 1880 and 1894

In the George Grantham Bain Collection of the Library of Congress

von Bülow would study the score, but von Bülow asked Mahler to play it at the piano. Mahler obliged. Looking up from the piano after a while, Mahler saw von Bülow with his hands clasped over his ears. When Mahler finished playing the movement, a deathly silence set in, followed by von Bülow's exclamation: "If what I have just heard is music, then I no longer understand anything about music."[21] Mahler wrote further of the incident to his friend

---

[21] The story of this encounter is related in La Grange, *Gustav Mahler: The Arduous Road to Vienna*, 470–471. La Grange draws upon the contemporary account of the incident reported by Mahler's

Fritz Löhr: "When I played my 'Todtenfeier' to him [von Bülow], he became quite hysterical with horror, declaring that compared with my piece [Wagner's] *Tristan* was a Haydn symphony."[22]

Like many musicians of the day, Mahler idolized von Bülow. In 1884, after hearing a performance by the Meiningen Court Orchestra under von Bülow's direction, Mahler wrote him an embarrassingly fawning letter, offering to leave his post at the Kassel Opera and serve him in any apprentice role he might deem possible.[23] Von Bülow's reaction to the *Todtenfeier* movement had to have left Mahler devastated. Mahler could deal with an excoriating review from a conservative critic of whose judgment he was dismissive, but this harsh rejection from an object of Mahler's unqualified esteem must have been extraordinarily painful.

Thus, a variety of factors accounts for the long hiatus in completing the Second Symphony, which was to go on for several years after the incident with von Bülow. Many of the causes that contributed to the delay are of a practical nature. As we reflect on his serious case of writer's block, however, we should not ignore the impact on Mahler of the crippling effects of von Bülow's annihilating criticism. Whatever the reasons for the long gap, it was not until 1893 that Mahler resumed work on the Second Symphony.

To gain an understanding of this movement, we have necessarily broken it into many small fragments. It needs to be reassembled so that the reader may appreciate its wholeness. It is vital that you encounter the movement in an uninterrupted presentation, and now is the ideal time to confront the music in this form. You will find an uninterrupted audio file of the first movement, along with light annotations, in Appendix 4A. Its presence in an appendix arises from my wish to keep the complete audio files of the various movements together and does not signify any diminishment in the importance of studying the movement intact.

---

friend, the composer Josef Bohuslav Förster. Förster's narrative appears in his wide-ranging memoire, *Der Pilger: Erinnerungen eines Musikers. Einleitende Studie von František Pala* (Prague: Artaria, 1955), 356–357.

[22] Knud Martner, ed., *Selected Letters of Gustav Mahler: The Original Edition Selected by Alma Mahler*, trans. Eithne Wilkins, Ernst Kaiser, and Bill Hopkins (New York: Farrar, Straus, Giroux, 1979), no. 99.

[23] An English translation of the letter appears in Blaukopf, *Mahler*, 170. In a move that can only have been motivated by a strain of gratuitous nastiness, von Bülow forwarded this letter, with callous disregard for its sensitive content, to the management of the Kassel opera, the employer Mahler was offering to leave for the apprenticeship to von Bülow he had proposed in his letter. The document is preserved in the archives of the Kassel Opera, in Mahler's personnel file.

4

The Second Movement

Mahler Returns to Composing Songs: *Des Knaben Wunderhorn*
(*Youth's Magical Horn*) •
Cognitive Fatigue • Two Themes Sketched Earlier
are Incorporated into a New Movement •
Theme One: One of the Melodies Conceived Five Years Earlier •
Theme Two: A Restless Theme in the Minor Mode (also from 1888) •
First Variation of Theme One: An Expressive Countermelody is Added •
First Variation of Theme Two: A Variation Becomes Developmental •
Second Variation of Theme One: A Climactic Moment •
Mahler's Misgivings about the Second Movement

*Before reading this chapter, you should avail yourself of the introduction to the
forms traditionally used for second movements of symphonies in Appendix 2.*

Mahler Returns to Composing Songs: *Des Knaben Wunderhorn* (*Youth's Magical Horn*)

Mahler put aside the Second Symphony in September 1888 and returned to
it five years later, in the summer of 1893. He may not have worked on the
Second Symphony during these years, but he did not set aside musical composition altogether. During this period, he returned to the composition of
songs, of which he had composed more than a dozen before 1887. A principal
source of poetry for them is of interest. In 1805, the first edition appeared of
a landmark collection of the verses of German folksongs purported to be of
medieval origin. It was coedited by the poet Clemens Brentano and the folk-
lorist and antiquarian Achim von Arnim. They entitled the anthology *Des
Knaben Wunderhorn* or *Youth's Magical Horn* (Fig. 4.1).

Brentano and von Arnim's editorial work in producing this anthology
was faulted on philological grounds. Not all the poetry they included is

Inside Mahler's Second Symphony:. Lawrence F. Bernstein, Oxford University Press. © Oxford University Press 2022.
DOI: 10.1093/oso/9780197575635.003.0004

Fig. 4.1. The title page of *Des Knaben Wunderhorn*
Wikipedia Photograph © H. P. Haack. Reproduced with the permission of the copyright holder

genuinely of medieval origin, and they took considerable liberties in "improving" some of the texts they selected. Nevertheless, *Des Knaben Wunderhorn* played a seminal role in fostering the great enthusiasm for folk poetry that arose within the literary traditions of German Romanticism. No less a figure than Johann Goethe—to whom the anthology was dedicated—maintained that no German home should be without its copy of this collection.

Mahler came across a copy in 1887 at the Leipzig residence of Karl and Marion von Weber.[1] It is thought that he composed some of his earliest songs set to poetry from *Des Knaben Wunderhorn* for their children, of whom he

---

[1] Henry-Louis de La Grange, *Gustav Mahler: The Arduous Road to Vienna (1860–1897)*, completed, rev., and ed. by Sybille Werner (Turnhout: Brepols, 2020), 328. Mahler visited the residence of Karl and Marion von Weber often in 1887 while he worked at completing an unfinished opera by Carl Maria von Weber, Karl's grandfather. He entered into a serious romantic relationship with Marion von Weber at the same time.

was especially fond.[2] He must have had access to the book earlier, however, because he modeled the poem he wrote for the first of his *Wayfarer Songs* (1884) on verses from two of the *Wunderhorn* poems.[3] Indeed, according to an interview Mahler gave in 1905, his earliest contact with this anthology goes back to the days of his childhood.[4] *Des Knaben Wunderhorn* provided the poetry for twenty-two of Mahler's songs, composed between 1887 and 1898. Some of the earlier songs were set only for voice and piano; the later ones were provided with orchestral accompaniment, too.

The years 1892 and 1893 saw a flurry of activity in Mahler's composition of *Wunderhorn* songs. This is significant for his resumption of work on the Second Symphony in the summer of 1893. Two of the *Wunderhorn* songs were to become part of the Second Symphony in the third and fourth movements, respectively. The second movement also relied on music that was conceived earlier. In January 1888, while Mahler was working fervently to complete the First Symphony, he sketched two themes that he would later incorporate in the second movement of the Second Symphony.[5]

Cognitive Fatigue

Try to recall your feelings as you listened while the first movement of this symphony came to an end. This twenty-one-minute voyage attained extraordinary levels of intensity. The blistering musical representation of Mahler's fervent existential concerns led us down a fiery and circuitous path, made even more treacherous by its frequent and unpredictable shifts in direction. An underlying road map, sonata form, was present. That was strong enough

---

[2] Stephen E. Hefling, "Zweite Symphonie," in Peter Revers and Oliver Korte, eds., *Gustav Mahler: Interpretationen seiner Werke* (Laaber: Laaber-Verlag, 2011), 1:213, quoting Alma Mahler and Natalie Bauer-Lechner.

[3] Jens Malte Fischer, *Mahler*, trans. Stewart Spencer (New Haven, CT: Yale University Press, 2011), 126–128.

[4] Alma Mahler, *Gustav Mahler: Memories and Letters*, ed. Donald Mitchell and Knud Martner, trans. Basil Creighton, 4th ed. (London: Sphere Books, 1969), 93.

[5] Natalie Bauer-Lechner, *Recollections of Gustav Mahler*, ed. Peter Franklin, trans. Dika Newlin (New York: Faber & Faber, 2013), 29; and Donald Mitchell, *Gustav Mahler: The Wunderhorn Years. Chronicles and Commentaries* (Woodbridge: Boydell Press, 2005), 166. The sketches are discussed in Hefling, "Zweite Symphonie," 1:237–238. The first of the two themes bears a slight resemblance to the melody of a Serenade in F Major by Robert Fuchs, Mahler's harmony teacher at the Vienna conservatory. See Rudolf Stephan, *Gustav Mahler: II. Symphonie c-moll*, Meisterwerke der Musik, 21 (Munich: Wilhelm Fink Verlag, 1979), 48 and Plate 3 (opp. p. 92).

to lend an essential shape to the movement, but the alterations to that conventional design were extensive and required us to struggle at sorting out the balance between adherence to the model and departure from it. Musical quotations from a wide range of sources appeared; the reasons for their presence, however, were not made explicit. As a result of these ambiguities, many questions remained unanswered at the end of the movement, denying us—even as the last notes sounded—the kind of closure we associate with the feelings of comfort that accompany complete resolution and understanding. Engaging seriously with a movement like this one is very hard work, and the range of feelings apt to surface at its end includes uncertainty, frustration at all the unanswered questions, and—perhaps most importantly—a withering sense of exhaustion.

We often experience a level of cognitive fatigue at the end of the first movement of a symphony. As symphonies proliferated during the eighteenth century, composers strove to expand their length, and, in doing so, they often tended to concentrate much of their energy on the first movement. Increasingly, they exploited within that movement the potential for complexity and dynamism that is inherent in sonata form. The complexity grew, as did the demands on the listeners' cognition. Leaving the listener enervated at the end of the first movement was not inherently undesirable, but heavy demands on the listeners' perceptive powers could not continue unabated in subsequent movements without running the risk of exhausting them and, as a result, losing their attention.

A conventional solution to this dilemma emerged during the evolution of symphonic form. At the onset of the second movement of a symphony, the composer often signals a fresh start by drawing sharp contrast with the opening movement. The symphony proceeds in a key other than that of the first movement and foregoes the robust rapid tempo of the preceding movement for a slower and more leisurely pace. This contrast is meant to signal the possibility of a departure from the complexity of the first movement. The composer goes on to render the movement more accessible by invoking a formal design that is much simpler—more transparent and more predictable—than that of the preceding movement.

Simplifying the form for the second movement depended on reducing in intensity, or avoiding altogether, some of the most dynamic features of sonata form like the transition and development. The rationale for sharply reducing complexity and tension in the second movement might be characterized as a reward of sorts for the listener: "You worked so hard in trying to absorb and understand the first movement," the composers seem to be saying, "now, just relax, and enjoy a more accessible kind of music." Several formal paradigms were applied to second movements to achieve the desired move toward greater simplicity. These included abridged sonata form, theme and variations, and alternating variation form; the latter is a design invented and used almost exclusively by Joseph Haydn. If you already familiarized yourself with Appendix 2, you will have encountered an introduction to these formal designs.

Two Themes Sketched Earlier are Incorporated into a New Movement

In late June 1893, Mahler turned to two melodies he sketched in 1888 and began to expand them into a full movement—the second movement of the Second Symphony.[6] He was able to complete this movement in only one week. Its tempo marking is *Andante moderato*, equivalent, roughly, to the pace of a slow walk. Mahler adds another performance direction: *Sehr gemächlich*, "very leisurely." The relaxed character of this music serves the very traditional role in the multi-movement symphonic cycle of providing vivid contrast with the first movement. The second movement is in a different key, and its nature is altogether different from that of the first movement, much of it reflecting a gentle, dance-like character. This movement focuses the listener's attention on transparent and relatively simple melodies. For its form, it depends on one of the variation designs favored for the more relaxed second movement, Haydn's alternating variation form. The recipe for this structural template calls for the following: two themes appear; they are in the same key, but in opposing modes; they are presented and varied alternately; and each of the themes and variations comprises a discrete section. The shape of Mahler's second movement may be outlined in the following schema (where superscript numbers indicate the presence of a variation):

$$A - B - A^1 - B^1 - A^2$$

---

[6] See the sources cited in the preceding note.

Theme One: One of the Melodies Conceived
Five Years Earlier

The first theme—one of the two Mahler originally sketched in 1888—is a placid, dance-like melody in triple meter and in the key of A♭ Major {▶ Audio Ex. 4.1}. It captures the feeling of a *Ländler* but is more delicate in character than are many examples of this dance type. Mahler marks the string lines *grazioso*, which calls for an elegant, flowing style of performance. The lines project a stylized character that is enhanced significantly by the ornaments that frequently adorn them. These include grace notes (quick notes, played lightly to introduce and embellish a main note) and *glissandi* (sliding gestures, often executed on string instruments by sliding a finger along the fingerboard to connect one note to another). Mahler introduces frequent changes in dynamics (loudness or softness) and articulation (the degree of incisiveness with which notes are attacked). At the very end of the theme (01:27), a French horn and harp enter, repeating a single note that will help Theme One to elide smoothly into Theme Two.

The fluid nature of this melody is one of its most important features. Bauer-Lechner attributes to Mahler a comment in which he described how it "pours forth in a full, broad stream [to create] one broad sweep."[7] She goes on to perceive in this flowing melodic style the influence of Franz Schubert, among the greatest song writers of the romantic period.[8]

Theme Two: A Restless Theme in the Minor Mode
(also from 1888)

As we have seen, Theme One is in A♭ Major. Mahler wants to keep the same tonic in Theme Two, while switching to the minor mode {▶ Audio Ex. 4.2}. This "monotonal" approach is a standard feature of alternating variation form. He does this, but he writes the second theme in G♯ Minor. (G♯ is just another way of writing A♭, but G♯ Minor can be notated more simply than A♭ Minor.) The E♭ (the same note as D♯) sounded by the harp and French horn at the end of Theme One and the beginning of Theme Two is of equal

---

[7] Bauer-Lechner, *Recollections of Gustav Mahler*, 29.

[8] This appears in Natalie Bauer-Lechner, "Aus einem Tagebuch über Mahler," *Der Merker*, 3, no. 5 (1912): 184; cited in Hefling, "Zweite Symphonie," 1:240.

importance to both themes. It is the dominant, a tone, along with the harmony based on it, that often signals and demands the forthcoming appearance of the tonic. That is why the focus on this note facilitates so smooth a transition between Theme One and Theme Two. The French horn continues to emphasize this dominant at the beginning of the second theme, repeating it many times.

₁Although the two themes share the same tonic, they are in different modes, which also accords with the protocols of alternating variation form. Still more contrast distinguishes the two themes. Theme Two replaces the calm balance of the first theme with a pervasive restlessness. This commences with the introduction of a nervous figure in relentless triplets right after the repeated notes begin in the French horn {⊙ Audio Ex. 4.2}. Both the repeated notes and triplets continue, after which a listless melody is introduced. It is played first by a flute (**00:10**), then taken over by a clarinet (**00:14**). The melody loses ground almost immediately as the triplets prevail in a thick string texture (**00:18**). Clarinets reintroduce the melody (**00:50**), and a fuller orchestra switches briefly to the major mode (**00:58**), but the continuing, determined triplet figure gains prominence again (**01:10**) until it begins to come apart (**01:16**). First, it is reduced to a three-note returning-note figure that moves back and forth between the upper and lower strings. Ultimately, that figure is further reduced to a single note (**01:27**). It is the same tone ($D\sharp = E\flat$) that provided the elision between the first theme and this one, and its function here will be to provide a similar pivot to the first variation.

First Variation of Theme One: An Expressive Countermelody is Added

After the jittery restlessness of the G♯ Minor theme, we welcome the return to the balanced serenity of Theme One {⊙ Audio Ex. 4.3}. The section begins with isolated repetitions of the transitional E♭, which then turn into a harbinger of the reappearance of Theme One by taking on its opening rhythm (**00:06**). The theme itself returns soon thereafter (**00:13**), but it is not alone. A wonderfully expressive countermelody in the violincellos joins the theme. Theme One and the new violoncello line fit together suavely. The new melody commands our attention, but not at the expense of diminishing our sense of the presence of Theme One. Theme and countermelody continue in this symbiotic relationship throughout the rest of the variation.

Theme One is presented intact. What makes this section a variation—besides the important addition of the countermelody—is the recasting of the original melody in a much higher range. It is projected more luminously as a result, which is one reason it can "compete" so successfully with the new and very conspicuous countermelody in the violoncellos. At the end of the passage (01:24), the music begins to trail off, ending eventually on E♭, the note used to connect all the individual sections so far. The theme and this variation are nearly the same in length.

The violoncello countermelody in this variation appears to have stimulated the expressive impulses of some musicians at one early performance. Describing the approach of the violoncellists to this passage at the Vienna performance of the Second Symphony that took place in April 1899, Bauer-Lechner suggests that "Mahler wanted them to play quietly, restrainedly, and without 'sentimental indulgence,' [but they] could not be held in check at the performance, so irresistibly were they carried away [by this melody]."[9] Bruno Walter appears to have reined in the violoncellists in our recording of this passage more effectively than Mahler is said to have done at the Vienna performance of 1899. Quiet restraint is often a cornerstone of Walter's interpretations, and that is precisely the way in which the violoncellists perform here. The result is that their elegant countermelody blends perfectly with Theme One, neither challenging it nor detracting from it.

First Variation of Theme Two: A Variation Becomes Developmental

From its blustery onset we suspect immediately that this will turn out to be more than a simple variation {▶ Audio Ex. 4.4}. The orchestra expands suddenly to a full complement of winds and strings, with the nervous triplet figure that appeared early in Theme Two converted now into a forceful gesture, played *fff*, mainly in the strings. The listless melody that followed in Theme Two is now blared out stridently by six French horns (00:05). These are major changes to the character of Theme Two, which now reflects a much higher level of energy than it originally displayed. Indeed, Mahler's performance direction for this passage is *Energisch bewegt*, "moving energetically." Energy and change are among the standard features of symphonic

[9] Bauer-Lechner, *Recollections of Gustav Mahler*, 126.

development, and that seems to be the stamp that Mahler wants to imprint on this variation. In a symphonic development, such intensity and mutability generate a need for resolution in a return to something simpler, more familiar, and more predictable. That is precisely the objective in this section of the second movement.

This variation breaks out of the boundaries of a conventional variation in several ways beyond those already cited. It is longer than Theme Two by a factor of nearly two-thirds. Unlike the theme, which remained in G♯ Minor throughout, this variation is tonally active. It begins to modulate (**00:13**) and then breaks down the once listless melody into separate motives, but it does so this time in D♯ Minor (**00:28**). Fragments of the melody continue to be juxtaposed to the running triplets, and another modulation begins (at **00:48**), which culminates in a return to G♯ Minor (**01:05**). In a surprising move, the music touches on A♭ Major (**01:28**). After a while, this turns into a passage of more highly anticipatory music (**01:44**). Eventually, the process of disintegration that marked the end of Theme Two sets in again (**02:09**), but more extensively and more forcefully than before.

This section of the second movement does serve as a variation, but its developmental properties are of paramount importance. Its length, intensity, changes to the melodic material, modulations, and heightened anticipatory power all generate a strong need for a return to music cast in the more accessible manner of Theme One.

Second Variation of Theme One: A Climactic Moment

As we suggested, the developmental energy of the preceding section is intense enough to demand resolution in a musical event of consequence. What appears in the wake of the developmental variation on Theme Two turns out, in fact, to be the culminating section of the movement {▶ Audio Ex. 4.5}. It embodies the steady balance we noted in Theme One, but the highly engaging manner in which Mahler varies this material is exceptional to a degree that seems to vindicate the high expectations for a moment of importance that were brought on by the tense and anticipatory developmental character of the variation on Theme Two.

Like every other section of this movement, this variation begins with repeated E♭s, played this time by the second violin. As was so in the first variation of Theme One, these repeated notes assume the rhythm of the melody being varied (**00:06**). An important distinction immediately sets in: the violins do not bow this music but, rather, play it *pizzicato*, which is accomplished by plucking the stings, as one would when playing a guitar.[10] At first, this does not seem particularly unusual; *pizzicato*, after all, is called for frequently. As more and more string instruments enter, however, we become aware of a unique and particularly rich sonority (beginning at **00:12**). Normally, the string section of a symphony orchestra provides five separate lines of music: first and second violins, violas, violoncellos, and string basses. Here, Mahler has divided the strings so that they provide nine discrete lines of music. The *pizzicato* playing, therefore, becomes part of a particularly lush string texture.

Mahler's orchestration continues down this innovative path (**00:17**), as the plucked strings of the harp enhance further the richness of the *pizzicato* sound. A flute and piccolo come in at the same time, their crisp and light articulation offering a remarkable simulation for woodwinds of the *pizzicato* sound of the strings. This passage provides an experience that is delectable for the sheer ingenuity of the orchestral sonority. It also wraps the music of Theme One in a cloak of delicate intimacy. Together, these features mark this variation as something quite special—a worthy successor to the high levels of anticipation that preceded it and an appropriately singular note on which to end the movement.

The *pizzicato* continues until the music of Theme One is stated fully, at which point (**01:04**), the string players begin to take up their bows again. The first to do so are two groups of first violins. They play something familiar: the expressive countermelody that appeared in the violoncellos in the first variation of Theme One. This time, Mahler enriches the countermelody with a fuller measure of lyricism, allowing it to soar above the orchestra in a high register and encouraging the lyrical impulses of the first violinists who play this line by marking their part *sehr gesangsvoll*, "very songful."

The elegant fit between this countermelody and Theme One that Mahler introduced in the first variation on that theme is preserved here, too. The music of Theme One is played along with the countermelody—this time, by a full complement of woodwind instruments. In the first variation, Mahler

---

[10] Early-on (before performance decisions were finalized in the printed score), Mahler suggested that the violinists and violists hold their instruments at this point as one would hold a guitar and pluck the strings gently with the thumb. See Gustav Mahler, *Symphonie Nr. 2*, ed. Renate Stark-Voit and Gilbert Kaplan, Gustav Mahler: Neue kritische Gesamtausgabe, 2 vols. (Vienna: Universal Edition and the Kaplan Foundation, 2010), Partitur, 107.

struck a perfect balance between Theme One and the countermelody in the context of a relatively subdued string orchestra. Here, we continue to be able to focus equally on both the theme and the countermelody, but in a greatly expanded orchestral texture. That augmentation in the orchestral sound helps to endow this variation with a climactic sense.

Theme One and its countermelody are played in full, after which (beginning at **02:16**), Mahler concludes the movement with a brief closing section. It is a model of airiness and understatement. At first, a brief motive, consisting in a turning-note figure followed by a downward leap is tossed back and forth between two groups of violins, all of whom play very softly (*PPP*). At the end of this passage (**02:33**), the first violin plays a slow ascending scale that culminates in a high A♭ (the tonic), played even more softly (*PPPP*). The arrival on the tonic is coordinated with the rolling out of an A♭ Major chord in the harp (**02:38**). Brief and subdued references to the opening motive of Theme One follow (beginning at **02:40**), and the movement then draws to a close with two leisurely chords (beginning at **03:05**), played *pizzicato* in the strings. Mahler ends this movement on a note of matchless intimacy.

In fashioning this movement, Mahler brought about a wonderful synthesis of two markedly different musical influences: the highly fluid quality of the Schubertian melody he fashioned for the first theme and the structural design of Haydn's alternating variation form, which, in its strict emphasis on pervasive segmentation, seems to offer the very antithesis of fluidity. Mahler adheres very closely to Haydn's protocols for alternating variation form. His movement is laid out almost entirely in one key; it presents and alternates consistently its themes and their variations in opposing modes; and the sectional divisions of the piece are regular and strong. In bringing about the synthesis of melody and form, however, Mahler allows the Schubertian character of the flowing melody to prevail over the more rigid regularity of Haydn's alternating variation form.

How did Mahler know Haydn's alternating variation form? His interest in conducting Haydn's symphonies appears to have begun in 1891 with a performance in Lübeck of Symphony H. I:101, the "Clock" Symphony. All told, he went on to direct five of them.[11] One of these—Symphony H. I:103, "The Drumroll"—offers in its second movement a textbook example of alternating variation form. Admittedly, the first known performance Mahler conducted of this work was in 1900, seven years after he composed the second movement

---

[11] Knud Martner, *Mahler's Concerts* (New York: Overlook Press, 2010), 79ff.

of our symphony, but this work was then among Haydn's most celebrated symphonies,[12] and it seems unimaginable that Mahler would not have been acquainted with it even in the years before he is known to have conducted it.

Mahler's Misgivings about the Second Movement

After a very brief burst of self-confidence with respect to this Andante, Mahler began to grow increasingly unhappy with it.[13] He agonized endlessly over the movement, beginning with a deep-rooted ambivalence that emerged right after he completed it during the summer of 1893. Bauer-Lechner quotes Mahler's reaction to the movement at that time:

> Of course, God alone knows whether my movement will turn out to be as good as I believe it to be at the moment. While I was working on it, with everything coming straight from the heart, it showed every sign of turning into something altogether new and much improved—although I admittedly fell back again to being dissatisfied afterwards, and was stricken with agonies to think that I might still not have succeeded in the way that I had hoped.[14]

Over the years, Mahler's reservations about the second movement grew more intense, as he worried that its tone set it apart too vividly from that of the first movement. At the time of the Vienna performance of the Second Symphony in 1899, Bauer-Lechner attributes the following reservation to Mahler:

> One mistake in the C Minor Symphony is the excessively sharp (hence inartistic) contrast between the Andante, with its cheerful dance rhythm, and

---

[12] The "Drumroll" Symphony appeared in numerous editions and in many arrangements for chamber ensembles. As evidence of the attention this symphony gained among composers in the nineteenth century, consider that, in 1831, Richard Wagner sent his arrangement of it for piano four hands to the publishing firm of Breitkopf & Härtel. The arrangement was never published, however, and is lost. See John Deathridge, Martin Geck, and Egon Voss, *Wagner. Werk-Verzeichnis (WWV): Verzeichnis der musikalischen Werke Richard Wagners und iherer Quellen* (Mainz: Schott, 1986), 76 (WWV 18).

[13] This is not the first time Mahler had second thoughts about the slow movement of a symphony; he demonstrated a prolonged ambivalence about the *Blumine* movement of the First Symphony, ultimately deciding to excise it altogether.

[14] Bauer-Lechner, *Recollections of Gustav Mahler*, 29, 231.

the first movement. It is because I originally planned both movements independently, without a thought of integrating them.[15]

In a letter dated March 25, 1903, to the conductor, Julius Buths, who was to direct the Second Symphony in Düsseldorf on April 2, Mahler amplified this negative assessment, assuming a tone of even harsher self-criticism:

[T]he second movement does *not* have the effect of a *contrast*, but simply of a discrepancy after the first. This is my fault, not inadequate appreciation on the listener's part. Perhaps you have already felt this after rehearsing the two movements consecutively. The andante was composed as a kind of *intermezzo* (as the echo of *long* past days in the life of the man borne to his grave in the first movement—"when the sun still smiled on him").[16]

There is no sign that Mahler's misgivings about this movement abated over the years. Indeed, his concerns could only have sharpened after the Paris performance of the symphony in 1910, when he learned from his wife, Alma, that Claude Debussy and Paul Dukas left the performance during the second movement. Afterwards, they explained that it was too "Schubertian" for them. This characterization suggests that they grasped the nature of the melodic style of Theme One. Their concerns about the movement, in general, however, seem to have had more to do with its failure to adhere to an adequately modernist agenda than with any of the reservations Mahler voiced.[17]

Notwithstanding Mahler's qualms about the second movement, many early listeners liked it. The audience applauded the second movement warmly when it was performed in Berlin on April 4, 1895, at a preview of three movements of the symphony.[18] Similar approval of the second movement was registered by the audiences at the performances in Vienna (1899)[19] and Munich (1900).[20]

Positive reaction to the second movement came from a fellow composer, too. Ernest Bloch attended the performance of the Mahler Second in Basel

[15] Bauer-Lechner, *Recollections of Gustav Mahler*, 127.
[16] Knud Martner, ed., *Selected Letters of Gustav Mahler: The Original Edition Selected by Alma Mahler*, trans. Eithne Wilkins, Ernst Kaiser, and Bill Hopkins (New York: Farrar, Straus, Giroux, 1979), no. 297.
[17] Alma Mahler: *Gustav Mahler*, 169–170.
[18] La Grange, *Gustav Mahler: The Arduous Road to Vienna*, 608.
[19] Bauer-Lechner, *Recollections of Gustav Mahler*, 126.
[20] Henry-Louis de La Grange, *Gustav Mahler, Volume 2, Vienna: The Years of Challenge (1897–1904)* (New York: Oxford University Press, 1995), 301.

in June 1903 and offered a review essay about it in *Le Courrier musical*. He praised the second movement for its charming naïveté and for transporting the listener into "another world, a world of dreams, tranquility, and sweetness, [providing] a delicate melody [that is] revisited in variations."[21]

Mahler is, of course, entitled to his reservations about the Andante. Nonetheless, it does seem somewhat perplexing that he should have been so deeply troubled over a movement that simply adhered to the normative conventions for a second movement and that had met with widespread approval in performance. His misgivings seem very intense. In his letter to Julius Buths, for example, he goes so far as to characterize himself as blameworthy. The discrepant nature of the movement, he suggests, "is *my fault*"; he sounds guilt-ridden about his perceived missteps in this movement. Why? Several possible reasons for the magnitude of his concerns come to mind.

First, as we have seen, Mahler's need to support himself by conducting left him relatively little time to compose and forced to cram all his compositional activity into the few summer months when the opera was closed. His predilection to incorporate previously composed music in new works—like the melodies he used for the two themes in the movement under discussion—may sometimes have resulted from an expedient way to work around the shortness of time available for composition. Usually, Mahler skillfully integrates the pre-composed material into the new work. Relying on pre-existent material in this way, however, may not always have been his first choice. Thus, sensing what he perceived to be a substantial disparity in tone between the first and second movements of the Second Symphony may have conjured up for Mahler a host of misgivings about ways in which he might have kept the light tone of a traditional second movement and still made it a better match to the first movement. "If only I had had more time to work on this problem," he may have rued.

Second, Mahler struggled intensely over the balance he achieved in his music between purely musical decisions and compositional choices that arose from an extra-musical agenda. A concern about this surfaces in his letter to Julius Buths, in which he characterizes the second movement as "the echo of *long* past days in the life of the man borne to his grave in the first movement—'when the sun still smiled on him.'" This morsel of programmatic

---

description seems altogether forced in the context of a simple movement in alternating variation form, which shows little, if any, sign of programmatic intent. It may have come about because of an overwrought sense of obligation on Mahler's part to link every movement of the Second Symphony to the extra-musical agenda he set forth in the opening movement. Does the extra-musical agenda have to be operative all the time? The first movement, as we have seen, suggests otherwise. Mahler bases some of the compositional strategies in that movement on his existential agenda, others, on purely musical requirements. Thus, a measure of the intensity of his dissatisfaction with the second movement may be linked to this somewhat inflexible sense of obligation to reflect the programmatic agenda in every movement.

Mahler struggled, early on, to ameliorate the problems he perceived in the juxtaposition of the first and second movements. His first solution was to exchange the positions of the second and third movements. (Placing the scherzo second, moreover, would offer yet another way in which to emulate the design of Beethoven's Ninth Symphony.) When he completed the manuscript of the second movement, a few weeks after he finished the scherzo, he numbered the Andante "4." Presumably, he entertained the possibility that the scherzo would serve as the second movement, to be followed by "Urlicht" (what is now the fourth movement), or something else, and only then would the Andante be played, directly before the finale. The present order of the movements was established in time for the premiere of the first three movements in March 1895.[22] In the end, in a prescription that seems the musical equivalent of serving sorbet as a palette cleanser between courses, Mahler mandated that a pause of at least five minutes should separate the second movement from the first. Conductors rarely, if ever, observe this direction for the full five minutes.

At this point, the reader should listen to the second movement uninterrupted. A complete performance (with light annotations) appears in Appendix 4B.

---

[22] Mahler, *Symphonie Nr. 2*, ed. Renate Stark-Voit and Gilbert Kaplan, Textband, 94.

5

A Song Serves as a Study for the Third Movement

A Frenzy of Compositional Activity •
The Legend of St. Anthony Preaching to the Fish •
Mahler Seeks to Realize the Spirit and Essence of the St. Anthony Poem •
Mahler Considers the Form of his Poem • The Critical Role of the Piano

A Frenzy of Compositional Activity

Turning our attention to the third movement of the Second Symphony, we focus on the summer of 1893 and the period of feverish creative work that accompanied Mahler's return to work on the Second Symphony after a hiatus of five years. Mahler was First Conductor of the opera at Hamburg in 1893, and the intense pressures of that position made it more necessary than ever for him to take full advantage of the summer months to compose. In June of that year, Mahler escaped to Steinbach, a small, bucolic village on the Attersee, the largest lake in Upper Austria that lies within the borders of the country. There he rented five rooms in a rustic inn at the water's edge. He arrived there with an entourage that included several of his siblings and Natalie Bauer-Lechner. One of the rooms was outfitted by the Bösendorfer Company with a baby grand piano, and it became Mahler's study.[1] Everything about this venue—the privacy it afforded, the barrier it provided from the pressures of work, the arcadian setting, and the presence of family and of his trusted confidante Bauer-Lechner—seemed to advance the cause of Mahler's creative work.[2] Not only did he finish several songs on texts from *Des Knaben*

---

[1] Kurt Blaukopf with contributions by Zoltan Roman, *Mahler: A Documentary Study*, trans. Paul Baker et al. (London: Thames and Hudson, 1976), 196, citing Alfred Rosé, "Intimes aus Gustav Mahlers Sturm- und Drangperiode," *Neues Wiener Journal*, August 19, 1928.

[2] Henry-Louis de La Grange, *Gustav Mahler: The Arduous Road to Vienna (1860–1897)*, completed, rev., and ed. by Sybille Werner (Turnhout: Brepols, 2020), 524–525.

Inside Mahler's Second Symphony:. Lawrence F. Bernstein, Oxford University Press. © Oxford University Press 2022.
DOI: 10.1093/oso/9780197575635.003.0005

Wunderhorn and the second movement of the symphony, but he completed the third movement, too, orchestrated what would eventually become the fourth movement, and at least gave thought to the all-important finale.

As we learned in Chapter 1, the line that generally separates song from symphony was often drawn indistinctly by Mahler: two songs from his *Lieder eines fahrenden Gesellen* (*Songs of a Wayfarer*), we discovered, found their way into the First Symphony. This fusion of genres carries over into the Second Symphony, in which two *Wunderhorn* songs were used in the third and fourth movements, respectively. The third movement, a scherzo and trio, incorporates the *Wunderhorn* song "Des Antonius von Padua Fischpredigt" ("St. Anthony of Padua Preaches to the Fish") in the scherzo; the trio was newly composed. In the scherzo, Mahler brings into the symphony the music of the song, but not its words. A second *Wunderhorn* song, "Urlicht" ("Primeval Light"), on the other hand, is sung by a contralto soloist in the fourth movement. Thus, during a remarkably short time, from the end of June till the beginning of August, Mahler worked simultaneously on different versions of these *Wunderhorn* songs—with piano or orchestral accompaniment—and on the second, third, and fourth movements of the symphony.

The chronology of Mahler's work during these weeks demonstrates vividly how closely dovetailed the songs and symphonic movements were in his conception and throughout the course of his composition of these movements of the Second Symphony. It also offers a valuable glimpse into how Mahler, so desperate for time to compose, was compelled to make the most efficient use of the summer months:

ca. June 21, 1893	Sketch for the second movement completed
July 8, 1893	Version of the St. Anthony song with piano accompaniment completed
July 16, 1893	Orchestral score of the scherzo completed
July 19, 1893	First orchestration of "Urlicht" completed
July 30, 1893	Second movement completed
August 1, 1893	Orchestral version of the St. Anthony song completed[3]

[3] Donald Mitchell, *Gustav Mahler: The Wunderhorn Years. Chronicles and Commentaries* (Woodbridge: Boydell Press, 2005), 171, 184.

The interdependence of the songs and symphonic movements Mahler composed during those frenzied weeks in 1893 and the intermingling of preexistent and new material call to mind one the principles of musical composition he espoused early-on: "Composing is like playing with bricks, continually making new buildings from the same old stones."[4] The starting point for the third movement of the symphony is the version of the St. Anthony song for voice and piano (which Mahler may have begun as early as 1892). In the manuscript, Mahler made note that it was intended as a "preliminary study" for the scherzo of the Second Symphony.[5]

The Legend of St. Anthony Preaching to the Fish

The song Mahler integrates into the scherzo of the Second Symphony relates a story about St. Anthony of Padua (1195–1231), a Portuguese-born Franciscan friar and the most celebrated follower of St. Francis of Assisi. What is it about the narrative related in this song that led Mahler to make it a part of the Second Symphony? The tale is a very old one, going back, at least, to the end of the fourteenth century, when it appeared in the *Fioretti* [Little Flowers] *di San Francesco*, a small anthology of stories about the life of St. Francis of Assisi.

In this version of the tale, St. Anthony comes to Rimini to preach to the many heretics who lived there. When they shun his sermon, St. Anthony goes down to the river's bank and preaches to the fish, who turn out in droves to hear him, and who accept his homily enthusiastically. Witnessing this miracle, the townsfolk of Rimini, including the heretics, throw themselves at St. Anthony's feet to hear and accept his exhortation.[6] A portrayal of this story on painted tiles may be seen in the Sé Cathedral in Lisbon, the city of which Anthony was the patron saint (Fig. 5.1). The cathedral is situated just a few blocks from St. Anthony's birthplace.[7]

---

[4] Natalie Bauer-Lechner, *Recollections of Gustav Mahler*, ed. Peter Franklin, trans. Dika Newlin (New York: Faber and Faber, 2013), 131.

[5] Mitchell, *Gustav Mahler*, 251, n. 19.

[6] For the entire story, as it is related in the *Fioretti* of St. Francis, see *The Little Flowers of Saint Francis of Assisi, First English Translation*, rev. and emended by Dom Roger Hudleston, intro. by Arthur Livingston (New York: The Heritage Press, 1965), chap. 40, available at: https://ccel.org/ccel/ugolino/flowers/flowers.i.html.

[7] Elizabeth Abbate suggests that Mahler might have known a particular painting on the theme of St. Anthony preaching to the fish, the portrayal by Arnold Böcklin (1892) now in the Kunsthaus in Zürich. See Elizabeth T. Abbate, "Myth, Symbol, and Meaning in Mahler's Early Symphonies" (Ph.D. diss., Harvard University, 1996), 119. For a reproduction of this painting, consult the

Fig. 5.1. *St. Anthony Preaching to the Fish.* Painting on tile in the Sé Cathedral in Lisbon

Zoomar GmbH / Alamy Stock Photo

Mahler set to music the version of the story from *Des Knaben Wunderhorn*. When we first introduced this collection of German folk poetry (in Chapter 4), we alluded to the widely censured practice in which its compilers (Clemens Brentano and Achim von Arnim) engaged: emending and "improving" some of the texts they included in the anthology. Their version of "St. Anthony Preaching to the Fish" is among the texts they altered freely. They acknowledge having based their version of the poem on one in a multi-volume didactic treatise by Johann Urlich Megerle, known as Abraham a Sancta Clara (1644–1709), a preacher at the court of the Holy Roman Emperor, Leopold I.[8] Brentano and von Arnim omitted two stanzas from the St. Anthony poem as it was published by Megerle, and they invented some new ones. In the first and last two stanzas of the poem, the editors fashioned their own poetry out of Megerle's introductory and closing remarks about the

website of the Mahler Foundation: https://mahlerfoundation.org/mahler/personen-2/arnold-bocklin-1827-1901.

[8] Megerle's work, entitled *Judas der Erzschelm* (*Judas the Arch-Rogue*), was published in Salzburg between 1686 and 1695 and reprinted several times thereafter.

poem.[9] Mahler's setting of the poem generally follows the reading in *Des Knaben Wunderhorn* with a few changes, mainly omissions (set off within square brackets in the following transcription of the poem, and to be addressed below). Here is the poem as it appears in *Des Knaben Wunderhorn*.[10]

1	Antonius zur Predig	St. Anthony, about to preach,
	Die Kirche findt ledig,	finds the church empty.
	Er geht zu den Flüssen,	He goes to the rivers
	Und predigt den Fischen.	and preaches to the fish.
2	Sie schlagen mit den Schwänzen,	They beat with their tails,
	Im Sonnenschein glänzen.	glistening in the sunshine.
3	Die Karpfen mit Rogen	The carp with roe
	Sind all hieher zogen,	all came near,
	Haben d' Mäuler aufrissen,	their mouths agape,
	Sich Zuhörens beflissen.	to become his attentive listeners.
4	Kein Predig niemalen	No sermon ever
	den Karpen so gfallen.	pleased the carp so much.
5	Spitzgoschete Hechte,	Pointy-nosed pike,
	Die immerzu fechten,	who are constantly fencing,
	Sind eilend herschwommen,	swam up quickly
	Zu hören den Frommen.	to hear the devout one.
6	[Kein Predig niemalen	[No sermon ever
	Den Hechten so gfallen.]	pleased the pike so much.]
7	Auch jene Phantasten	Also, those dreamers
	So immer beim fasten,	who are constantly fasting—
	Die Stockfisch ich meine,	I mean the dried cod—
	Zur Predig erscheinen.	appear for the sermon.

[9] Jon W. Finson, "The Reception of Gustav Mahler's *Wunderhorn* Lieder," *The Journal of Musicology*, 5 (1987): 97–100.

[10] The German text generally follows the authoritative modern edition: Heinz Rölleke, ed., *Des Knaben Wunderhorn: Alte deutsche Lieder gesammelt von Achim von Arnim und Clemens Brentano* (Frankfurt am Main and Leipzig: Insel Verlag, 2007), 326–328.

8   Kein Predig niemalen
     Den Stockfisch so gfallen.

     No sermon ever
     pleased the cod so much.

9   Gut Aalen und Hausen
     Die Vornehme schmausen,
     Die selber sich bequemen,
     Die Predig vernehmen.

     Fine eels and sturgeons,
     on which aristocrats feast,
     who relax
     to hear the sermon.

10   [Kein Predig niemalen
     den Aalen so gfallen.]

     [No sermon ever
     pleased the eels so much.]

11   Auch Krebsen, Schildkroten,
     Sonst langsame Boten,
     Steigen eilend vom Grund,
     Zu hören diesen Mund.

     Also crabs and turtles,
     usually slow couriers,
     climb hastily from the deep,
     to hear this voice.

12   Kein Predig niemalen
     den Krebsen so gfallen.

     No sermon ever
     pleased the crabs so much.

13   Fisch große, Fisch kleine,
     Vornehm' und gemeine
     Erheben die Köpfe
     Wie verständge Geschöpfe.

     Big fish, little fish,
     aristocratic and common,
     raise their heads
     like sentient creatures.

14   Auf Gottes Begehren
     Die Predig / [Antonium]
         anhören.

     At God's bidding
     they listen to the sermon /
         [St. Anthony].

15   Die Predigt geendet,
     Ein jedes sich wendet,
     die Hechte bleiben Diebe,
     Die Aale viel lieben.

     With the sermon at an end,
     each one turns away;
     the pikes remain thieves,
     the eels make love a lot.

16   Die Predig hat gfallen.
     Sie bleiben wie alle.

     Though the sermon pleased them,
     they remain as they were.

17   Die Krebs gehn zurücke,
     Die Stockfisch bleiben dicke,

     The crabs walk backwards;
     the cod stay fat;

| Die Karpfen viel fressen, | the carp stuff themselves; |
| Die Predig vergessen. | the sermon is forgotten. |

| **18** Die Predig hat gfallen. | Though the sermon pleased them, |
| Sie bleiben wie alle. | they remain as they were. |

The differences between the St. Anthony story in the *Fioretti* of St. Francis and that of *Des Knaben Wunderhorn* are striking. In the early version of the tale, the fish listen attentively to every word of the sermon and alter their ways, which, in the end, leads the heretics to repent. The *Wunderhorn* redaction offers a poem that takes an abrupt and sardonically ironic turn just before its end. (Poems with this kind of sudden, late reversal of meaning are sometimes called epigrams.) All through the poem, the fish listen earnestly to the sermon and approve of it. Their ability to respond to St. Anthony's exhortation as the original human targets of the sermon did not is charming. The image of the fish listening attentively to the sermon with their heads raised out of the water offers delectable humor, as do the specific behaviors attributed to each species of fish. However, beginning at No. 15 in the transcription of the poem given above, charm and humor give way to a tone of irony when, at the sermon's end, the fish just slip away from the river's bank to fall back immediately into their routine behaviors. There is no mention of the heretics repenting. Despite the miracle that transformed the fish into sentient creatures, despite the wondrous ability of the fish to surpass their human counterparts by attending to the sermon and approving it enthusiastically—when the sermon is over, all they do is revert to their old ways. St. Anthony's efforts are thus reduced to an essay in futility. In the mordant conclusion of the poem as it is transmitted in *Des Knaben Wunderhorn*, the failure of St. Anthony's pious project renders his saintly exercise utterly meaningless.

Mahler Seeks to Realize the Spirit and Essence of the St. Anthony Poem

We turn first to the "original" version of the St. Anthony song for voice and piano. Obviously, every song takes its lyrics as its point of departure. The composer must assess the words to make appropriate choices about the mood and atmosphere the music will project and about how it will reflect the essential rhetorical thrust of the poetry. As he read this text in pursuit of ideas about how to express it in music, Mahler is apt to have focused on its epigrammatic contour—especially on the moment, late in the poem, when its tone of affable humor turns into caustic irony.[11] He surely will also have taken note of the central point of the poem: its bleak conclusion that, notwithstanding valiant efforts at achieving progress, real change is altogether elusive. How did he go about expressing these sentiments in his song?

Often, the performance directions Mahler provides in his music open a window on his broad intentions for it. Recall, for example, his direction that the opening of this symphony be played "fiercely" (wild in German). That instruction helped to generate the agitated tone that served as an indispensable marker of the terrifying existential questions that were prefigured in this important introductory passage. Mahler heads the St. Anthony song with the marking Behäbig. Mit Humor ("Stolid. With humor"). Calling for a stolid quality in the performance is telling. "Stolid" can mean stationary, suggesting a quality of unmitigated uniformity, a sluggish resistance to variation and change. Mahler seems to be admonishing the performers to restrain any impulses they may have to emphasize or add contrast as they perform this song. In so doing, he appears to be calling for a performance style that goes to the heart of this version of the St. Anthony poem by echoing musically its embittered conclusion about how elusory change can be. The emphasis on humor in the performance direction is of equal importance in Mahler's reading of this poem. It shows the composer's sensitivity to both the charming and ironic components of the poetry. How does Mahler go on to emphasize these two qualities—immutability and humor—in his musical setting?

Both are carefully built into the music. We can see this most clearly in some of the passages played by the piano alone. The piano is used to reflect the poem's focus on St. Anthony's failure to bring about change. It echoes this focus by reaching for an exaggerated sense of homogeneity. Mahler achieves this by casting the piano accompaniment largely as a moto perpetuo, a kind of music characterized by perpetual motion, in which the same rhythmic

---

[11] It does not matter that the epigrammatic turn is the invention of the editors of Des Knaben Wunderhorn, their realization in poetry of a conclusion that had been added in prose by the compiler of their source of the St. Anthony poem. Mahler worked from the verses he encountered in Des Knaben Wunderhorn, and that version of the poetry must be regarded exclusively as the source from which Mahler gained his understanding of the text.

patterns are used relentlessly. Examine the piano part in Music Ex 5.1 and note the incessant reliance on sixteenth notes in the right-hand, set against the equally invariable eighth notes in the left-hand. The music proceeds in this way for a long time.

Humor puts in an early appearance in the brief piano introduction to our song {▶ Audio Ex. 5.1}. The introduction begins as do many by Mahler with the presentation of a distinct musical interval—the one he often endows with an important structural role: the perfect fourth (**00:00**). Almost immediately (**00:03**), two notes are added, and the three of them together prefigure the melody with which the song itself will begin moments later. Music like this is standard fare in introductions. What follows is not. At **00:05**, a single note appears four times, introduced each time with a grace note, a lightly played and very short note just above the pitch of the main note that embellishes the note that follows it. The repetitions of the main note seem redundant, and the grace notes that introduce them add a silly, flippant quality. Then (**00:08**), the two pitches—those of the main note and the grace note that is attached to it—continue to be played, but successively, oscillating in a steady sequence that begs to take off and cover more expansive melodic ground, but the entrance of the voice interrupts, and the introductory melody never goes

Music Ex. 5.1. Rhythmic homogeneity in the piano part of "Des Antonius von Padua Fischpredigt"

anywhere. The humor in this brief passage resides in the stubbornly prosaic quality of the music, which results from its failure to expand into an even minimally substantial melodic compass.

Mahler intersperses in this song several piano interludes that are equally expressive of the underlying atmosphere of the poem. The first of them is specifically marked "mit Humor," and it is obviously meant to reflect the comical content of the poem that will later take a critical epigrammatic turn {⊙ Audio Ex. 5.2}. This passage is very different from the piano introduction. It is highly heterogeneous, tightly packed with many snippets of greatly disparate material. At first (00:00), the higher notes played by the right-hand wind sinuously up and down, offering a melodic line that progresses in a wide variety of strange-sounding intervals that change rapidly. They fail to relate comfortably to each other or to any standard scale, which produces a bizarre effect. Against this, the left-hand offers exaggeratedly wide leaps. Then (00:05), the higher melody proceeds with the same continuous motion with which it began, but it adds another line in parallel to the highest one at the interval of a third. Here, the left hand provides dense, dissonant, and starkly punctuated chords, emphasizing—in contrast to the higher line—the third beat of each measure. Finally (00:08), a series of chromatic descending lines is launched.

There is more than considerable heterogeneity in the rich mixture of materials just described. Many fragments of different material—some of it rather weird in its intervallic content—are juxtaposed in a very short time frame. The overriding impression is of a level of incongruity so highly discrepant as to seem almost absurd. Incongruity bordering on the absurd calls to mind what has become a dominant theory of humor among philosophers and psychologists, known as the *incongruity theory*. As early as 1779, James Beattie, the Scottish poet and essayist, suggested in his "Essay on Laughter and Ludicrous Composition" that laughter is brought about by "two or more inconsistent, unsuitable, or incongruous parts or circumstances, considered as united in one complex object or assemblage. . . ."[12] Later in the song, the same piano interlude is repeated and expanded. This time, Mahler marks it "mit Parodie." Presumably, the pianist is meant to exaggerate even more the incongruities of the passage, causing them to approach the level of satire.

At the very end of the song, it is the piano again that serves to project musically the final outcome of the poem. In place of the strong and emphatic

---

[12] "Philosophy of Humor," *Stanford Encyclopedia of Philosophy*, Section 4, "The Incongruity Theory," available at: https://plato.stanford.edu/entries/humor/#IncThe.

closure we might have expected had St. Anthony's mission succeeded, as the fish slink away and return to their old habits, the piano ends the song in a markedly understated manner. Its chromatic melody descends fleetingly, as its dynamic level fades to **PPP**, landing, soon and inevitably, on an achingly isolated, very low *D* {⊙ Audio Ex. 5.3}. This passage does bring a level of closure to the song, but the sense of completion it provides is weak. The ending is so swift, so mechanical, and so unceremonious as to leave the impression that the music simply stops, where most compositions celebrate with a greater measure of emphasis the moment when the musical narrative draws to a final close. The intentional weakness of Mahler's "ending" may be interpreted as a musical image of the outcome of St. Anthony's mission, which fails to reach a meaningful conclusion. Here, the music inches its way stealthily to a weak close, just as the fish slink away from the river's bank forgetting St. Anthony's admonitions and returning to their old behaviors.[13]

Mahler Considers the Form of his Poem

The content and meaning of a poem are important factors a composer needs to consider as he contemplates putting words to music, but another dimension of the poetry must also be taken into account: its structure. The musical setting ultimately will have a shape of its own, and the extent of concurrence between the structure of the poetry and what will emerge as that of the music needs to be thought out carefully. In formulating this correspondence, composers often consider two factors: (1) any formal framework that seems apparent in the poetry; and (2) the ways in which this design might fit into one or another of various standard musical forms that are traditionally used in setting poems to music. We shall examine both these parameters, turning first to the structure Mahler is apt to have detected in the poem about St. Anthony.

(1) It may be possible to reconstruct Mahler's initial reaction to the form of the poetry by examining the specific source he used for it in pursuit of any hints its layout on the page might offer about the shape of the poem. Here is the beginning of the St. Anthony poem as it is printed in the 1806 edition of *Des Knaben Wunderhorn* (Fig. 5.2).

---

[13] We shall have more to say in the next chapter about the musical content of this concluding passage and a musical source Mahler quoted in it.

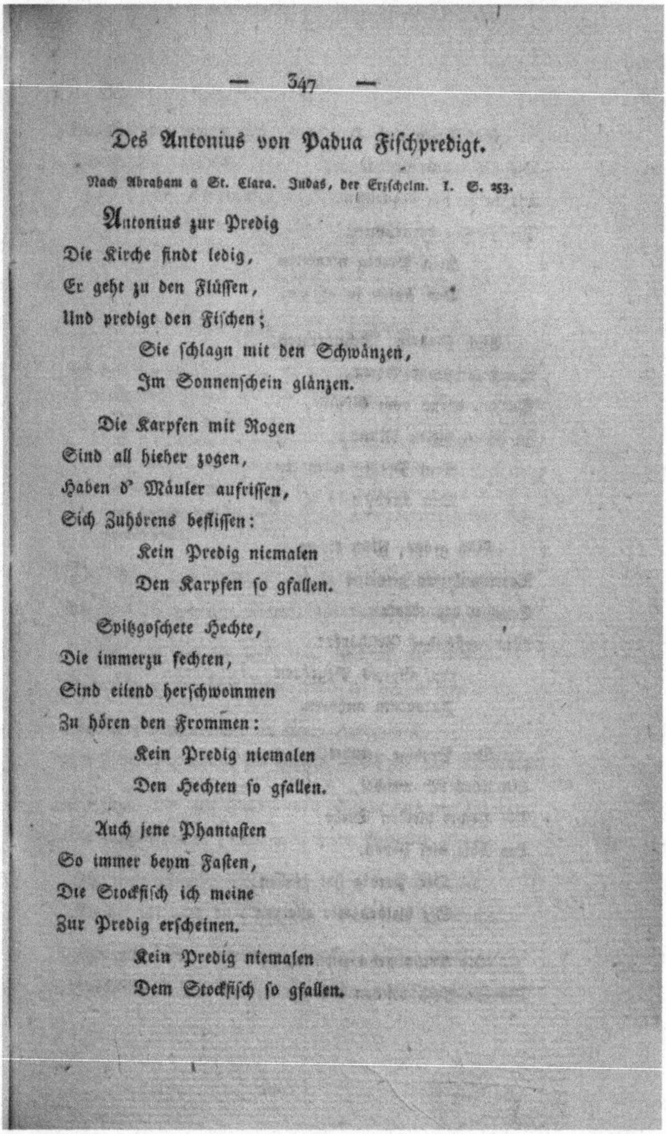

Des Antonius von Padua Fischpredigt.

Nach Abraham a St. Clara. Judas, der Erzschelm. I. S. 253.

Antonius zur Predig
Die Kirche findt ledig,
Er geht zu den Flüssen,
Und predigt den Fischen;
    Sie schlagn mit den Schwänzen,
    Im Sonnenschein glänzen.

Die Karpfen mit Rogen
Sind all hieher zogen,
Haben d' Mäuler aufrissen,
Sich Zuhörens beflissen:
    Kein Predig niemalen
    Den Karpfen so gfallen.

Spitzgoschete Hechte,
Die immerzu fechten,
Sind eilend herschwommen
Zu hören den Frommen:
    Kein Predig niemalen
    Den Hechten so gfallen.

Auch jene Phantasten
So immer beym Fasten,
Die Stockfisch ich meine
Zur Predig erscheinen.
    Kein Predig niemalen
    Dem Stockfisch so gfallen.

Fig. 5.2. The opening of the St. Anthony poem as it appears in the 1806 edition of *Des Knaben Wunderhorn*, p. 347

Bayerische Staatsbibliothek München, BVD 42631692. Reproduced with permission

When Mahler cast his eyes on this very page, he is most likely to have noted first the distinction between divisions of the poetry into units of two and four lines, respectively (what we often call couplets or distichs, on the one hand, and quatrains, on the other). This dichotomy leaps out vividly from the typographical layout of the page.[14] Upon examining the poetry more closely, Mahler would have gone on to perceive that the units of four lines are all different from one another with respect to both content and rhyme, while most of the distichs are essentially the same. It will be helpful to refer to the complete transcription and English translation of the poem provided a little earlier in this chapter. There you will see that the two-line units numbered 4, 6, 8, 10, and 12 are virtually the same with respect to both content and rhyme; the only differences that occur are the mentioning in each of them of a different species of marine life. The two-line units numbered 2, 14, 16, and 18, on the other hand, offer different content; they depart from the recurrent couplets, each of which mentions a different fish that was pleased by the sermon. With our knowledge of how the editors of *Des Knaben Wunderhorn* tampered with the poem, we can account for the divergent couplets—the ones that offer different content instead of replicating each other. The first of them and the last two are not in the original poem; the editors fashioned them. And we should not be surprised by some variation in No. 14, in the lines that constituted the concluding words of the original poem.

(2) Having noted these traces of a formal shape in the poem, Mahler could proceed, at this point, to devise a musical framework that, to a greater or lesser extent, reflects this configuration of the poetry. He may, however, have taken another step first, as many composers do. He might first have made a mental note of the repertoire of standard musical designs traditionally used in setting poetry to music. This was generally done to find a match between one of those formal approaches and the poem he aims to set to music. It behooves us to examine these standard designs briefly. Gaining a grasp of how they work can help us understand the decision-making process a composer deploys in moving from words to music and, more specifically, how Mahler went about designing the musical form for the St. Anthony poem.

---

[14] This typographical layout is not unique to the 1806 edition; it became the standard and is preserved in later editions of *Des Knaben Wunderhorn*, too, including those printed in Berlin (1916), Halle (?1891), and Leipzig (1857, 1878, and 1906), among others.

A roster of forms used traditionally in composing songs may be culled from the vast repertory of German songs from the romantic era known as *Lieder*. The list of specific formal designs used most widely is not very long. We mention here four of the designs encountered most often. (What follows may seem like a lengthy digression, but please be patient in reading it. A clear understanding of how these traditional forms work will help us understand some of the decisions Mahler made as he approached his setting of the St. Anthony poem.)

1. *Ternary form* (related to *Song form*). This is a closed, tripartite form (A–B–A), in which the music of the opening section (A) returns after a contrasting middle section (B) that is usually in a different key. The return of A is a particularly satisfying moment as it provides simultaneously the return of the tonic and of the signature material with which the song began. Sometimes, the verses of the opening section return, too, in which case the structure is sometimes designated *song form*. (That is not so in the example provided here.)

Franz Schubert's "An den Mond" (D. 193) serves as an example of a song in ternary form {▶ Audio Ex. 5.4}.[15] Its form may be charted as follows, followed by the text and translation:

Introduction	**00:02**
A	**00:15**
B1	**01:02**
B2 (the music of **B1** set to a different strophe)	**01:21**
A	**01:42**

A

Geuss, Lieber Mond, geuss deine Silberflimme	Beloved moon, shed your silver radiance
Durch dieses Buchengrün,	through these green beeches,
Wo Phantasien und Traumgestalten	where fancies and dreamlike images
Immer vor mir vorüberfliehn.	forever flit before me.

[15] Franz Schubert serves, in many ways, as the quintessential *Lieder* composer, having written more than 600 of them. A great number of his songs exhibit a paradigmatic level of skill and taste in combining words and music. Schubert's *Lieder* can be easily sampled by way of the Schubert Lieder Project (https://schubertlied.de/de/). This site, directed by the baritone Peter Schöne, aims to offer online performances of all the Schubert Lieder by 2028. Mr. Schöne graciously allowed me to use two of his performances of Schubert songs to illustrate formal design in the *Lied*.

B1

Enthülle dich, dass ich die Stätte finde,	Unveil yourself, that I may find the spot
Wo oft mein Mädchen sass,	where my beloved sat, where often,
Und oft, im Wehn des Buchbaums und der Linde,	in the swaying branches of the beech and lime,
Der goldnen Stadt vergass.	she forgot the gilded town.

B2

Enthülle dich, dass ich des Strauchs mich freue,	Unveil yourself, that I may delight in the whispering
Der Kühlung ihr gerauscht,	bushes that cooled her,
Und einen Kranz auf jeden Anger streue,	and lay a wreath on that meadow
Wo sie den Bach belauscht.	where she listened to the brook.

A

Dann, lieber Mond, dann nimm den Schleier wieder,	Then, beloved moon, take your veil once more,
Und traur um deinen Freund,	and mourn for your friend.
Und weine durch den Wolkenflor hernieder,	Weep down through the hazy clouds,
Wie dein Verlassner weint!	as the one you have forsaken weeps.[16]

The B–sections offer stark musical contrast to the A–sections that serve as bookends for the medial sections. This contrast extends to key, mode, meter, tempo, and mood.

  2. *Refrain form.* In refrain form, a musical section (the refrain) returns again and again, usually without alteration and always in the same key. It is interspersed with sections of music, most of which are new and often in different keys from that of the refrain. In the following schema for this design, **A** stands for the refrain:

A–B–A–C–A.

[16] Translation © Richard Wigmore, author of *Schubert: The Complete Song Texts*, published by Schirmer Books, reprinted here courtesy of Oxford Lieder (https://www.oxfordlieder.co.uk/).

Franz Schubert's "Der Einsame" (D. 800) provides an example of a song in refrain form {▶ Audio Ex. 5.5}. The musical structure of the song can be tracked in the following outline. The refrain (A) appears three times: at the beginning, middle, and modified at the end of the song, with different material (B, B' and C) interspersed between the refrains. One stanza follows the first refrain, and two after the medial refrain. The design pertains, once again, to the music, but not to the poetry.

Introduction	00:00
A	00:13
B	00:42
A	01:12
B'	01:40 (begins like B but becomes something new)
C	02:06
A'	02:28 (varied and extended to provide forceful closure)

A

Wenn meine Grillen schwirren,	When my crickets chirp
Bei Nacht, am spät erwärmten Herd,	at night, by the late-glowing hearth,
Dann sitz' ich mit vergnügtem Sinn	I sit contentedly,
Vertraulich zu der Flamme hin,	confiding in the flame,
So leicht, so unbeschwert.	so light-hearted and untroubled.

B

Ein trautes, stilles Stündchen	For one cozy, peaceful hour
Bleibt man noch gern am Feuer wach,	it is pleasant to stay awake by the fire,
Man schürt, wenn sich die Lohe senkt,	kindling the sparks when the blaze dies down,
Die Funken auf und sinnt und denkt:	musing and thinking,
"Nun abermal ein Tag!"	"Well, yet another day!"

A

Was Liebes oder Leides	What joy or grief
Sein Lauf für uns dahergebracht,	its course has brought us
Es geht noch einmal durch den Sinn;	we run once again through our mind.

Allein das Böse wirft man hin,	But the bad is discarded
Es störe nicht die Nacht.	lest it disturb the night.

B'

Zu einem frohen Träume,	We gently prepare ourselves
Bereitet man gemach sich zu,	for pleasant dreams.
Wenn sorgenlos ein holdes Bild	When a sweet image
Mit sanfter Lust die Seele füllt,	fills our carefree soul with gentle
	pleasure,
Ergibt man sich der Ruh.	we succumb to rest.

C

Oh, wie ich mir gefalle	Oh, how happy I am
In meiner stillen Ländlichkeit!	with my quiet rustic life.
Was in dem Schwarm der lauten Welt	What in the bustle of the noisy world
Dar irre Herz gefesselt hält,	keeps the heart fettered
Gibt nicht Zufriedenheit.	does not bring contentment.

A'

Zirpt immer, liebe Heimchen,	Chirp on, dear crickets,
In meiner Klause eng und klein.	in my narrow little room.
Ich duld' euch gern: ihr stört	I like to hear you: you don't
mich nicht,	disturb me.
Wenn euer Lied das Schweigen	When your song breaks the silence
bricht,	
Bin ich nicht ganz allein.	I am not completely alone.[17]

3. *Strophic form.* In strophic form, each stanza is set to the same music.

4. *Through-composed.* Often the structure of choice in setting long, narrative poems, through-composed designs rely on no pre-determined design, but offer, instead, an ongoing, continuous flow of music, which often attempts to match the progression of events in the narrative.

If we return now to picturing Mahler reading the St. Anthony poem in his copy of *Des Knaben Wunderhorn* and searching the poem for markers of how

[17] Translation © Richard Wigmore, author of *Schubert: The Complete Song Texts*, published by Schirmer Books, reprinted here courtesy of *Oxford Lieder* (https://www.oxfordlieder.co.uk/).

it might best fit one of the standard formal designs used in the *Lieder* repertory, only one potential match comes to mind. The strain of uniformity in the couplets and the persistent diversity in the quatrains are suggestive of refrain form. As we have seen, the refrain structure in the poem is irregular, owing to the additions the editors made to the poem. And Mahler, who was surely ignorant of the role editorial intervention played in corrupting the regular structure of the poetry, must have found the poem an unusually irregular example of refrain form. Nonetheless, if Mahler wanted to match the St. Anthony poem to one of the standard musical forms, refrain form—its irregularities notwithstanding—offers the best fit.

Now, let's see if Mahler did set the St. Anthony poem in refrain form. The poem of Mahler's song follows, coordinated with an outline of its form and with time stamps from a performance of the entire song {▶ Audio Ex. 5.6}. Listen to the complete song and pay close attention to the five numbered couplets marked in the first column with boldface capital letters. These are the two-line units of poetry that offer opportunities to be treated as refrains. As you listen to these sections, make note of whether or not the same music is used for any or all of them (as would be standard procedure in refrain form).

Piano introduction (00:01)
Quatrain 1 (00:11)

Antonius zur Predig	St. Anthony, about to preach,
Die Kirche findt ledig.	finds the church empty.
Er geht zu den Flüssen	He goes to the rivers
Und predigt den Fischen.	and preaches to the fish.

Quatrain 1 extension (00:20)

Sie schlagen mit den Schwänzen,	They beat with their tails,
Im Sonnenschein glänzen.	glistening in the sunshine.

Quatrain 2 (00:33)

Die Karpfen mit Rogen	The carp with roe
Sind all hieher zogen,	all came near,
Haben d' Mäuler aufrissen,	their mouths agape,
Sich Zuhörens beflissen:	to become his attentive listeners.

Piano interlude 1 (00:42)
COUPLET 1 (00:46)

Kein Predig niemalen	No sermon ever
Den Karpfen so gfallen.	pleased the carp so much.

Piano interlude 2—"*mit Humor*" (00:56)
Quatrain 3 (01:12)

Spitzgoschete Hechte,	Pointy-nose pike,
Die immerzu fechten,	who are constantly fencing,
Sind eilend herschwommen	swam up quickly
Zu hören den Frommen.	to hear the devout one.
Mahler omits the couplet that originally followed this verse.	

Quatrain 4 (01:21)

Auch jene Phantasten	Also, those dreamers
So immer beim fasten,	who are constantly fasting—
Die Stockfisch ich meine	I mean the dried cod—
Zur Predig erscheinen.	appear for the sermon.

COUPLET 2 (01:30)	**Slightly varied version of the music for Couplet 1**
Kein Predig niemalen	No sermon ever
Den Stockfisch so gfallen.	pleased the cod so much.

Piano interlude 3—"*mit Parodie*" (01:39)
Piano introduction to music in a new key (01:52)
Quatrain 5 (02:04)

Gut Aalen und Hausen	Fine eels and sturgeons,
Die vornehme schmausen,	on which aristocrats feast,
Die selber sich bequemen,	who relax
Die Predig vernehmen.	to hear the sermon.
Mahler omits the couplet that originally followed this verse.	

Quatrain 6 (02:13)

Auch Krebsen, Schildkroten,	Also crabs and turtles,
Sonst langsame Boten,	usually slow couriers,
Steigen eilend vom Grund,	climb hastily from the deep,
Zu hören diesen Mund.	to hear this voice.

COUPLET 3 (02:25) — **Altogether different from the music of Couplets 1 and 2**

Kein Predig niemalen	No sermon ever
Den Krebsen so gfallen.	pleased the crabs so much.

Quatrain 7 (02:32) **Music of Quatrain 4**

Fisch große, Fisch kleine,	Big fish, little fish,
Vornehm' und gemeine	aristocratic and common,
Erheben die Köpfe	raise their heads
Wie verständige Geschöpfe.	like sentient beings.

Quatrain 7 extension (02:41) **Music from Couplets 1 and 2 but in A Major**

Auf Gottes Begehren	At God's bidding
Die Predig / [Antonium] anhören.	they listen to the sermon / [St. Anthony].

Piano interlude 4—"*mit Parodie*" (02:50)

Quatrain 8 (03:03) **Return of the music of Quatrain 1**

Die Predigt geendet,	With the sermon at an end,
Ein jedes sich wendet,	each one turns away;
Die Hechte bleiben Diebe,	the pikes remain thieves,
Die Aale viel lieben.	the eels make love a lot.

COUPLET 4 (03:16)	Altogether different from the music of earlier couplets	
	Die Predig hat g'fallen,	Though the sermon pleased them,
	Sie bleiben wie alle.	they remain as they were.
Quatrain 9 (03:20)		
	Die Krebs gehn zurücke,	The crabs walk backwards;
	Die Stockfisch bleiben dikke,	the cod stay fat;
	Die Karpfen viel fressen,	the carp stuff themselves;
	Die Predig vergessen.	the sermon is forgotten.
COUPLET 5 (03:31)	Altogether different from the music of earlier couplets	
	Die Predig hat gfallen,	Though the sermon pleased them,
	Sie bleiben wie alle.	they remain as they were.
Piano postlude (03:39)	Music fades away and stops abruptly.	

Clearly, Mahler was aware of the suggestion of refrain form inherent in the poem. At first, he signals the listener an intention to pursue this suggestion by using essentially the same music for the first two couplets. Thereafter, however, his interest in pursuing refrain form wanes strikingly. The music for Couplets 1 and 2 reappears only one more time, and not in one of the poetic refrains, but in the two-line extension to Quatrain 7. It fails to resurface for any of the other couplets. And, as we suggested earlier, Mahler further denigrates the importance of refrain form in this song by omitting altogether the couplets that originally followed Quatrains 3 and 5. We need to wonder why, after using the same music for the first two couplets and thereby demonstrating to the listener the likelihood that he is embarking on some kind of refrain structure, Mahler goes on to abandon a design that seems implicit in the poem. Moreover, this is not the only example of such a contradictory posture with respect to his treatment of form. A parallel mystery involving another one of the standard formal designs also needs to be examined.

In addition to his aborted flirtation with refrain form, Mahler grafts onto his setting of these verses a tripartite song form with a modified return (A–B–A'). This seems odd at the outset because nothing at all at the end of the poem even hints at a return to its opening. There is no repetition of the initial verses or of any of the ideas they contain. In fact, traditional song form seems inappropriate as a design for setting an epigrammatic poem, which, by definition, calls for change, rather than return, at the end of the poem. In the outline of the song given below, boxed letters A–B–A' are used to define the loose, modified ternary form that Mahler created in his setting of the poem. Several important ingredients of song form are, indeed, present:

- A tripartite tonal design begins and ends in D Minor, with a contrasting middle section in G Major.
- The near literal repetition in Quatrains 2 and 3 of the opening melody from Quatrain 1 endows the opening melody with a level of importance that suggests it might warrant a return later in the piece.
- That melody does, indeed, return in the third section of the modified three-part form, but not, as we shall see, at its beginning.

Listen to the complete song again {▶ Audio Ex. 5.6}, noting carefully the ways in which Mahler imprints these attributes of three-part song form on the poem. Take note especially of the sections marked A, B, and A'. Do the music and poetry align to define a closed, ternary form clearly? Do you detect a coordinated return of the tonic and the opening material in the third section of the form A'?

A (of three-part   D Minor
    form: A–B–A')
Piano introduction (00:01)
Quatrain 1 (00:11)

Antonius zur Predig	St. Anthony, about to preach,
Die Kirche findt ledig.	finds the church empty.
Er geht zu den Flüssen	He goes to the rivers
Und predigt den Fischen.	and preaches to the fish.

Quatrain 1 extension (00:20)

Sie schlagen mit den Schwänzen,	They beat with their tails,
Im Sonnenschein glänzen.	glistening in the sunshine.

Quatrain 2 (00:33) **Nearly literal repeat of the music of Quatrain 1**

Die Karpfen mit Rogen	The carp with roe
Sind all hieher zogen,	all came near,
Haben d' Mäuler aufrissen,	their mouths agape,
Sich Zuhörens beflissen.	to become his attentive listeners.

Piano interlude 1 (00:42)

Couplet 1 (00:46)

Kein Predig niemalen	No sermon ever
Den Karpfen so gfallen.	pleased the carp so much.

Piano interlude 2—"*mit Humor*" (00:56)

Quatrain 3 (01:12) **Slightly varied repeat of the music of Quatrain 1**

Spitzgoschete Hechte,	Pointy-nose pike,
Die immerzu fechten,	who are constantly fencing,
Sind eilend herschwommen	swam up quickly
Zu hören den Frommen.	to hear the devout one.

Quatrain 4 (01:21)

Auch jene Phantasten	Also, those dreamers
So immer beim fasten,	who are constantly fasting—
Die Stockfisch ich meine	I mean the dried cod—
Zur Predig erscheinen.	appear for the sermon.

Couplet 2 (01:30)

| Kein Predig niemalen | No sermon ever |
| Den Stockfisch so gfallen. | pleased the cod so much. |

Piano interlude 3—"*mit Parodie*" (01:39)

B̄ (of three-part	G Major
form: A–B–A′)	
Piano introduction (01:52)	
Quatrain 5 (02:04)	

Gut Aalen und Hausen	Fine eels and sturgeons,
Die vornehme	on which aristocrats
schmausen,	feast,
Die selber sich bequemen,	who relax
Die Predig vernehmen.	to hear the sermon.

Quatrain 6 (02:13)

Auch Krebsen,	Also crabs and turtles,
Schildkroten,	
Sonst langsame Boten,	usually slow couriers,
Steigen eilend vom Grund,	climb hastily from the deep,
Zu hören diesen Mund.	to hear this voice.

Couplet 3 (02:25)

| Kein Predig niemalen | No sermon ever |
| Den Krebsen so gfallen. | pleased the crabs so much. |

Ā′ (of three-part	D Minor
form: A–B–A′)	
Quatrain 7 (02:32)	**D Minor returns suddenly, but with the music of Quatrain 4.**

Fisch große, Fisch kleine,	Big fish, little fish,
Vornehm' und gemeine	aristocratic and common,
Erheben die Köpfe	raise their heads

	Wie verständige Geschöpfe.	like sentient beings.

Quatrain 7
extension (02:41)   Set to the music of
                        Couplets 1 and 2

Auf Gottes Begehren	At God's bidding
Die Predig / [Antonium]	they listen to the
anhören.	sermon / [St. Anthony].

Piano interlude 4—"*mit Parodie*" (02:50)

Quatrain 8 (03:03)   Return of the music of
                         Quatrain 1 in D Minor
                         (well after D minor
                         itself returned)

Die Predigt geendet,	With the sermon at an end,
Ein jedes sich wendet,	each one turns away;
Die Hechte bleiben Diebe,	the pikes remain thieves,
Die Aale viel lieben.	the eels make love a lot.

Couplet 4 (03:16)

Die Predig hat g'fallen,	Though the sermon
	pleased them,
Sie bleiben wie alle.	they remain as they were.

Quatrain 9 (03:20)

Die Krebs gehn zurücke,	The crabs walk backwards;
Die Stockfisch bleiben	the cod stay fat;
dikke,	
Die Karpfen viel fressen,	the carp stuff themselves;
Die Predig vergessen.	the sermon is forgotten.

Couplet 5 (03:31)

Die Predig hat gfallen,	Though the sermon
	pleased them,
Sie bleiben wie alle.	they remain as they were.

Piano postlude   **Music fades away and**
(03:39)   **stops abruptly.**

This three-part form functions most clearly as such in the realm of to-nality. The framing outer sections are in D Minor, while the middle section is in G Major. The melodic material, however, is not coordinated with the tonal design. A seamless ternary form would have brought back the music of Quatrain 1—the opening melody that earlier had exhibited potential for return—at Quatrain 7, at the same point at which D Minor is reinstated. Instead, the return of D Minor is linked to a reappearance of the music of Quatrain 4, which hardly connotes a sense of a return to the beginning. The actual return of the opening material is delayed till Quatrain 8, well after the reinstatement of D Minor. This lack of coordination between thematic mate-rial and tonality in a putative ternary design inevitably causes confusion for the listener.

How do we account for the disjunction between tonal and melodic return in this "three-part" form? And, similarly, why did Mahler hint that he would rely on refrain structure in this song, only to abandon that design early on? Considering the broader picture of Mahler's approach to musical form may be of help in answering these questions. His tendency to alter and stretch traditional formal templates has surfaced more than once in these pages. Moreover, it is worth reporting that Mahler harbored a distinct aversion to large-scale repetition, which may be relevant to the discontinuities in the formal design of this song. Mahler articulated this antipathy most emphati-cally (surely *too* emphatically) in the context of an unreasonably harsh char-acterization of the music of Franz Schubert:

How easily he takes things when it comes to developing his ideas! ... No elab-oration, no artistically finished development of his original idea! Instead, he repeats himself so much that you could cut out half the piece without doing it any harm. For each repetition is already a lie. A work of art must evolve perpetually, like life. If it doesn't, hypocrisy and theatricality set in.[18]

Mahler held the same position about repetition in the songs of Carl Loewe, the prolific composer of *Lieder* sometimes called the "north German Schubert":

Nor can he quite free himself from the old style; he repeats individual stanzas, whereas I have come to recognize a perpetual evolution of the

---

[18] Bauer-Lechner, *Recollections of Gustav Mahler*, 147.

song's content—in other words, through-composition—as the true principle of music.[19]

Thus, Mahler's music tended to favor variation and development over wholesale repetition.[20] And his sense of how that balance should be struck could account for the formal dislocations in his treatment of both refrain structure and ternary form in the St. Anthony song.

There is apt to be more to the matter than that, however, especially if we consider how Mahler manipulates the listener's expectations in his setting of the St. Anthony song. He leads the listener to anticipate refrain structure and then works hard at undermining that promise. Similarly, he lays the groundwork for a ternary design, but uncouples the melodic return from that of the tonic in ways that seriously impair the clarity of the three-part form.

Why would he do this? A possible explanation comes to mind. Of the various levels of meaning music can convey, one is the meaning inherent in musical form. As we observe in our engagement with sonata form (Appendix 1), for example, the journey from the uncertainties of the development to the clarity and resolution that accompany the recapitulation evokes the sense of meaning intrinsic in a dramatic outcome. Perhaps, by preparing the listener for both refrain form and ternary design and then undercutting each of them in turn, Mahler is purposely muting the capacity of this song to project such a clear sense of abstract musical meaning. Why would he go down this convoluted path? Possibly, he wanted to provide a musical metaphor for a principal message of his poem. The poem narrates the degeneration of St. Anthony's mission into a meaningless effort. Mahler invites the listener to consider two formal templates as vehicles for lending abstract musical meaning to his setting of the St. Anthony poem. By torpedoing *both* these designs and depriving the listener of a sense of the musical meaning inherent in either of them, Mahler may have attempted to reflect the meaninglessness of St. Anthony's venture in purely musical terms.[21]

---

[19] Bauer-Lechner, *Recollections of Gustav Mahler*, 130.

[20] For additional discussion of Mahler's avoidance of repetition, particularly in his songs, see Zoltan Roman, "Structure as a Factor in the Genesis of Mahler's Songs," *The Music Review* 35 (1974): 157–166; and Stephen E. Hefling, "Gustav Mahler: Romantic Culmination (after the original essay by Christopher Lewis)," in Rufus Hallmark, ed., *German Lieder in the Nineteenth Century*, 2nd ed. Routledge Studies in Musical Genres (New York and London: Routledge, 2010), 297.

[21] By this, I do not mean to suggest that the music is incoherent. On the contrary, as we have seen, there is a great deal that holds this piece together convincingly (e.g., the ternary tonal form,

The Critical Role of the Piano

It may seem strange that, in attempting to explain how Mahler conveys a sense of the poetry in his setting of the St. Anthony song, we have emphasized so much the role of the piano, as opposed to that of the vocal line that transmits the words. That choice arises, in part, from the nature of this piano part. In the *Lieder* repertoire, some piano parts serve a distinctly subservient role, offering harmonic accompaniment that may seem to be an accessory to the more riveting melody that projects the poetry. Others behave that way except in introductions and instrumental interludes. In still others, the piano becomes more a coequal of the voice. The piano part in Mahler's setting of the St. Anthony song belongs to the latter category. It projects a powerful presence, attaining ear-catching prominence with its unique, often strange, music. It sometimes challenges the singer contrapuntally. It never recedes from its state of conspicuousness, offering a relentless source of potent nervous energy. In the next chapter, we shall see how Mahler capitalizes on the unique nature of the piano part as he expands the St. Anthony song into a scherzo and integrates it into the existential agenda that lies at the heart of the Second Symphony.

the regular appearances of the piano interludes, and the satisfying homogeneity of the reliance on perpetual motion). It is only in the realm of hinting at distinct formal templates and then intentionally frustrating them that Mahler robs the song of a measure of abstract musical meaning at the level of form.

6

The Third Movement: Scherzo and Trio

The Form of the Movement •
A Song without Words for Two Categories of Listeners •
The First Iteration of the Scherzo: The St. Anthony Song without Words •
The Trio: Beethoven Addressed Once Again • Hans Rott • The Trio Continues •
First Return of the Scherzo • The Second Trio •
The Final Section of the Movement

*Before reading this chapter, you should avail yourself of the introduction to the
form and origins of the scherzo in Appendix 3.*

The Form of the Movement

The conventional form of a scherzo (as you will have learned from the introduction to that design in Appendix 3) normally falls into one or the other of
two designs, one of them tripartite, the other in five sections. The former of
these consists of the scherzo, a trio, and a return of the scherzo (a closed three-
part form, A–B–A, like that of the song form we discussed in the last chapter).
In the five-part design, the tripartite structure is followed by another return
of the trio, after which a final iteration of the scherzo ends the movement
(A–B–A–B–A). The later "returns" of the scherzo and trio need not be literal;
changes can be, and often are, incorporated in these sections. Mahler opts for
the five-part plan in the second Symphony, and the last two sections differ
markedly from the first iterations of the scherzo and trio. They use music from
the trio and scherzo, respectively, but introduce substantial alterations to the
original sections and include some important new material, too. Mahler does
not specify exactly where the trio begins, and, as we shall see, this has given
rise to some controversy. We know from the last chapter that the scherzo is
based on the St. Anthony song from *Des Knaben Wunderhorn*, while the trio

Inside Mahler's Second Symphony:. Lawrence F. Bernstein, Oxford University Press. © Oxford University Press 2022.
DOI: 10.1093/oso/9780197575635.003.0006

is newly composed. In addition, the first trio also incorporates an important nod in the direction of a preexistent musical composition.

A Song without Words for Two Categories of Listeners

Of the two *Wunderhorn* songs incorporated in the Second Symphony, the one that appears in the brief fourth movement is sung, which affords the listener the opportunity to know from its text much of what inspired Mahler to incorporate the song in the symphony. The St. Anthony song, however, is performed in the scherzo as a free orchestral arrangement and expansion of the song—that is, *without* the words. As a result, the reason behind incorporating the song in the symphony is less explicit than it would be, were the words present. This raises some questions about exactly what the listener is expected to take away from the presence of the music of the St. Anthony song in this movement.

Imagine you and a friend are attending a performance of the Second Symphony to hear the work for the first time. You are familiar with the St. Anthony song. Your friend is not. How might each of you be expected to react to the implications inherent in the presence of the St. Anthony song in this movement? Is your friend at a serious disadvantage for lack of knowledge of the song, especially of its words? On the other hand, should you, perhaps, try to suppress what you know of the significance of a song, the words of which have not been made a part of this symphony—presumably for a good reason the composer had in mind? And what can we say about Mahler's intentions vis-à-vis the role of the song in the scherzo?

Answers to these questions do not lie within easy reach, but a few reasonable assumptions may provide some guidance about what Mahler is apt to have expected of his listeners regarding their understanding of the connection between the song and the symphony:

- The essence of the St. Anthony song, including its text, cannot but have been at the forefront of Mahler's consciousness when he wrote the scherzo. He composed the song and the scherzo virtually in tandem, as we have seen. Moreover, recall his annotation to the autograph of the song in the version for voice and piano specifying that it was meant to serve as a preliminary study for the scherzo. Including its music— but not its words—in the symphony, thus, should not be taken as an indication that the content of the poetry of the St. Anthony song was not of importance to Mahler as he fashioned the scherzo, even if the words are not performed in the symphony.

- Mahler would not have been so naïve as to assume that listeners who attended his Second Symphony would *necessarily* know the song. Thus, he could not realistically plan on how listeners might react to the scherzo based on a presumption that they were familiar with the song.
- At the same time, he was savvy enough to know that some listeners *would* know the song. Under such circumstances, would he not have been willing to capitalize on their ability to use this knowledge to advantage as they attempt to understand the meaning of the scherzo?
- And we should not discount the strength of Mahler's likely conviction that the great power of music includes its capacity to convey, at least partially, the essential message and underlying feelings of the song even in the absence of its words.

These assumptions—all of them plausible, I believe—suggest that, as he envisioned how the third movement of this symphony would be grasped and understood, Mahler had in mind *both* listeners who knew the song and those who did not. They would fall (ever so roughly) into two groups, each of which will interpret in its own way the presence in the symphony of music from the St. Anthony song. Clearly, Mahler had to factor in the needs of both categories of listeners as he planned the scherzo. This will not have been an easy task, for, as we shall see, Mahler wanted the scherzo to convey the essence of the song to his listeners, even in the absence of its words. Let us explore how he accomplished this.

The First Iteration of the Scherzo: The St. Anthony Song without Words

To gain a preliminary insight into how Mahler infused the meaning of the St. Anthony song into a version of it that lacks the words, we return first and briefly to the opening of the song with piano accompaniment {⊙ Audio Ex. 6.1}. The introduction with which the excerpt begins offers, as we have seen, humorous gestures in its frivolous grace notes (**00:05**) and in the seemingly aimless oscillation between two notes (**00:08**) with which it ends. If the opening of the passage seems somewhat empty, it assumes that guise purposefully because its primary objective is to look ahead at what is about to happen more than to encourage us to engage deeply with the introduction itself. In this sense, it serves as a "music of becoming," presaging the arrival of a musical event of greater substance and integrity than itself: the beginning of the melody that serves as the vehicle for the words (00:10).

Now, compare what we have just heard to the version of this material that appears in the symphony {⊙ Audio Ex. 6.2}. If anything, the anticipatory force of the introduction is sharper in the orchestral version, which is slightly longer than its counterpart in the version for voice and piano. At the beginning of the passage, the opening interval seems more dramatic played by the timpani than it was in the piano version, and the flippant grace notes are rendered more pungent and more piquant as they are rendered by the English horn and clarinet (beginning at 00:09). The two-note oscillation, played quietly by the clarinet, is folded into the grace-note passage beginning at 00:12. Vivid orchestral sonorities thus render the watchfully expectant quality of the introduction more acute than it was in the version for voice and piano. Our need for the arrival of something sturdy and robust like the melody that is introduced by the singer is more pressing in the orchestral version. When the moment for the arrival of that melody or something equally stable comes, however (00:13), Mahler does not provide it. Instead, he introduces in the violins the piano accompaniment for the first quatrain of the song, followed by the piano accompaniment for the extension of that quatrain in the clarinets (beginning at 00:21). In place of something like the hardy melodic material from the song we have been led to expect, we are given music that emphasizes rhythmic energy and conveys a distinctly nervous quality that results from the highly animated nature of that rhythmic vitality. Mahler continues to rely exclusively on music drawn from the piano accompaniment for a long time (through 00:46). True, this focus on rhythmic energy is compatible with the generic nature of scherzos, which, as we point out in the discussion of the scherzo in Appendix 3, are often defined by the lively and nimble quality of their rhythm. But scherzos need a significant amount of stability, too, of the sort that is often embodied in a melody, as opposed to its accompaniment. We shall have to determine how Mahler goes about striking this balance.

Listen to the entire first scherzo {⊙ Audio Ex. 6.3} in conjunction with Table 6.1. It identifies the source of the music of the scherzo in the version of the St. Anthony song for voice and piano, distinguishing between material

Table 6.1. Source of the music in the first iteration of the scherzo (melody vs. piano accompaniment of the original song)

Time	Form	Vocal Melody	Piano Accompaniment	New or Developed Material
00:00	Introduction		12 mm.	
00:14	A—C Minor		8 mm.	
00:22			12 mm.	
00:35			8 mm.	
00:43			4 mm.	
00:47		8 mm.		
00:56			16 mm.	
01:12		4 mm.		
01:16			4 mm.	
01:20		4 mm.		
01:24			4 mm.	
01:28		8 mm.		
01:37			12 mm.	
01:51	B—F Major		8 mm.	
02:00		4 mm.		
02:05			8 mm.	
02:13		4 mm.		
02:18			8 mm.	
02:27		4 mm.		
02:31		4 mm.		
02:36				New transition, 4 mm.
02:40	A′—C Minor	8 mm.		
02:49				Transition, 20 mm.
03:10		4 mm.		
03:14				New closure, 10 mm.

Note: mm. = measures.

drawn from the vocal melody and from the piano accompaniment, respectively. A few passages of new or developed material are identified, too.

As he incorporated music from the St. Anthony song into the scherzo of the Second Symphony, Mahler distributed material from the vocal melody and the piano accompaniment very unevenly, greatly favoring the piano part. Excluding some thirty-four measures devoted to new transitional material, he fills more than 100 of the 189 measures of the scherzo with music from the piano accompaniment, while limiting references to the vocal melody to a mere fifty-four bars. More importantly, the emphasis on the less melodically oriented piano music is not merely quantitative. The opening of a composition often declares the essential character of a work compellingly, but the scherzo follows its brief introduction with thirty-two measures of material taken directly from the piano accompaniment. It is the longest continuous swath of material preserved from the song in this section of the scherzo, and it marks the composition indelibly with a conspicuous sense of avoiding a "real" melody.

Melodic material from the song *is* quoted in the scherzo, but, often, only fragments of it appear. The reduction of extended melodies from the song into mere snippets produces in the scherzo a somewhat episodic and disjointed melodic landscape. Consider Mahler's treatment in the scherzo of the opening melody, and of the particularly well-defined melodies of the fourth and sixth quatrains (offered in succession in {⊙ Audio Ex. 6.4}). Each of the three excerpts is limited to a scant four measures. Sometimes, moreover, Mahler uses orchestral sonority in ways that contribute to a further erosion in the melodic integrity of the St. Anthony song as it is quoted in the scherzo. Here again is the smidgen he quotes of the important opening melody {⊙ Audio Ex. 6.5}. Mahler relegates this fleeting reference to the frail and brittle sonority of the piccolo, while the violins compete with the tune and deflect our attention from it by overlaying the melodic quotation with an excerpt from the piano accompaniment for this melody. The lower strings also divert attention from the melody with a series of incessant repeated notes.[1]

Thus, Mahler plays down the role of melody in the scherzo, just as he accentuates the nervous rhythmic energy inherent in the passages of the piano accompaniment from the St. Anthony song. Mahler highlights this largely a-melodic music in various ways. When the third piano interlude of the song—one of the passages Mahler identifies as a representation of ironic humor—appears in the scherzo, Mahler assigns it to the screeching sonority

---

[1] The rhythm in the lower strings is duplicated by an unusual percussion instrument, the *Ruthe*, a bunch of sticks or twigs used to strike the rim of the bass drum. I believe that this exotic sound is meant to distract us even more from the melody at hand. Unfortunately, the sound of the *Ruthe* is inaudible in our recording.

of the high E♭ clarinet (an instrument he proudly imported from its use in military bands like those he heard in his hometown of Iglau).[2] The shrillness of this sonority alone greatly accentuates one's sense of the importance of the passage—a line that favors bizarre intervals and restless rhythmic motion over any attempt at conventional melodic cogency. Thus, the raucous sound of the E♭ clarinet serves to reinforce the freakish quality of the music in this passage {▶ Audio Ex. 6.6}. All told thus, it seems that, in this section of the scherzo, Mahler offers not only a song without words, but a song whose melodic content has been substantially attenuated.

Another important difference between the scherzo and its model in the version of the song with piano accompaniment needs to be mentioned. In our discussion of the latter version of the song in Chapter 5, we alluded to the misalignment of the return of the tonic and of the opening melodic material. We interpreted this dislocation as Mahler's attempt to deprive a tripartite song form of the traditional structural meaning inherent in the standard coordinated return of tonic and opening melody. This debasement of the musical meaning of a traditional form, we suggested, was meant to be a musical metaphor for the concept of meaninglessness inherent in the poem. In the Scherzo, the opening melody *does* reappear with the return of the tonic, C Minor, at **02:40** in {▶ Audio Ex. 6.3}. This seems puzzling. Has Mahler stepped back from the musical expression of meaninglessness as a central pillar of this movement as he presented it in the version of the song for voice and piano? It turns out that Mahler has a special reason for realigning the tonal and melodic returns in the scherzo, but we will be able to understand it only when we encounter the first return of the scherzo later in this movement.

It is one thing to report on the de-emphasis of melody in the scherzo section of Mahler's Second Symphony. It is quite another—and more difficult— task to explain why Mahler opted to proceed down this path. The degree of difficulty varies, depending on whether the scherzo is interpreted from the

---

[2] Mahler told Bauer-Lechner in 1896 that he had borrowed the E♭ clarinet from military band music, going on to suggest that, even as a boy, he was thrilled by the sound of the instrument. Natalie Bauer-Lechner, *Recollections of Gustav Mahler*, ed. Peter Franklin, trans. Dika Newlin (New York: Faber and Faber, 2013), 46. Further on the widespread use of the E♭ clarinet in wind bands, see Donald Mitchell, *Gustav Mahler: The Wunderhorn Years. Chronicles and Commentaries* (Woodbridge: Boydell Press, 2005), 369–370, n. 18; and Timothy David Freeze, "'Fit for an Operetta': Mahler and the Popular Music of his Day," in Erich Wolfgang Partsch and Morten Solvik, eds., *Mahler im Kontext / Contextualiziung Mahler* (Vienna: Böhlau Verlag, 2011), 377.

perspective of a listener who has knowledge of the St. Anthony song, or from that of one who does not. Apparently, in the scherzo, Mahler is building on an approach inherent in the version of the song with piano accompaniment. As we observed in Chapter 5, the piano part already challenges the vocal melody for preeminence in the song, resulting in a ubiquitous sense of disquieting, nervous energy. The rhythm tends to be relentless and unvarying, and the larger form internally self-contradictory. Seen as reflections of the poem, these musical features underscore the sense of futility and meaninglessness inherent in St. Anthony's failure to bring about lasting change in the fish, who miraculously understand and heartily approve of his sermon, but who ironically only revert to their old ways thereafter.

The listener who knows the song can readily transfer this account of its meaning to the scherzo. But what of the listener who lacks this knowledge? Much of what we have observed about the scherzo thus far may be perceived as Mahler's attempt to awaken in this listener, too, a more generalized awareness of what lies behind the meaning of the St. Anthony song. The rhythmic perpetual motion suggests an unsettling measure of relentlessness and conveys a disturbing aura of nebulous nervous energy. The absence of a substantial, integrated melodic framework leaves the impression of melodies that are pointlessly vacant, precisely where the listener is prone to seek a *meaningful* melodic shape. The devices that give rise to a sense of irony and satire in the song are, if anything, stronger as they are orchestrated in the scherzo. Mahler's scherzo, thus, aims to defeat the listener's natural penchant to seek order and meaning in melody, and the scherzo—*even without the words*—seems, in this sense, reflective of a sense of meaninglessness.

We need not rely entirely on our own devices to understand the relationship between the musical character of the scherzo and the concept of meaninglessness. Mahler set forth some of his ideas about what he was trying express in the Second Symphony in a conversation with Bauer-Lechner in January 1896. Here is her account of what he said about the scherzo:

> The experience behind the Scherzo I can describe only in terms of the following image: if, at a distance, you watch a dance through a window, without being able to hear the music, then the turning and twisting movement of the couples seems senseless, because you are not catching the rhythm that is the key to it all. You must imagine that to one who has lost his identity and

his happiness, the world looks like this—distorted and crazy, as if reflected in a concave mirror.[3]

In a letter to the music critic Max Marschalk written in March 1896, Mahler also engages in a description of his intentions for the Second Symphony. On addressing the scherzo, he repeats the image of the silent dance as a metaphor for life, concluding that, as it is reflected in the scherzo, "life then becomes meaningless, an eerie phantom state."[4] A song devoid of words is comparable to the image of the silent dance—all the more so when that song is, to an extent, further stripped of one of the most palpable elements of its meaning: cogent melody.

The Trio: Beethoven Addressed Once Again

The scherzo ends abruptly, and the music elides into new material. Listen {⏵ Audio Ex. 6.7} to the final moments of the scherzo (**00:00**), followed immediately by the beginning of the trio (**00:07**). Although no interruption separates the scherzo from the trio, the beginning of the new section brings with it a sea change in musical style. The mode changes from C Minor to C Major, and a thin orchestral texture replaces the fuller orchestral complement with which the previous section ended. These changes are conventional hallmarks of the onset of a trio.[5] Most importantly, a special kind of theme—we call it a subject—enters in the lower strings here. Its contour is sharply defined, and Mahler directs that it be played very powerfully (*sehr wuchtig*), which also helps to delineate this music as the beginning of a new section. Although many violoncellos and double basses play this line, they all play the same notes, which leads us to expect and await an expansion of the musical texture. The features described here—sharp contour and decisive performance of a single line of music—are suggestive of a unique musical texture: imitative counterpoint. In this kind of music, a subject

---

[3] Bauer-Lechner, *Recollections of Gustav Mahler*, 43–44.

[4] Knud Martner, ed. *Selected Letters of Gustav Mahler: The Original Edition Selected by Alma Mahler*, trans. Eithne Wilkins, Ernst Kaiser, and Bill Hopkins (New York: Farrar, Straus, Giroux, 1979), no. 158.

[5] Mahler does not identify this or any other section as the trio in the published score, which has led to controversy in the literature about where the trio begins in this movement. Some writers place it at this point; others, at the junctures discussed subsequently at {Audio Exx. 6.10 and 6.15}. This literature is summarized in Claudia Maurer Zenck, "Technik und Gehalt im Scherzo von Mahlers Zweiter Symphonie," *Melos / NZ. Neue Zeitschrift für Musik*, 2 (1976): 179–184.

(theme) is introduced, and its melody is imitated by a different instrument a little later, usually at a different pitch level, at which time the first line to have entered continues with something else that competes with the subject for our attention. Listen to the beginning of the trio again {⊙ Audio Ex. 6.8} and take note of the imitative entry at **00:12**. This entry in the violas and bassoon, in the wake of what preceded it, enables us to identify the passage definitively as an example of imitative counterpoint. Examples in which the imitation is carried out strictly are called *fugues*; when the imitation is somewhat more loosely defined, as in this example, we call the music that results a *fugato*.

Now, fugue or fugato is a rare choice of texture for the opening of the trio section of a symphonic scherzo, but there is a famous example in which it does appear: in the trio of the third movement of Beethoven's Fifth Symphony. This is a work Mahler knew well, having conducted it numerous times, beginning in Budapest in 1890 and including a cluster of performances in 1892 and 1893—in close proximity, that is, to his work on the scherzo of the Second Symphony.[6] Here is the opening of the trio from Beethoven's Fifth Symphony {⊙ Audio Ex. 6.9}. It has a lot in common with Mahler's trio: both are in C Major; both are couched in an imitative texture; both begin with a powerful subject in the low strings; both give the first imitation to the violas and bassoon. These seem not to be coincidental resemblances, particularly because imitative counterpoint is not the musical texture with which one normally begins a symphonic trio. Mahler seems to be paying homage to Beethoven here, much as he did with the ways in which he emulated the beginning of Beethoven's Ninth Symphony in the opening of our symphony (see the section "Echoes of Beethoven" in Chapter 1).

Important differences also distinguish the two trios. Listen again to the first section of the Beethoven trio (which is repeated) {⊙ Audio Ex. 6.9} and note the precise and systematic symmetry reflected in the counterpoint.

Brief subject on the note C	00:01 / 00:14
Brief imitation on the note G	00:05 / 00:18
Brief imitation on the note C	00:09 / 00:22
Immediate imitation on the note G and closure	00:10 / 00:24

---

[6] Knud Martner, *Mahler's Concerts* (New York: Overlook Press, 2010), 69ff.

Beethoven's counterpoint is quite strict, which results in a taut, concise, robust, and predictable passage. Mahler's counterpoint is nothing like this. Listen to it again {▶ Audio Ex. 6.8}. The opening subject trails on for a much longer time than we expect it to. This leaves the listener somewhat bewildered in the absence of a way of sensing exactly where the imitations will enter. When the first imitative entry finally occurs (**00:12**), it is on the note *A*, not on *G* where such imitation usually occurs when the subject begins on *C*. Moreover, above much of the imitative activity, the flute and piccolo sustain a long, inverted pedal on the tonic. Such emphasis on the tonic gives added weight to the first entry, which is also on the tonic, and it diminishes the integrity of the second imitative entry on *A*. Mahler's approach here seems to fly in the face of the strict rules of counterpoint that so importantly inform Beethoven's trio.

The contrapuntal anomalies of Mahler's trio have scarcely had a chance to register with us when the passage is brashly interrupted by an abrupt shift in key and the sudden appearance in the full orchestra of an audacious fanfare (Music Ex 6.1 and {▶ Audio Ex. 6.10}). The material that brashly interrupts Mahler's counterpoint at **00:06** could hardly offer more decisive contrast to what preceded it. Everything changes: without preparation, D Major takes the place of C Major, and the texture, sonority, and melodic material are radically different from that of the preceding imitative passage.[7]

Music Ex. 6.1. Mahler's paraphrase of Hans Rott's fanfare

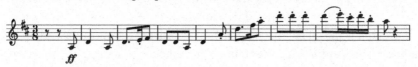

In fact, another reason the fanfare sounds so starkly different from what precedes it is that it is not limited to music by Mahler. It is his free paraphrase of a passage from the scherzo of the Symphony in E Major by Hans Rott, which we can confirm by comparing the fanfare we just heard to this excerpt from the Rott symphony {▶ Audio Ex. 6.11}.[8] Who was Hans Rott, and why

---

[7] Some writers favor this fanfare as the initiation of the trio, but this seems untenable because the fanfare is introduced specifically to interrupt a musical process already in progress.

[8] James L. Zychowicz, "Gustav Mahler's Motives and Motivation in his 'Resurrection' Symphony: *The Apotheosis of Hans Rott*," in Darwin F. Scott, ed., *For the Love of Music: Festschrift in Honor of Theodore Front on his 90th Birthday* (Lucca: Libreria musicale italiana, 2002), 145.

does Mahler invite his voice into the Second Symphony, allowing it to interrupt the trio of the scherzo so obtrusively?

Hans Rott

Hans Rott was a fellow student of Mahler at the Vienna Conservatory. Like Mahler, his concentration was in composition—both studied with Franz Krenn—and the two young men shared devotion to the ideals of the avant-garde, an allegiance reflected in their membership in the Viennese Academic Wagner Society. Rott submitted a score for the coveted Beethoven prize for composition awarded at the conservatory. The conservative wing of the faculty openly scoffed at Rott's entry (probably the symphony that Mahler paraphrases in the scherzo under consideration), prompting the avant-garde composer Anton Bruckner to come to Rott's defense by admonishing his colleagues not to mock a composer who obviously was on the brink of a distinguished career. The latter prediction never became a reality, however. The faculty at the conservatory, along with Johannes Brahms, discouraged Rott from pursuing a life as a composer. He tried unsuccessfully to find work as an organist in Vienna, finally accepting a position as a choral conductor in Strasbourg at a time when he deeply felt that leaving Vienna would mean the end of his career. He was already showing signs of mental illness. For a likeness of Hans Rott, see Fig. 6.1.

In October 1880, Rott grudgingly boarded a train for Strassburg to assume his new conducting responsibilities, at which time a combination of pressure, despair, and an encroaching mental disorder overcame him, leading to a bizarre incident aboard the train. When a fellow passenger attempted to light a cigar, Rott is said to have pointed a gun at him, admonishing him not to light the cigar because "Brahms has filled the coach with dynamite." Rott was removed from the train and returned to Vienna, where he spent the last four years of his life in a series of psychiatric institutions. He died of tuberculosis in June 1884 at the age of twenty-six.[9]

Critical to any assessment of Mahler's purpose in paraphrasing Rott's material in his own symphony would be an appreciation of what he thought of

---

[9] Jens Malte Fischer, *Gustav Mahler*, trans. Stewart Spencer (New Haven, CT: Yale University Press, 2011), 57–58. For more information on Hans Rott, see the website of the International Hans Rott Society: http://www.hans-rott.de/indexe.htm.

Fig. 6.1. A photograph of Hans Rott (1858–1884)
© Professor Uwe Harten. Reproduced with his kind permission

the man and of his music. In the summer of 1900, sixteen years after Rott's death, Mahler visited his composing hut in Maiernigg. He brought along a score of Rott's symphony, planning to study the work in preparation for a possible performance under his baton with the Vienna Philharmonic.[10]

---

[10] That performance never took place, and it was not until 1989 that Rott's symphony had its premiere in Cincinnati, Ohio. Zychowicz, "Gustav Mahler's Motives and Motivation in his 'Resurrection' Symphony," 142.

Bauer-Lechner attributes to Mahler the following comment about Rott made that summer:

> What music has lost in him is immeasurable. His First Symphony, written when he was a young man of twenty, already soars to such heights of genius that it makes him—without exaggeration—the founder of the New Symphony as I understand it. . . . His innermost nature is so much akin to mine that he and I are like two fruits from the same tree, produced by the same soil, nourished by the same air. We would have had an infinite amount in common. Perhaps we two might have gone some way together towards exhausting the possibilities of this new age that was then dawning in music.[11]

Thus, Mahler viewed Rott as a close ally—a true comrade in arms—in what was surely the central artistic objective of his life: the transformation of the symphony into the New Symphony. By giving voice to Rott's music in his own symphony, Mahler makes in the scherzo a powerful statement in support of this artistic goal. Juxtaposing this reference to the allusion to the scherzo of Beethoven's Fifth enhances the force of Mahler's statement greatly. Earlier (in Chapter 1), we alluded to the plight of composers who wrote symphonies in the shadow of Beethoven. They could not escape from confronting Beethoven's powerfully influential symphonic production. Often, they would feel compelled to mirror his achievements and, at the same time, demonstrate their artistic independence by striving to overcome them. That seems to be precisely what Mahler is about at this point in the Second Symphony. He alludes overtly to a celebrated moment in a Beethoven symphony, which seems to be a way of acknowledging and emulating his predecessor's achievements. But then he throws caution to the wind and violates the very rubrics of counterpoint and symmetry that lie at the heart of the Beethoven trio. Surely, this must be taken as a mark of Mahler's effort to transcend Beethoven's accomplishment. The reference to Hans Rott's music—emblematic, in Mahler's view, of the New Symphony—then flagrantly interrupts both the emulation and surpassing of Beethoven, as if to proclaim: "The day of the New Symphony has arrived; we have ample license to go as far beyond Beethoven as we may wish to!"

---

[11] Bauer-Lechner, *Recollections of Gustav Mahler*, 146.

This interpretation of the allusion to Rott's music in the trio addresses a global agenda with which Mahler was preoccupied throughout his creative life. For Mahler, the quest for the New Symphony was a lifelong passion. At the more local level of what he is trying to tell us in the Second Symphony, the appearance of Rott's music in it is even more significant. From the St. Anthony song and Mahler's own comments about his scherzo to Bauer-Lechner and Max Marschalk, we know that the central theme of this movement concerns life's meaninglessness. For Mahler, what more poignant and more potent emblem of life devoid of meaning could there be than a musical allusion to a brilliant young composer who lost his mind and died at the age of twenty-six without his major contribution to the emergence of the New Symphony having come before the public?

Thus, the brief fanfare-like motive adapted from Rott's symphony is of profound significance. It serves as a major turning point in the Second Symphony, providing a critical opportunity for Mahler to elevate the topos of meaninglessness as it appears in the St. Anthony song to the level of an existential concern. Apparently, the "dreadfully serious voice" that lies at the center of the musical narrative in the first movement, awakening terrifying existential questions, has returned, and its reoccurrence is vividly underscored by the reference to Rott's fanfare.

The Trio Continues

We return to the explosive entry of Mahler's paraphrase of the Rott fanfare {▶ Audio Ex. 6.12}. Note the prominent appearance in Mahler's version of this theme of the uneven rhythm (the dotted figure) that appears twice in the brief fanfare. (You can consult the music for this passage in Music Ex. 6.1, above; the dotted figure appears in the second and fifth complete measures of the passage.) Mahler makes much of this rhythmic figure, using it first in a closing gesture he appends to the fanfare {▶ Audio Ex. 6.13}. The dotted figure will reappear before long. First, however, after the closing gesture winds down, Mahler resumes the imitative counterpoint—both the texture and the subject—with which he began the trio {▶ Audio Ex. 6.14}. The music is gentle, as before, and it remains free and unpredictable in contrast to the more rule-bound counterpoint in the Beethoven trio to which it alludes. The texture is a little busier here than it was at the beginning of the trio. Two new subjects are introduced: one in the oboe at the very beginning of the passage, and another in the clarinet (at **00:04**). This imitative passage meanders casually for a while, but, like its predecessor at the start of the trio, it, too, is glaringly interrupted (at **00:23**) by Mahler's paraphrase of the Rott fanfare—this time in yet another key, E Major (the key of Rott's symphony).

Next, the dotted figure derived from the fanfare reappears prominently in a prolonged and very lyrical melody, first introduced by a solo trumpet {(▶) Audio Ex. 6.15}.[12] It appears initially at **00:02**, then at **00:08**, and four times thereafter. Mahler marks this passage "Very stately and songful" ("Sehr getragen und gesangvoll"). He held this melody in particularly high esteem, commenting to Bauer-Lechner in 1899:

> [I]n the Scherzo, the most beautiful passage—the quiet theme of the middle section which forms an interlude between the surging wave of the piece—occurs once and never again. At first sight, this seems an incredible waste. The pleasure of exploiting the lovely fresh motif and repeating it in a different key or variation is, indeed, one that one would not readily forego. But that would have gone against the essence of this passage, which—like the aloe—should blossom but once.[13]

The passage stands out for its melodic elegance—an aspect of music that has been assiduously avoided in the movement so far. That avoidance, as we have seen, is placed in the service of projecting a sense of meaninglessness, one of Mahler's principal objectives in this movement. There comes a point, however, when the listener's craving for at least a small measure of melodic contrast seems to cry out for satisfaction. That purely musical aim seems to be the essential purpose underlying this passage. Yet Mahler clearly has not lost sight of his principal objective, and this is probably another reason he resisted what he described as his temptation to repeat this lovely theme. And,

---

[12] According to several writers, this lyrical melody should be designated the trio. Supporters of this assertion allude to the significant degree to which this melody contrasts with the music that precedes it. Furthermore, they call attention to two contemporaries of Mahler (Richard Sprecht and Ferdinand Pfohl) who designated this section the trio (Maurer Zenck, "Technik und Gehalt im Scherzo von Mahlers Zweiter Symphonie," 180). On the other hand, the lack of a clear sense of initiation at the beginning of this section, the remote and unconventional key in which the section is written (E Major), and the failure of this putative trio to fit comfortably into any of the standard large-scale repetition schemes of the five-part scherzo argue compellingly against viewing this material as the initiation of the trio.

[13] Bauer-Lechner, *Recollections of Gustav Mahler*, 141–142.

even in the single appearance of this lovely melody, Mahler quotes the dotted rhythmic figure in common with Rott's fanfare six times, which seems to link the quintessentially graceful passage to his principal musical metaphor for meaninglessness, the reference to the Rott fanfare. An elegant close is provided for the lyrical melody (**00:55**).

At the very end of this graceful music {⊙ Audio Ex. 6.16}, Mahler slips deftly back into C Major (**00:04**) and resumes the imitative counterpoint. The new passage is very short, however, and it swiftly builds in rhythmic intensity, dynamic level, anticipatory power, and in the size of the orchestra. It serves to end the trio and as a brief transition back to the scherzo, albeit to a significantly altered and foreshortened version of it.

First Return of the Scherzo

Once again, we have mapped out the relationship between the St. Anthony song and this portion of the scherzo in a table that shows the distribution between material taken from the vocal melody and that drawn from the piano accompaniment. Listen to this section of the scherzo, noting the nature of its relationship to the song as outlined in Table 6.2. For reasons that will become clear presently, I have identified the section of the original song from which the music of this portion of the scherzo derives {⊙ Audio Ex. 6.17}. (Note that this version of the scherzo is truncated suddenly and severely at the end of this example.)

At first, this section of the third movement does not convey a strong impression of the return of the scherzo. Mahler opted to mute the return by choosing to open the section with free developments of material from several sections of the piano accompaniment. Beginning at **00:26** with the arrival of the music for Quatrain 3 (= Quatrain 1), however, this version of the scherzo gradually begins to present the melody of the song more transparently, which does enhance the sense of a return of the scherzo. The entire section is shorter and more concise than the opening scherzo, and more sections follow each other in the original sequence of the song. Some of the sections drawn from the piano accompaniments, moreover (like those from Quatrain 6), are among the most tuneful of the accompaniments. Thus, the overall sense of melodic presence in this section of the movement is greater than it was at the beginning of the movement. Indeed, this

Table 6.2. Source of the music in the first return of the scherzo (melody vs. piano accompaniment of the original song)

Time	Form	Vocal Melody	Piano Accompaniment
00:00	A⎯C Minor		10 mm. (Q1)
00:11			10 mm. (Q1 extension)
00:22			4 mm. (Pn. Interlude-1)
00:26		8 mm. (Q3 = Q1)	
00:34		4 mm. (Q4)	
00:39			4 mm. (Q4)
00:43		8 mm. (C1)	
00:52			13 mm. (Pn. Interlude-3)
01:05	B⎯F Major		8 mm. (Pn.-Introduction)
01:15		4 mm. (Q6)	
01:19			8 mm. (Q6)
01:28		4 mm. (Q6)	
01:33			8 mm. (Q6)
01:40	Swift modulation back to C Minor to prepare for the return of A, but this section of the scherzo is abruptly cut off here and interrupted by the material that appears in the next Audio Ex.		

Note: C = couplet; mm. = measures; Pn. = piano; Q = quatrain.

"reprise" of the scherzo gives the impression of offering a somewhat more faithful replica of the melodic content of the song than we encountered in the first scherzo.

All these features imbue this section with a more relaxed, more accessible character than that of the original iteration of the scherzo, which leads us to wonder if Mahler has lost sight of a central musical strategy: limiting the amount of melodic and formal clarity in the scherzo as a means of capturing a sense of the meaninglessness the movement is meant to convey. In this context, it is worth returning to a point we made earlier but left open: that, in the closed form of the scherzo in the symphony, Mahler brings about the return of the tonic and of the opening melody simultaneously, as he did *not* in the original version of the song with piano accompaniment. This choice, too, could be taken to be a step back from the use of various musical devices in the original song to portray the concept of meaninglessness. In fact, however, Mahler remains unwaveringly on track with respect to this objective. Although the level of melodic clarity may be higher in the second scherzo, and its tonal design more conventional, these attributes are starkly nullified by the way the section ends. In the first section of the scherzo, we heard a coordinated return of the tonic and the opening melody. Naturally, we expect to hear it again in this second iteration. In its last moments {⊙ Audio Ex. 6.18} at **00:04**, we hear a very brief modulation from F Major back to C that prepares us for a return of the A-section of the scherzo. At precisely this moment, however, the scherzo is abruptly suspended—interrupted, yet again, by a sudden return of the paraphrase of the Rott fanfare, this time in C Major. The course of musical events here results in a dramatic surprise. We are stunned, in equal measure, by the music we do not hear (the expected return of the opening of the scherzo) and what we do hear (another paraphrase of the Rott fanfare). This most powerful musical token of meaninglessness at an existential level keeps the paramount emphasis on this quality viable, and the disruptive failure to return to the opening of the scherzo as expected buttresses the same impression. Without ending this section "naturally," it throws us, without preparation, directly into the fourth section of the movement, the second trio.

The Second Trio

In its two earlier appearances, the paraphrase of the Rott fanfare broke into the middle of a section, each time interrupting the gentle, imitative flow of the first trio with the poignant and weighty reference it makes to the senseless tragedy of a promising artistic life unfathomably cut short. This time, after again interrupting the scherzo, it also serves to *initiate* the second trio, which places it in a very different perspective vis-à-vis the music that follows. Beginning a section with material we associate with interruption appears to portend a redoubling of the seriousness and intensity implicit in the fanfare.

This is precisely the plan Mahler follows {▶ Audio Ex. 6.19}. Right after the fanfare is played, the music presses forward with an increasing sense of agitation and ferocity, combining high dynamic levels, tremolando in the lower strings, and powerful accents. The sense of impending upheaval culminates (**00:23**) in a terrifying and utterly grisly outburst that is often called "the orchestral scream."

Many components contribute to the frightful effect of this moment, its high dynamic level (*fff*) and thunderous writing for percussion instruments among them. But it is the harmony at the beginning of this eruption that contributes most vividly to the listener's sense of the horror Mahler means to convey in this passage. The harmony emphasized here is a chord built on $B\flat$, but this sonority is superposed on the note C. C and $B\flat$ clash harshly when played together. They form the interval we call a major second {▶ Audio Ex. 6.20}, a particularly astringent dissonance that is amplified monumentally by Mahler's massive orchestration.

Mahler explained the intended meaning of this passage in very specific terms. Addressing the way his scherzo portrays the world as distorted and senseless, he commented to Bauer-Lechner about how this music expresses the pain anyone living in such a world feels. He goes on to add: "The Scherzo ends with the appalling shriek of this tortured soul."[14] In the letter to Max Marschalk in which he describes the Second Symphony, Mahler characterizes what the orchestral scream is meant to depict a little differently: "Life then becomes meaningless, an eerie phantom state out of which you may start up with a cry of disgust."[15]

The listener needs to recover from a musical moment as intense as this one. We begin with the orchestral scream again and follow how the music unfolds thereafter {▶ Audio Ex. 6.21}. After the shock of the scream registers, the intensity of the music begins to recede (**00:08**), first with a gradual reduction in dynamic level. The main subject of the imitative counterpoint of the trio enters vividly in the violoncellos and basses (**00:16**), and we know that we are in the midst of the second trio. The counterpoint quickly retreats from the spotlight, however, as another, and very different, musical affect is introduced (**00:26**). Our focus of attention shifts from the bustling activity of the imitation to soft and sustained sonorities in the

---

[14] Bauer-Lechner, *Recollections of Gustav Mahler*, 44.
[15] Martner, ed., *Selected Letters of Gustav Mahler*, no. 158.

winds and violins that evoke an aura of calm and serenity. The imitative material continues unabated, but the need to recover from the sheer intensity of the orchestral scream is so great that we are apt to focus more intently on the sense of tranquility that is emerging in this passage. That feeling assumes a more specific guise (00:34) when a trumpet contributes to the halo-like effect of this passage with a lyrical, descending melody. (The abrupt shift in mood could hardly be more compelling.) This is followed (00:40) in the first violins with an equally placid theme: a calm and gentle descent through the octave. The welcome sense of calm continues for a few moments.

We characterized this passage as the provider of needed comfort in the wake of the shocking orchestral scream, but there must be more to the extraordinary polarization inherent in this section of the second trio. If the orchestral scream evokes the sense of despair brought about by confronting a world without meaning, surely the music that follows it—a music that seems to be the very antithesis of the scream—offers a glimmer of hope that such meaning may not, in fact, lie beyond our reach. This is only a fleeting prospect, however, and one that will have to await the last movement for true resolution. Indeed, the newfound serenity of this passage evaporates just after the point at which the last example concluded.

We return to the movement as the restful music comes to an end {▶ Audio Ex. 6.22}. Immediately after a harp glissando (00:12), the main subject of the imitative trio attempts a return, but its entries are fitful, stridently accented, and quite dissonant. The motive almost disintegrates (00:18–00:22) as it becomes increasingly fragmented. The counterpoint appears to resume (00:23), but the passage takes on a markedly anticipatory character (00:32), culminating in the same gesture—a rapid, downward cascade (00:39)—that catapulted us into the second scherzo. This brings the second trio to a close. As we have seen, it makes little effort to provide a recognizable repeat of the first one. Rather, it introduces something new and shocking—the orchestral scream—and uses other elements primarily derived from the first trio to address issues that go beyond the essential form of a scherzo and trio: issues like the pain of experiencing a world without meaning and the pressing question of whether there may be a remedy for that grim reality. The last section of the movement follows. It is based largely, but not entirely, on material from the scherzo.

The Final Section of the Movement

We may survey the first four sections of this five-part scherzo and trio as follows:

- **Scherzo-1.** Based on the voice-and-piano version of the St. Anthony song from *Des Knaben Wunderhorn*. Mahler privileges the piano accompaniment of the song in his symphonic arrangement.
- **Trio-1.** Incorporates an allusion to the trio of Beethoven's Fifth Symphony and two paraphrases of a fanfare from Hans Rott's Symphony in E Major.
- **Scherzo-2.** A reasonably faithful return of material from the scherzo, albeit altered significantly and with the expected return of the opening material at the end of the section truncated.
- **Trio-2.** Mahler begins this section with a third paraphrase of the Rott fanfare and moves on to music that is increasingly anticipatory and agitated, culminating in a terrifying orchestral outburst that is meant to resemble a scream. The horrific character of this music eases with a brief return of the principal thematic material of the trio—the imitative counterpoint—and goes on to offer several motives that reflect an aura of celestial serenity.

With a great deal of the material of the opening scherzo already clearly reiterated in **Scherzo-2**, Mahler saw no need to repeat this in the last section of the movement, which traditionally returns to material from the initial scherzo in a five-part scherzo and trio. Instead, he offers a very brief section (a mere forty-five seconds in our performance) that contains a highly telescoped synopsis of motivic material, followed by a short passage that brings the movement to an abrupt halt.

The last section of the movement appears in {ⓘ Audio Ex. 6.23}, beginning with the rapid downward cascade at the end of the second trio that leads into it. Initially, we hear (at **00:01**) music from the florid piano accompaniment of the song. At **00:10**, this flowing figure continues, but Mahler adds to it the rapid-fire sixteenth notes played in the low strings and by the *Ruthe* that he used earlier to distract us from the melodic content of the song when it appeared in the first scherzo.[16] Mahler also broadens the synoptic

---

[16] See note 1, above.

scope of this passage by adding another motive into the mix at the same moment (00:10). In the oboe and clarinet, we hear a motive taken from the first trio—one of several new contrapuntal subjects that were introduced therein. The conspectus Mahler is providing here, thus, spans the whole movement, not just the scherzo. The additive thematic process continues to expand at 00:18. Here, the motive from the trio is taken over by a flute and piccolo while the violins play the flowing accompaniment passage. Newly added also is a melody from near the end of the song that is played here by a variety of woodwind instruments and the lower strings (00:22).

Finally (00:29), the concluding couplet of the song enters prominently and loudly, moving directly into the music of the piano postlude (00:36) that brought the St. Anthony song to an abrupt end. In discussing the ending of the song (in Chapter 5), we commented on its brevity and its unceremonious character. The music ends brusquely, where we might expect a more emphatic and dramatic closure for the end of the musical narrative. In discussing the St. Anthony song, we associated this abrupt and weak close with Mahler's effort to reflect in music the failure of the holy man's spiritual efforts, which rendered his mission meaningless. In addition, depriving the end of this movement of a more assertive completion results in the inability of the over-arching narrative of this symphony to attain any semblance of real closure at the end of the third movement.

Bauer-Lechner records the unusual response of the audience to the end of the movement at the Vienna performance of the symphony on April 9, 1899. She describes it as a "deathly silence"—a momentary absence of applause, where the convention was to applaud at the end of every movement—brought on by the wholly unexpected nature of the closure. Some "scattered applause" followed, according to her account.[17]

The St. Anthony song, its reflection in the scherzo, and the paraphrases of the Rott fanfare convey a powerful sense of the meaninglessness of life. In so doing, they reawaken and embolden the narrator of this symphony—the "dreadfully serious voice" that, from the initial moments of the first movement, forces us to confront that most terrifying existential question: How can a life that must end in death be meaningful? Like the first movement, the scherzo is not without its glimmerings of hope. We sense this in the quintessentially graceful melody near the end of the first trio (the one Mahler had to resist repeating) and in the blissfully celestial motives that follow

---

[17] Bauer-Lechner, *Recollections of Gustav Mahler*, 126.

immediately the grisly orchestral scream in the second trio. Clearly, we need to take note of the optimistic potential inherent in these melodies. The way Mahler ends the movement, however, cautions us not to invest too seriously in that potential, at least not yet.

The weakness of this ending appears to have been so important to Mahler that he took special precautions to ensure its effectiveness. To the end of the third movement, he attaches a performance direction: "The fourth movement follows without any break" ("folgt ohne jede Unterbrechung der 4. Satz"). Had any prolonged silence followed the last note of the third movement, it would have enhanced somewhat any sense of resolution we detect in the ending. The immediate segue into the next movement helps to deny the third movement truly meaningful closure.[18] Our struggle with that "dreadfully serious voice," Mahler seems to be telling us, continues, powerfully and unabated.

Despite the anemic quality of this closing and the way in which Mahler uses that quality to refocus our attention on core existential issues, Mahler embeds within it an extraordinary intertextual reference. The last few measures of the scherzo present a direct quotation from the piano postlude at the end of "Das ist ein Flöten und Geigen" ("There is a fluting and fiddling"), a song from Robert Schumann's song cycle, *Dichterliebe* of 1840.[19] Compare the two endings in the following example {▶ Audio Ex. 6.24}.

The scene described in the poem by Heinrich Heine that Schumann set to music in this song is the dancing at a wedding celebration, narrated from the perspective of a rejected lover. In Heine's poem, no visual aspects of his dance scene appear; the poem refers exclusively to sounds, those of flutes and fiddles, trumpets, drums, and shawms, interspersed with the sobbing and groaning of lovely angels (the latter image adding a note of poignancy that relates to the narrator's sorrow). Inevitably, Heine's poem calls to mind another dance scene: the one in the metaphor for meaninglessness Mahler used to describe the scherzo of the Second Symphony. In it, as we have learned, the motions of the dance can be seen, but without the music being heard,

---

[18] If Bauer-Lechner's account of the audience's reaction to the end of the scherzo at the Vienna performance in 1899 is accurate—she reported on its uncertainty regarding the appropriateness of applause, followed by sporadic applause—Mahler, who conducted that performance, would appear to have violated his direction that there be no pause between the scherzo and the fourth movement. That instruction had appeared in the published score two years before the Vienna performance.

[19] Robert S. Hatten, "The Place of Intertextuality in Music Studies," *The American Journal of Semiotics*, 3 (1985): 73, 79.

resulting in an image that seems, to use Mahler's words, "senseless, distorted, and crazy."

The total concentration on aural imagery in Heine's poem offers an anti-pode of Mahler's metaphor for meaninglessness, which relies exclusively on visual imagery. The two tableaux thus stand in stark contrast. But Mahler brought them together conspicuously, which implies that there must be some meaning to the juxtaposition. What could it be? And for whose benefit did Mahler intersperse them here? Perhaps, where the silent dance of Mahler's metaphor is designed to evoke meaninglessness, the omnipresence of sound in the conceit from the *Dichterliebe* song was perceived by Mahler not only as an antipode of his image for meaninglessness, but as an antidote, signifying a means of lighting a path to meaning.

Mahler cannot have expected his listeners to grasp this connection. Doing so would require them to know his metaphor of the silent dance, which he circulated only in closed, private circles. In addition, they would have to rec-ognize the musical linkage between the endings of Schumann's song and Mahler's scherzo and go on to take a position on the meaning of the contrast between the focus on visual imagery in Mahler's metaphor and aural sym-bolism in Heine's poem. Few, if any, listeners would be up to making all these connections. That circumstance, however, does not rob this exceptional quo-tation of its power.

If the relatedness of these metaphors is so important, and yet necessarily beyond the listener's grasp, for whom was this quotation from Schumann's song intended? I suggest that it may well have been for his own benefit that Mahler incorporated the excerpt from Schumann's song. The parallelism in the metaphors seems designed to be of help in the arduous and painful quest to find meaning in life. Think back on the autobiographical thread in Mahler's first two symphonies. "My [first] two symphonies contain the inner aspect of my whole life; I have written into them *in my own blood* every-thing that I have experienced and endured," he told Bauer-Lechner.[20] These words suggest that the preoccupation with existential angst that pervades the Second Symphony is not merely a reflection of an abstract concern. It is Mahler's own deeply personal fears that are driving this symphony. The image of aspects of Mahler's life being transcribed into the two symphonies "in his own blood," moreover, suggests that the process of imbuing the sym-phonies with this autobiographical thread was not without pain. In this light,

---

[20] Bauer-Lechner, *Recollections of Gustav Mahler*, 30, 231 (emphasis added).

his quotation of the Schumann song may well have filled an intimate need for *self*-assurance. "Perhaps there can be meaning in life after all," Mahler may have needed—so intensely—to remind himself with this remarkable quotation from Schumann. The listener, however, remains firmly in the grip of the symphony's narrator, "the dreadfully serious voice."[21]

At this point, the reader should listen to the third movement uninterrupted. A complete performance (with light annotations) appears in Appendix 4C).

---

[21] Carolyn Abbate offers an engaging and broad interpretation of the role of "deafness" as it is reflected in Mahler's metaphor of the silent dance. Her account considers several other literary texts that use the metaphor of a man peering into a ballroom, including Heine's "Das ist ein Flöten und Geigen" and Adam Mickiewicz's *Todtenfeier* (a work closely related to the Second Symphony, as we have seen). See Carolyn Abbate, *Unsung Voices: Opera and Musical Narrative in the Nineteenth Century* (Princeton, NJ: Princeton University Press, 1991), 124–130.

7

The Fourth Movement: "Urlicht"

Another Song from *Des Knaben Wunderhorn* •
The Poem: A Private Prayer at the Deathbed •
The Music: A Devotional Tone and an Anomalous Intensification •
The Contralto Soloist: Maureen Forrester • The Role of "Urlicht" in the Symphony

Another Song from *Des Knaben Wunderhorn*

For the fourth movement of the Second Symphony, Mahler used another song he had already composed—this one to be sung in the symphony by a contralto soloist. He turned once again to *Des Knaben Wunderhorn* for its text. The poem he selected was "Urlicht" ("Primeval Light"). Mahler's taste in poetry was impeccable. Beyond the quality of his literary judgment, moreover, he exhibited an uncanny ability to find poems that suited his own artistic needs and objectives to a tee. We shall see presently that "Urlicht" is among these, especially in the way it is made to fit Mahler's broad plan for the Second Symphony.

The chronology of the incorporation of this song within the symphony is complicated because the autograph of the first version, that for voice and piano, is lost. The Czech composer and close friend of Mahler Josef Bohuslav Foerster maintained that the song was composed in 1892.[1] Mahler finished the orchestral setting of this song (i.e., the version for contralto and orchestra separate from the symphony) on July 19, 1893, in Steinbach. Typically, he completed the piano and orchestral versions of his songs in close succession, which suggests that "Urlicht" may have been composed in

---

[1] Donald Mitchell, *Gustav Mahler: The Wunderhorn Years. Chronicles and Commentaries* (Woodbridge: Boydell Press, 2005), 137.

Inside Mahler's Second Symphony:. Lawrence F. Bernstein, Oxford University Press. © Oxford University Press 2022.
DOI: 10.1093/oso/9780197575635.003.0007

1893.[2] It is not clear exactly when Mahler decided to incorporate this song as the fourth movement of the symphony, but he appears to have done so relatively late in the compositional process. To do so, he had to bring the orchestral version of "Urlicht" as a separate song into line with the orchestral resources he used for the symphony. This may have been done as late as 1894.

The Poem: A Private Prayer at the Deathbed

The poem, which the editors of *Des Knaben Wunderhorn* suggest was culled from an oral tradition, addresses the speaker's impending death and hopes for immortality:[3]

O Röschen rot,	O little red rose,
Der Mensch liegt in grösster Not,	Man lies in the greatest need,
Der Mensch liegt in grösster Pein,	Man lies in the greatest pain,
Je lieber mögt ich im Himmel sein.	I would prefer to be in heaven.
Da kam ich auf einen breiten Weg,	Then I came on a broad path,
Da kam ein Engellein und wollt mich abweisen,	An angel came and sought to turn me away,
Ach nein ich liess mich nicht abweisen.	Ah no! I would not be turned away.
Ich bin von Gott, ich will wieder zu Gott,	I am from God and wish to return to God,
Der liebe Gott wird mir ein Lichtchen geben,	Dear God will give me a little light,
Wird leuchten mir bis an das ewig selig Leben.	Will light my way to everlasting blessed life.

[2] Gustav Mahler, *Symphonie Nr. 2*, ed. Renate Stark-Voit and Gilbert Kaplan, Gustav Mahler: Neue kritische Gesamtausgabe, 2 vols. (Vienna: Universal Edition and the Kaplan Foundation, 2010), Textband, 91.

[3] Heinz Rölleke, ed., *Des Knaben Wunderhorn: Alte deutsche Lieder gesammelt von Achim von Arnim und Clemens Brentano* (Frankfurt am Mein and Leipzig: Insel Verlag, 2007), 445. Our reading of the poem follows Rölleke's edition. The English translation is after that of Renate Stark-Voit and Thomas Hampson in Mahler, *Symphonie Nr. 2*, Partitur, 279.

The poem is really a prayer, a very private prayer, of a sort that was traditionally read at the deathbed, just before or after the demise of a loved one or friend. In Germany, a prayer like this one was known as a *Todesgebet*.[4] This genre of personal devotional expression emanates from a venerable tradition going back to the fifteenth century. About 1415 and 1450, respectively, two versions of an important Latin treatise were composed—first a long version, then a shorter one. We don't know who the author of either was, but it appears that the longer tract was written by a Dominican friar. This was entitled *Tractatus artis bene moriendi*, or the *Treatise on the Art of Dying Well*.

The work was very widely disseminated, having been translated into many European languages, and it was among the first books to be printed with movable type. The treatise took as its point of departure the Christian notion that man dies to live, that death, carried out properly, is a preparation for the hereafter. Thus, it advises that death is not to be feared, cautions against various temptations that beset the dying man, and offers questions to be put to him that can bring him closer to Christ's redemptive powers. It instructs family and friends on proper behavior at the deathbed, and—most importantly from the perspective of "Urlicht"—it includes prayers to be said before and after death.[5] This background helps us to understand the functional use to which a poem like "Urlicht" would have been put.

"Urlicht" consists in an opening motto, "O Röschen rot" ("O little red rose"), followed by three stanzas of three lines each.[6] The argument of each of the stanzas seems clear:

- The protagonist (who may be perceived both as an individual and as a representative of all mankind) has experienced the greatest need and anguish and would relish a place in paradise.
- An angel attempts to block his way on his journey to God, but he will not give up.

<hr />

[4] Hampson Song Foundation, *Mahler's "Urlicht" and the Second Symphony: A Conversation between Thomas Hampson and Renate Stark-Voit*, Part VI, https://hampsongfoundation.org/resource/mahlers-urlicht-and-the-second-symphony/, beg. at **00:29**.

[5] "Ars moriendi," *New World Encyclopedia*, https://www.newworldencyclopedia.org/entry/Ars moriendi.

[6] Despite the symmetry in the stanzaic structure of the poem (three stanzas of three lines each), Mahler makes no attempt to reflect it in his musical setting. His song is through composed, which is in line with the aesthetic preferences he expressed for setting poetry to music. See his critique of the songs of Franz Schubert and Carl Loewe reported above, pp. 106–107.

- He remains steadfast in his resolve to return to God, notwithstanding the angel who stands in his way, and will receive directly from God primeval light, to illuminate the path to eternal life.

The Music: A Devotional Tone and an Anomalous Intensification

The opening motto commands our attention immediately.

O Röschen rot	O little red rose

It must have symbolic significance. In the context of a Christian prayer, the red rose traditionally represents the blood shed by Jesus on the cross. Indeed, in a contemporary, longer poem that includes most of the lines of "Urlicht," the opening motto reads more specifically "O Jesu, Jesu rosenrot" ("Oh Jesus, Jesus of the red rose").[7] That symbolism goes beyond the color of the rose; it extends to the presence of thorns on the stems, which is reminiscent of the crown of thorns Jesus wore during the crucifixion. Viewed this way, the flower is linked to the purpose underlying Christ's death: the immanent resurrection, which, in turn, facilitates redemption and an opportunity for life after death for believers.

The motto is set musically as a particularly brief and sparse statement. However, it accomplishes much more than one might expect from its scant content. Beginning, as you may recall, with no pause after the scherzo, the first sounds of "Urlicht" bring about a sudden and complete reversal of the tone and mood of the third movement. In place of the frightening orchestral scream, the relentless driving rhythm, the void that arises from the de-emphasis of melody, and the bitterly sardonic irony we experienced in the scherzo, the opening notes of "Urlicht" provide a compelling sense of quietude and simplicity and a distinct aura of spirituality. The motto is declaimed gently and quietly by the contralto in D♭ Major, accompanied by muted

---

[7] Edward R. Reilly, "Sketches, Text Sources, Dating of Manuscripts—Unanswered Questions," *News About Mahler Research*, 30 (1993): 5–7. The longer poem was published in Georg Scherer, *Jungbrunner: Die schönsten deutschen Volkslieder*, 3rd ed. (Berlin: Wilhelm Herz, 1875), in which it is given pride of place as the concluding selection in the collection.

strings marked **PPP**. Mahler directs the contralto to sing tenderly throughout {⊙ Audio Ex. 7.1}.

What follows enhances the religious symbolism inherent in the opening motto {⊙ Audio Ex. 7.2}. This music has the character of a Lutheran chorale, richly orchestrated for trumpets, French horns, bassoons, and contrabassoon.[8] Beyond its explicit liturgical association, the stark and solemn simplicity of this chorale-like passage seems quintessentially tranquil. Then the first stanza begins {⊙ Audio Ex. 7.3}.

Der Mensch liegt in grösster Not,	Man lies in the greatest need,
Der Mensch liegt in grösster Pein,	Man lies in the greatest pain,
Je lieber mögt ich im Himmel sein.	I would prefer to be in heaven.

Mahler sets its successive expressions of need, pain, and the desire to enter paradise succinctly, but eloquently. For the first line, without abandoning the tonic of the preceding section, he switches to the minor mode to set off the gravity of mankind's "greatest need" from the simple piety reflected in the preceding chorale.[9] Mahler changes the orchestration, too; the ceremonial solemnity of the wind choir is replaced by strings alone, which resonate with a deep sense of austerity. For the "pain" mentioned in the second line, the music suggests a shift toward a new key, E♭ Major by hovering on the specific chord that portends the arrival of E♭ Major (beginning at **00:12**). E♭ Major arrives immediately thereafter, and that appearance is very brief (**00:22–00:25**).

For the third line (**00:28**), we are back in D♭ Major, the key of the chorale. The wish for paradise is articulated with two elegant examples of word painting. Both stress ascending motion, meant in a pictorial sense. The first is an expressive, upward leap of an octave to a high D♭ (the tonic) on "Himmel" ("heaven") (**00:36**). Then, after a brief descent, we hear a more gradual scalar ascent (**00:44**) to the same high D♭, which culminates in a second iteration of the same word (**00:51**). With these simple but exquisite touches of word painting, Mahler luxuriates on the word "Himmel," lending elegantly a sense of validity and importance to the concept of life after death.

---

[8] Mahler writes over this passage in the score *Choralmässig* (in the manner of a chorale).

[9] Mahler notates this brief passage in C♯ Minor, which is another way of writing D♭ Minor, a key that exists in theory, but which is rarely, if ever, used because of the extensive number of flats it would require.

The second stanza follows.

Da kam ich auf einen breiten Weg,	Then I came on a broad path,
Da kam ein Engellein und wollt mich abweisen,	An angel came and sought to turn me away,
Ach nein ich liess mich nicht abweisen.	Ah no! I would not be turned away.

This stanza has three components: (1) the protagonist encounters the path to paradise; (2) his way is blocked by an angel; and (3) he resists the angel. Mahler treats these elements separately. After the reflections on the dire nature of the human condition in the first stanza, the poem shifts into narrative mode, a transition that is vividly marked tonally by a stark change of key to B♭ Minor at the very beginning of the first line {⯈ Audio Ex. 7.4}. As the speaker describes encountering a broad path in this new key, the orchestra provides a host of different motifs: at the very beginning, triplets in the clarinets and open fifths in the French horns and harp, then a sweepingly expressive passage in a solo violin (**00:10**). In addition to these musical figures, a glockenspiel sounds seven times—at the beginning of each of the first seven measures of this passage. This array of material is so diverse that we have difficulty discerning within it any unified musical expression of the nature of the path the protagonist encounters. Perhaps that is precisely the purpose of the proliferation of material: to portray the speaker's initial bewilderment about the process that lies before him, one that will eventually lead to eternal life.

One of these musical elements, however, points us in a specific direction: the seven chiming tones of the glockenspiel. Concerning this passage, Mahler told Bauer-Lechner that the sound of a little bell in the chiming of the glockenspiel was for him childlike in nature. It reminded him of the old belief that a soul that found its way to heaven must, like a chrysalis, begin again as a little child.[10] Why precisely *seven* strokes on the glockenspiel? Perhaps to refer to the traditional seven ages of man that separate the soul of the deceased from the state of infancy to which it would initially return in paradise: infant, schoolboy, lover, soldier, wise judge, clueless old man, and corpse. Thus, in a mere seven measures, Mahler introduces the path, generates a sense of incipient bewilderment about where it leads, and then

---

[10] Constantin Floros, *Gustav Mahler: The Symphonies*, trans. Vernon and Jutta Wicker (Portland, OR: Amadeus Press, 1997), 67, quoting Natalie Bauer-Lechner, *Gustav Mahler in den Erinnerungen von Natalie Bauer-Lechner*, ed. Herbert Killian (Hamburg: K. D. Wagner, 1984), 168.

offers a musical and numerological hint that it might, indeed, be a path to immortality.

In the second line of the stanza, as we suggested, an angel appears to block the speaker's way along the path. The appearance of the angel is, at first, welcomed {⊙ Audio Ex. 7.5}. At the very end of the ornate solo violin passage that concludes the first line of the stanza, a modulation is deftly made from B♭ Minor to the warmer key of A Major (at **00:02**). The contralto's first description of the angel coincides with the arrival of A Major (**00:03**). It is bathed in a mantel of shimmering, if very quiet, triplet writing in the strings. The solo violin melody gives way to a flute, which plays a simpler version of it, this one clearly in A Major. However, a stark change in the music occurs when the angel attempts to turn away the speaker (**00:10**). Here, on the word "abweisen" ("to turn away"), the radiant shimmering suddenly stops, the mode changes from major to minor (**00:12**), the tempo slows, and (at **00:16**) the solo violin plays a poignant imitation of a sigh.

The speaker will not be turned away, however, as we learn in the last line of the stanza {⊙ Audio Ex. 7.6}. The refusal is made as a terse exclamation, which takes on added force from its stark repetition ("Ah no! I would not be turned away" sung twice). At the beginning of the passage, the key heads toward F♯ Minor, the tempo picks up, the refusal is set excitedly in rapid rhythms, and the strings accompany this with passages of tremolando, which add a touch of agitation to the music. Mahler calls upon the contralto to deliver this passage with a combination of passion and tenderness.

The image of the angel blocking the protagonist's way to God is very important. It suggests that salvation is not automatic. There is a stop along the way to it. Because it is an angel who interrupts the journey to redemption, the poem seems to condone this barrier as a legitimate component of the road to salvation. That component must be the apocalyptic Day of Judgment—the process that determines if salvation lies ahead for the departed soul. A reading of Chapters 8 and 9 of The Book of Revelations makes clear that it is angels who provide the primary instrumentation for meting out to mankind the suffering that is often a central part of the process of judgment. The longer poem cited above that includes most of the lines of "Urlicht" makes the connection to the Day of Judgment more explicit. It is entitled *Vom jüngsten Tage* (*Of the Last Judgment*).[11]

The angel may also be related to a famous biblical narrative, which can help us understand what this image meant to Mahler as he set the lines of

[11] Reilly, "Sketches, Text Sources, Dating of Manuscripts," 6.

"Urlicht" to music: the Old Testament story of the patriarch Jacob, who wrestled for an entire night with a determined opponent (Genesis 32: 25–33).[12] The identity of the adversary in this biblical narrative is unclear, but it seems to have been some sort of metaphysical being. In the copious literature that was spawned by this story, Jacob's opponent is most often characterized as an angel, as it is in Rembrandt's famous portrayal of the story (Fig. 7.1).[13] The adversary is, like the angel of "Urlicht," an impediment to an important objective, in this instance, a blessing that Jacob wishes to claim. He receives it ultimately, but only after persevering by demonstrating great tenacity in refusing to release his opponent from his hold until the blessing is his.

Mahler's close friend and intellectual mentor Siegfried Lipiner appreciated the symbolic meaning reflected in the figure of the angel, and he wrote about it.[14] As the philosopher Paul Natrop, a close friend of Lipiner, reported in his edition of Lipiner's play, *Adam*:

> From his first poem onward, Lipiner captured the problems of Christianity as few Christians had, as few had at all. To bring this problem in the height of perfection, as it stood before his eyes, also to an outer, life-like depiction, was his true and last artistic goal. Jacob Struggling with the Angel, one of his most beloved images from Rembrandt, is like a symbol of his own struggles with this great task, which almost bled him to death.[15]

We know, too, that Mahler identified with the narrative of Jacob's struggle at a very personal level. Opting to characterize Jacob's adversary as God Himself and focusing on man's creative efforts, Mahler saw in the story a

---

[12] Stephen E. Hefling, "Zweite Symphonie," in Peter Revers and Oliver Korte, eds., *Gustav Mahler: Interpretationen seiner Werke* (Laaber: Laaber-Verlag, 2011), 1:262.

[13] The mysterious figure is referred to as a man at the beginning of the biblical narrative in Genesis. At the end of the recounting of the incident there, Jacob is said to have struggled "with *Elohim* and with man," and his adversary is explicitly named as *Elohim* in a later reference to the narrative in the Book of Hosea (12:4). The Hebrew word *Elohim* is one of the names for God, but it also can connote some sort of generic divine being. The matter is further complicated because Jacob's name is changed in the wake of this incident to *Yisrael* (Israel), which is formed from the Hebrew words that mean "struggling with God." And Jacob names the place where the incident took place *Peniel*, which can be related to the Hebrew words that mean "encountering God face to face." Many of the traditional biblical commentators identify Jacob's antagonist as a form of divine being, an angel, perhaps. See *The Hebrew Bible: A Translation by Robert Alter* (New York: W. W. Norton, 2019), 1:121–122.

[14] Hefling, "Zweite Symphonie," 1:262.

[15] The translation is from Caroline A. Kita, "Jacob Struggling with the Angel: Siegfried Lipiner, Gustav Mahler, and the Search for Aesthetic-Religious Redemption in *Fin-de-siècle* Vienna" (Ph.D. diss., Duke University, 2011), 2, fn. 1.

Fig. 7.1. Rembrandt van Rijn, *Jacob Wrestling with the Angel*
Berlin, Gemäldegalerie. Reproduced under the Creative Commons Attribution-ShareAlike License

metaphor for his own struggles with the creative process. Bauer-Lechner attributes the following remark to Mahler:

> A magnificent symbol of the creator is Jacob wrestling with God until he blesses him. . . . God similarly withholds His blessing from me. I can only extort it from Him in my terrible struggles to bring my works into being.[16]

---

[16] Natalie Bauer-Lechner, *Recollections of Gustav Mahler*, ed. Peter Franklin, trans. Dika Newlin (New York: Faber and Faber, 2013), 76.

Thus, we can assume that Mahler would have been acutely sensitive to the role of the angel in the "Urlicht" poem. Whether viewed from the perspective of eschatology or that of the creative process, the angel is a formidable obstacle who needed to be overcome. In the final stanza, the speaker continues to bypass the angel, emphasizing a direct and personal connection to God, who will bestow upon him the manner of light that leads the way to eternal life.

Ich bin von Gott, ich will wieder zu Gott,	I am from God and wish to return to God,
Der liebe Gott wird mir ein Lichtchen geben,	Dear God will give me a little light,
Wird leuchten mir bis an das ewig selig Leben.	Will light my way to everlasting blessed life.

The speaker rejoices in asserting this immediate relationship to God, unintimidated by the intermediate stage represented by the angel, or, at the very least, unafraid of it. A wonderful goal is in plain sight—a clear path, divinely illuminated, to eternal life.

The speaker's reference to his oneness with God gives rise to a stark intensification of the musical setting {▶ Audio Ex. 7.7}. From the beginning of the passage through half of the second line, the music is disposed in short melodic units. They generate a charged, spasmodic quality that drives the music forward urgently. A chain of sequences underscores this sense of forward propulsion. In its combination of chromaticism and a high level of dissonance, the musical language of this passage contrasts sharply with all that precedes it in the song. Seemingly out of nowhere, a feeling of dramatic fervor envelops the listener. The music takes on an operatic character—one that sounds overtly passionate, perhaps even bordering on the sensual. We have gone from the sound of a Lutheran chorale to music that is distinctly reminiscent of Richard Wagner's music dramas. The contrast inherent in this passage is short-lived, but very powerful and equally mystifying. Mahler must have detected something in the poetry that signaled the need for this musical change. On the face of it, the speaker's expression of a oneness with God would not seem to require a sudden shift to music of this character, which prompts us to wonder what inspired Mahler to treat this brief passage in this way. The seminal motive of this passage—the one that is sequenced—will return at a decisive climactic moment in the last movement. That will shed light on Mahler's understanding of the oneness with God the speaker of "Urlicht" celebrates so intensely and on his reasons for portraying it with a musical setting that is, however briefly, as dramatic and sensual as this passage is. Yet again, Mahler raises an important question and delays its resolution for a considerable time. Not unusually, he seems to be demanding of us an ample measure of patience.

Our protagonist's journey has a clear goal—the attainment of eternal life (represented by "heaven" in the poem)—and reaching that goal is an important factor in the sequential organization of the melody in this intense section of "Urlicht." The sequential units are organized around the first notes of each measure (Music Ex. 7.1 and {▶ Audio Ex. 7.7}). The pattern is that of an upward, chromatic ascent: B♭, B♮, C. That is as far as the sequence goes, but it is not an accident that the next step along the sequential path would be D♭, the tonic of "Urlicht" and the melodic tone Mahler associated so elegantly with the attainment of heaven at the end of the first stanza.

When the sequence stalls on C midway through the second line of the poem, much changes, but only temporarily {▶ Audio Ex. 7.8}. The sequential pattern seems to be aborted, the melody descends, and the tempo slows. Thus, we suddenly seem to abandon the goal of the sequential passage, whose implicit ascent to a high D♭ was interrupted when the melody stalled on C, changed direction, and slowed down. But this turns out to be a momentary diversion, for the goal of the descending line turns out to be D♭ again, but a lower D♭, sung to the word "geben" ("give," at **00:07**)—that is, at the very moment in the poem at which God is described as conferring primeval light on the speaker. The advent of the D♭ when it *does* arrive is made even more satisfying owing to the brief postponement of its return. What is more, as the speaker denotes how that celestial radiance will "light his way to everlasting blessed life," ("wird leuchten mir bis in das ewig selig Leben"), the singer initiates the musical setting of that decisive conclusion with the same octave leap to a high D♭ (**00:10**) that "painted" the word "Himmel" so exquisitely in the first stanza of the song.

Music Ex. 7.1. A chromatic sequence near the end of "Urlicht"

Mahler treats this passage with considerable subtlety, embedding within it a protracted delay of the final arrival of the tonic that goes beyond its failure to appear directly at the apex of the chromatic ascent from $B\flat$ in the first phrase of the last stanza. It is the sort of delay that greatly enhances the sense of gratification we experience on its arrival, for having been made to await it just a little longer.[17] In the course of this delay, the vocal line and the orchestral music sometimes are made to work at cross purposes. When the soloist provides an arrival on $D\flat$, the orchestra does not always confirm it. The contralto's first strong landing on $D\flat$ (on "ge-*ben*" at **00:05**) is not accompanied by a harmony on $D\flat$ in the orchestra; nor is the second vocal arrival on $D\flat$ (on "*leuch*-ten" at **00:10**). In this way, Mahler builds into the passage continuing delay of a truly satisfying arrival of the tonic—that is, a coordinated arrival of the melodic $D\flat$ in the vocal line with a harmony on $D\flat$ in the orchestra. When that finally happens, Mahler adds yet another element of delay. The orchestra that at first avoided tonic harmony when the soloist provided arrivals on the tonic here reaches the tonic before the contralto does. On the final "Le-*ben*" (at **00:31**), the soloist overshoots the tonic by one scale degree just as the orchestra finally sounds the tonic harmony. She sings a standard non-harmonic tone called an *appoggiatura*, a note that lies a single scale degree above the desired point of arrival. It is dissonant with the tonic harmony and must achieve resolution thereafter (on the last syllable the contralto sings at **00:34**). Mahler has extended the delay in reaching full resolution on the tonic just a bit more.

This is a powerfully emotional moment in the song, one at which listeners have been known to shed tears. I am among them. With the grown men who cried openly at the premiere of the Second Symphony (according to Justine Mahler's account of that performance),[18] I often cry when I experience the matchless levels of satisfaction Mahler provides in the magical and broad sense of coalescence he brings about in the final few seconds of this song. The poem culminates in several compelling evocations of *return*, itself a potent source of satisfaction in both poetry and music. The speaker returns to God, and his soul to heaven. Both are portrayed most evocatively in the music, which goes on in the final moments of the song to offer yet another

---

[17] We observed the inner workings of this kind of delay in our discussion of binary forms in Appendix 1. In both examples of binary form, a gratuitous modulation to a more remote key was inserted before the final return to the tonic was gained. In both instances, the arrival on the tonic was ultimately strengthened owing to the listener's having to await it longer than was necessary.

[18] See Justine Mahler's remarks about the premiere of the Second Symphony in the preface to this guide.

important return: to the tonic, combined with a reappearance of the signi-
fication of heaven in the elegantly expressive upward octave leap to D_b. The
subtle elements of delay Mahler builds into these moments of return—the
ways in which he makes me wait just a bit longer for their greatly needed and
greatly anticipated arrival—brings these moments of satisfaction, for me, to
a level of exquisite refinement. In but a few seconds, I am made to experience
the deep satisfaction of return and resolution, coupled with an overpowering
sense of calm and optimism.

The Contralto Soloist: Maureen Forrester

The expressive power of this song, as we have experienced it here, cannot be
separated from the subtle interpretive impulses Maureen Forrester brings to
bear on her performance of it. These go beyond her meticulous observance
of Mahler's elaborate dynamic markings into the ways in which she alters her
vocal quality to achieve a subtly nuanced and highly expressive reading of the
song. In the first stanza {⊙ Audio Ex. 7.3}, the sharp contrast between "need"
and "pain" and the speaker's yearning to be in heaven is drawn sharply with
Ms. Forrester's full-throated rendition of the more harrowing sentiments of
the first two lines. This contrasts eloquently with the tone of delicate restraint
and understatement that she uses to convey the references to heaven in the
third line of the stanza.

In the brief chromatic and sensual passage {⊙ Audio Ex. 7.7}, Ms.
Forrester underscores the incisive quality of the melodic line by increasing,
ever so slightly, the intensity with which she renders each of the notes of the
systematic chromatic ascent: B_b (on "bin"), $B_\natural$ (on "wie-der"), and C (on "lie-
be"). Besides contributing importantly to the overarching intensity of the
passage, these graded increases in the earnestness with which each of these
notes is delivered help to underscore the important sense of direction inherent in the line.

It is in the last two verses of the song—in their refined portrayal of return,
rendered so much stronger by the forces of delay—that Ms. Forrester's interpretation shines most impressively {⊙ Audio Ex. 7.8}. As the orchestra
acts repeatedly to prevent harmonic corroboration of a fully satisfying arrival
on D_b, Ms. Forrester assures that the listener keeps the centrality of that goal
securely in mind. She highlights the first D_b ("ge-ben" at **00:05**) in a lushly
resonant tone, bringing out the next one ("leuch-ten" at **00:10**) through stark

contrast, by switching effortlessly to a tone of sublimely tender moderation in her high range. That register of Ms. Forrester's voice is one of her great assets, and she saves up a copious display of its radiant beauty for the last *D♭* at the very end of the passage ("Le-*ben*" at **00:31**), when the tonic is finally gained in both the vocal line and in the orchestra. These are but a few of the ways in which Ms. Forrester's interpretation has lent an iconic status to this performance of "Urlicht."

Some of the history that led to the collaboration between Bruno Walter and Maureen Forrester is germane. Walter had, for some years, maintained a special musical bond with the English contralto Kathleen Ferrier. In 1947, she sang in *Das Lied von der Erde* under his direction at the Edinburgh Festival, and with the New York Philharmonic the following year. Their collaboration in performances and recordings of Mahler's music flourished right up to the time of Ferrier's untimely death in 1953 at the age of forty-one. Walter wrote of her then: "The greatest thing in music in my life has been to have known Kathleen Ferrier and Gustav Mahler—in that order."[19] Walter was thereafter bereft of a unique partnership in performing Mahler's music. As he planned his performances and recordings of the Mahler Second in New York in 1957 and 1958, he needed to find a new Mahler contralto. Filling Ferrier's shoes would be no easy task.

Maureen Forrester was hardly known at this time; her reputation as an important artist in the United States dates only from an auspicious debut re-cital she gave at Town Hall in New York in November 1956, which received a rave review from Edward Downes in *The New York Times*.[20] Walter heard about Forrester, who was then twenty-seven years old, and asked her to sing for him. After listening to her sing Brahms's *Alto Rhapsody*, one of Kathleen Ferrier's signature pieces, he hired Forrester on the spot for the New York concert, which would form the basis for our recording of the symphony made in the following year.[21]

Although Forrester was to become noted for her interpretations of Mahler's music, including the Second and Third Symphonies and *Das Lied*

---

[19] George Henry Hubert Lascelles (Earl of Harewood), "Kathleen Mary Ferrier (1912–1953)," *Oxford Dictionary of National Biography*, online edition: https://www.oxforddnb.com/view/10.1093/ref:odnb/9780198614128.001.0001/odnb-9780198614128-e-33118;jsessionid=7539F2E00C525 101B2482D187FFEDCB2.

[20] Anthony Tommasini, "Maureen Forrester, Canadian Contralto, Dies at 79," *New York Times*, June 17, 2020, available at: https://www.nytimes.com/2010/06/18/arts/music/18forrester.html?searc hResultPosition=1.

[21] Maureen Forrester, with Marci McDonald, *Out of Character: A Memoir* (Toronto: McClelland and Stewart, 1986), 130–131.

von der Erde, she had sung no music by Mahler when Bruno Walter invited her to appear in his performances and recordings of the Second Symphony. Her own recollection of her relationship to Mahler's music at that time is of interest. In an interview she gave in *The Boston Globe* in 1986, she reflected on first singing "Urlicht": "That was the first time I had ever sung Mahler, and I thought to myself: 'What is this little piece? It's nothing!' Years later, as I teach it to young people, I realize how difficult it is. Ah, the rashness of youth."[22] Several inferences come to mind as we read this comment. One is that Forrester must have brought to bear on her reading of "Urlicht" powerful intuitive reflexes that inspired this extraordinary interpretation. Another is that she was receptive to the coaching that Bruno Walter surely offered her. Probably, both these interpretations reflect accurately what transpired. Indeed, Forrester's own recollections of how she worked together with Bruno Walter seem to substantiate the latter characterization of their joint effort:

> [I]n fact, he spoke very little, and I have come to the conclusion that great musicians are people of few words—you're either on their wave length or not. I picked up what Bruno Walter had to teach me almost by osmosis. I had an instinctive feeling of what he wanted or how I ought to correct a phrase and when I would hit what he was striving for, a smile would break over his face. I learned from that look. *"Ja, ja, mein kind,"* he would say, nodding.[23]

If this is how Walter and Forrester worked out their interpretation of "Urlicht," the somewhat muted but powerfully musical nature of how they interacted gave rise to an "Urlicht" of truly legendary status.

The Role of "Urlicht" in the Symphony

"Urlicht" displays an extraordinary level of elegance, but there is so much more to it than that. In the way it captures the spiritual essence of the poem, it resonates with a deep level of authenticity. It addresses the speaker's fundamental existential concerns with equal levels of honesty, conviction, forcefulness, and beauty. This makes of "Urlicht" a decisive moment in the trajectory

---

[22] Tommasini, "Maureen Forrester."
[23] Forrester, *Out of Character*, 150.

of the Second Symphony. Amid all the turbulent expressions of existential angst throughout this work, there have been periodic moments that gave cause for optimism: the gentle secondary theme in the first movement {⊙ Audio Ex. 7.9}, the quiet trumpet tune in the scherzo that Mahler regarded as its most beautiful melody {⊙ Audio Ex. 7.10}, and the lyrical descending melody in the violins that follows the orchestral scream in the scherzo and that is related to the trumpet melody{⊙ Audio Ex. 7.11}. All these melodies project a sense of solace and optimism—but, in the absence of words, none of them can do so in a specific way. In this respect, "Urlicht" differs; it offers a clear suggestion that the answer to the central existential question posed by the Second Symphony resides in the Christian concept of eternal life. Thus, "Urlicht" has taken us a long way toward resolving a question put forth nearly an hour earlier in the first movement.

We must exercise care, however, for aspects of "Urlicht" and their relationship to Mahler's broader plan for the Second Symphony remain unclear. The speaker's resistance to the angel raises questions about the role of judgment in the attainment of immortality, and the sudden introduction of a brief but intense chromatic passage with dramatic and passionate overtones requires explanation. At a live performance of the symphony, moreover, if we look at the stage and take note of a chorus of about 100 singers who have yet to sing a note, we know instantly that a long stretch of the road to final resolution of this symphony and its existential agenda still lies before us. We will set forth on that road soon because Mahler indicates that the finale should begin without pause after the conclusion of "Urlicht."

At this point, the reader should listen to the fourth movement uninterrupted. A complete performance (with light annotations) appears in Appendix 4D.

8

How to Complete the Symphony

Keeping the Finale in Mind • An Epiphany •
An Alternative View of the Epiphany

Keeping the Finale in Mind

After a long hiatus of five years, as we have seen, Mahler's intense work on the
Second Symphony during the summer of 1893 brought about the completion of the three inner movements (although it is not known for certain exactly when he decided to incorporate "Urlicht" in the symphony). He began
to make some sketches for the finale at this time but found them unsatisfying.
"Things have a nasty will of their own," he told Bauer-Lechner. "Instead of
the ideas in 4/4 time, which I need for my finale, I now have only ideas in 3/4
time, which are of no use to me at all."[1]

That Mahler committed little of the finale to paper at this time, however,
does not mean that it had not already become a major preoccupation for
him. His old friend Fritz Löhr visited him in Steinbach during that most pro-
ductive summer of 1893. Their conversations touched on many topics, one of
which was Mahler's prioritization of a union of the arts, best exemplified, he
thought, by Beethoven's Ninth Symphony, which, as Mahler told Löhr, "went
as far as it is possible to go in music, much as Goethe had done with words; he
then took the tremendous step of introducing speech—and to what effect!"[2]
Mahler's plan to make of the Second Symphony a massive choral symphony
in the manner of Beethoven's Ninth was at the forefront of his consciousness
at this time. Some years after the Second Symphony had been completed,

[1] Gustav Mahler, *Symphonie Nr. 2*, ed. Renate Stark-Voit and Gilbert Kaplan, Gustav Mahler: Neue
kritische Gesamtausgabe, 2 vols. (Vienna: Universal Edition and the Kaplan Foundation, 2010),
Textband, 92.
[2] Henry-Louis de La Grange, *Gustav Mahler: The Arduous Road to Vienna (1860–1897)*, completed,
rev., and ed. by Sybille Werner (Turnhout: Brepols, 2020), 533.

Inside Mahler's Second Symphony:. Lawrence F. Bernstein, Oxford University Press. © Oxford University Press 2022.
DOI: 10.1093/oso/9780197575635.003.0008

Mahler reflected on his quest for the right text for the finale. On February 17, 1897, he wrote to Arthur Seidl, a musician, music critic, and teacher at the Leipzig conservatory: "In the last movement of my Second I simply had to go through the whole world of literature, including the Bible, in search of the right word[s]."[3]

All this—the fruitless sketches and the exacting search for the perfect text—took place in the summer of 1893. Time ran out, however, and, by the end of August, Mahler had to return to Hamburg to prepare for performances of *Der Freischütz* and *Die Meistersinger*. Once the opera season was fully under way, there would be little time for work on the Second Symphony, and, when the new year of 1894 was ushered in, the symphony remained unfinished, now nearly six years after Mahler began working on it. A short time later, however, an event took place in Hamburg that would precipitate the advancement of the completion of the symphony.

An Epiphany

On February 12, 1894, Hans von Bülow, the great conductor, pianist, and composer, died in Cairo where he had gone to convalesce from a serious illness. A service for von Bülow was held at St. Michael's Church in Hamburg some weeks later, on March 29. Mahler attended the service. There he heard a chorale sung by a children's choir to a text by the important eighteenth-century German writer Friedrich Gottlieb Klopstock (Fig. 8.1). The chorale was called *Die Auferstehung* ("The Resurrection").

In an edition of Klopstock's sacred songs (*Geistliche Lieder*) published in 1758, the poem to which the chorale that was sung at von Bülow's funeral is accompanied by the rubric "Mel. Jesus Christus unser Heiland, der den Tod [überwand]," which informs the reader to sing the words to the tune ("Mel[odie]") of "Jesus Christus unser Heiland," a famous chorale melody set many times by composers, including J. S. Bach and Martin Luther. None of the known melodies used to set this text, however, will serve for Klopstock's "Auferstehen," which was written in an entirely different poetic meter.[4]

---

[3] Knud Martner, ed., *Selected Letters of Gustav Mahler: The Original Edition Selected by Alma Mahler*, trans. Eithne Wilkins, Ernst Kaiser, and Bill Hopkins (New York: Farrar, Straus, Giroux, 1979), no. 205.

[4] Donald Mitchell, *Gustav Mahler: The Wunderhorn Years. Chronicles and Commentaries* (Woodbridge: Boydell Press, 2005), 418.

Fig. 8.1. Friedrich Klopstock in a print by Lazarus Gottlieb Sichling
Washington, DC, Library of Congress, Division of Prints and Photographs

Hearing this chorale set to Klopstock's text about resurrection sung by a choir of children appears to have been something of an epiphany for Mahler in his struggle to find a way of ending the Second Symphony. Von Bülow's funeral is described movingly by Mahler's close friend, the Czech composer, Josef Bohuslav Foerster, who also attended it:

> Mahler and I were present at the moving farewell. . . . The strongest impression to remain was that of the singing of the children's voices. The effect

was created not just by Klopstock's profound poem but by the innocence of the pure sounds issuing from the children's throats. The resurrection hymn died away and the old, huge bells of the church opened their eloquent mouths . . . and their mighty threnody brought mourning to the entire port [city of Hamburg].[5]

Foerster tried to meet up with Mahler after the service but could not find him. He went to Mahler's apartment. His description of their encounter is a tribute to the warmth of their friendship. It also reflects beautifully the ability of a fellow-composer to grasp independently—almost telepathically—how a piece of music he heard might suggest a solution to a pressing compositional problem in a work by his colleague.

I opened the door and saw him sitting at his writing desk, his head lowered and his hand holding a pen over some manuscript paper. I remained standing in the doorway. Mahler turned to me and said: "Dear friend, I have it!" I understood. As if illuminated by a mysterious power I answered: "Auferstehen, ja auferstehen wirst du nach kurzem Schlaf" ["Rise again, yes you will rise again after a brief sleep"]. Mahler looked at me with an expression of extreme surprise. I had guessed the secret he had as yet entrusted to no human soul: Klopstock's poem, which that morning we had heard from the mouths of children, was to be the basis for the closing movement of the Second Symphony.[6]

Foerster's account of Mahler already at work on music that resulted from his encounter at the von Bülow funeral appears to be accurate. A sketch survives that seems to contain the music he worked out upon returning home from the service in Hamburg.[7]

Mahler himself described the memorial service some years later in the same letter to Arthur Seidl from which we quoted above:

Then the choir, up in the organ-loft, intoned Klopstock's *Resurrection* chorale.—It flashed on me like lightning, and everything became plain and

---

[5] Josef Bohuslav Foerster, *Der Pilger: Erinnerungen eines Musiker. Einleitende Studie von František Pala* (Prague: Artia, 1955), 404; English translation in Mitchell, *Gustav Mahler*, 169.

[6] Foerster, *Der Pilger*, 405; English translation in Mitchell, *Gustav Mahler*, 169.

[7] Stephen Hefling, "Content and Context of the Sketches," in Gilbert Kaplan, ed., *Mahler: The Resurrection Chorale* (New York: The Kaplan Foundation, 1994), 13. See also the facsimile of the sketch on p. 27.

clear in my mind! It was the flash that all creative artists wait for "conceiving by the Holy Ghost"![8]

However important the bolt of inspiration Mahler describes here was, we should not conclude from his rhapsodic account that the broad scheme for the last movement came to him in that instant. We know that he had been planning a choral finale for quite some time. What he seems to be describing is the utter exhilaration he experienced when, in a flash, he received the answer to the question he had been pursuing so earnestly: to what text would he set the choral finale? Given the existential issues Mahler raised in the Second Symphony, what more appropriate text could one imagine for the finale than one concerned with resurrection? And, with that text in hand, and a melody sketched for it, he had musical ideas on paper that allowed him to proceed with further work on the last movement.

An Alternative View of the Epiphany

An epiphany can come about for more than one reason. As we picture Mahler sitting in St. Michael's church in Hamburg at Hans von Bülow's funeral, we can readily imagine his having had deeply conflicted feelings about the decedent. On the one hand, Mahler revered von Bülow, and he did so from the perspective of one of the few musicians in Europe who was in von Bülow's league as a conductor. Mahler enjoyed reciprocal respect from von Bülow for his conducting. That was not, however, what he wanted most from him. He coveted von Bülow's approval for his music, but he never received it. Think back on the episode described in Chapter 3 when, in 1891, Mahler played his newly completed *Todtenfeier* at the piano for von Bülow, only to look up from the keyboard to see him covering his ears with his hands. Moments later, Von Bülow dismissed the work by suggesting that "If this is music, I no longer know what music is." Given the intensity of his respect and admiration for von Bülow, Mahler had to have been devastated by this response to his new work. Indeed, as we suggested, this episode may have contributed to a writer's block that delayed significantly the completion of the Second Symphony. It seems very unlikely that Mahler sat at von Bülow's funeral and mourned his passing unconditionally.

---

[8] Martner, ed., *Selected Letters of Gustav Mahler*, no. 205.

Theodor Reik, the Viennese psychoanalyst and student of Sigmund Freud, took into account how heavily this encounter with von Bülow must have weighed on Mahler. In 1953, he offered an alternative view of Mahler's "epiphany" at the memorial service. He suggests that Mahler had to have harbored deeply conflicted feelings about a man he admired greatly and who had shown the deepest appreciation for Mahler the conductor, yet who had dealt Mahler an annihilating blow with his outright rejection of his music. Yet Reik found no overt expression of outrage—scarcely any display of emotion at all—over this rejection in anything Mahler ever wrote about von Bülow's deep antipathy toward his music. He concludes that Mahler may well have suppressed these feelings and converted them into an unconscious death wish. The "epiphany" Mahler experienced at von Bülow's funeral, Reik suggests, had much to do with a sense of triumph over the elimination of the antagonist, at once revered and hated. In Reik's view, these feelings surfaced momentarily at the service, bringing Mahler a powerful sense of relief, which was then transferred into hopes for the success of the symphony:

> It is as if Mahler had thought: *As my unconscious wish that you who rejected me as a composer should die was fulfilled, so my symphony will be finished and become a masterwork. . . .* Not the intonation of the chorus struck Mahler "like a bolt of lightning," but the unconscious recognition that his wish had the power to kill the antagonist who had been an obstacle in his way.[9]

Reik came to this analysis of Mahler's "epiphany" by way of a set of personal circumstances strikingly similar to those that surrounded Mahler's relationship with von Bülow. On Christmas evening of 1925, Reik was informed of the death of his mentor and close friend, the distinguished Viennese psychoanalyst Karl Abraham. He spent most of the following days writing a eulogy for Abraham, which he read at the meeting of the Vienna Psychoanalytic Association on January 6, 1926. Throughout that time, Reik was haunted by a melody that surfaced in his consciousness, a tune he could not identify

---

[9] Theodor Reik, *The Haunting Melody: Psychoanalytic Experiences in Life and Music* (New York: Farrar, Straus, Young, 1953; repr. New York: Da Capo Press, 1983), 259–270, "In Search of the Finale." The quotation appears on 269–270. Years after Reik's study was published, evidence came to light that Mahler had, in fact, articulated feelings of rancor toward von Bülow, in his correspondence with his sister Justine and with Richard Strauss. See La Grange, *Gustav Mahler: The Arduous Road to Vienna*, 566. Whether or not Mahler repressed his feelings of antipathy toward von Bülow, they had to have had an impact on his reactions to von Bülow's funeral, just as they must have played an important role in delaying his completion of the Second Symphony.

and that remained omnipresent despite his many efforts to drive it off. (This provided the inspiration for the title of the study in which Reik discusses these matters, *The Haunting Melody*.) Only later, was he able to identify the music as the chorale melody Mahler wrote for Kloptsock's *Auferstehen*. Reik remained disquieted over the persistence of this melody as he wrote the eulogy for his friend and mentor, until he brought to the surface of his awareness a striking parallel between his relationship to Karl Abraham and Mahler's to Hans von Bülow. Reik had earned a Ph.D. He was not a physician. As a young man, when he informed Abraham of his intentions to practice psychoanalysis, Abraham strongly opposed Reik's plan out of his disdain for what he called "lay analysis." Only physicians, as opposed to psychologists, should engage in psychoanalysis, according to Abraham. Abraham supported and respected his student as a researcher, but not as a therapist. The analogy with von Bülow's divergent views of Mahler's conducting and his musical composition is compelling. Reik believed that, at the time he wrote the eulogy and focused so intensely on his memories and feelings about Abraham, he must have recalled his mentor's qualms about his competence as a therapist and momentarily felt a sense of relief at the news of his death.[10]

Whatever mechanism brought about Mahler's epiphany—be it the fortuitous discovery of the perfect text, or the momentary surfacing of the full extent of his hostility toward von Bülow, or both—the logjam that had inhibited the completion of the symphony broke in its wake. The opera season was at its height in February, and normally Mahler would have to await the summer to put his plans for the finale into play. By June 29, however, he had finished a short score of the finale, which means that he must have found time to compose even during the last months of the opera season.[11] Most of the finale was composed at Steinbach in the summer of 1894. On July 25, Mahler wrote to his friend Arnold Berliner "The last movement (score) of the Second Symphony is finished! It is the most important thing I have done yet."[12]

[10] Reik, *The Haunting Melody*, 292–297.
[11] Hefling, "Content and Context of the Sketches," 14.
[12] Martner, ed., *Selected Letters of Gustav Mahler*, no. 124.

9

The Last Movement, Part 1: References to Judgment and the Airing of Themes

A Return of the Orchestral Scream •
Symbols of Judgment Drawn from the Jewish Liturgy •
A Promissory Note • Symbols of Judgment Drawn from the Christian Liturgy •
More about an Old Enigma • Back to Christian Judgment •
Is this an Exposition?

A Return of the Orchestral Scream

With no pause after the end of "Urlicht," the finale erupts with a shock. We hear a modified statement of the fearful orchestral scream from the third movement, the one Mahler characterized as a cry of disgust in reaction to the lack of meaning in life. The two passages are not identical, but they share the same musical representations of catastrophe: frenzied rhythm and explosive dynamics, combined with the acrid dissonance that arises when C is pitted against $B\flat$, in an overwrought orchestration {▶ Audio Ex. 9.1}. A new addition to this passage is a stark motive played by the trumpets and trombones with the bells raised (beginning at **00:04**). It outlines an F Minor triad and has come to be known as the "terror motive." It will recur prominently later.

What is most shocking about this passage is its stark juxtaposition to "Urlicht," which had, just moments earlier, provided us with the most compellingly optimistic outlook until that point in the symphony. The quiet and sincere devotional tone of the fourth movement encouraged us to imagine that death might find meaning in the Christian doctrine of eternal life. That notion seems to evaporate with the outburst at the beginning of the finale. We might almost have expected this turn of events because, over the course of this symphony, Mahler has so often indulged in larger-than-life swings from

Inside Mahler's Second Symphony:. Lawrence F. Bernstein, Oxford University Press. © Oxford University Press 2022.
DOI: 10.1093/oso/9780197575635.003.0009

catastrophe to solace and back. He addresses the magnitude of this sort of contrast in a letter of January 31, 1895, to his friend the German physicist Arnold Berliner. He described a thought he had about the Second Symphony as he heard it in his initial rehearsals of a concert in Berlin that previewed the first three movements: "One is battered to the ground and then raised on angels' wings to the highest heights."[1] Grandiose musical contrast like that between the tranquility of "Urlicht" and the bombastic return of the orchestral scream with which the finale begins, thus, can originate in the dramatic emotional shifts Mahler traces in his symphony. The magnitude of the contrast and the suddenness with which it is introduced are suggestive of an operatic aesthetic.

Another reason we might have suspected that Mahler would return to the anxieties reflected in the orchestral scream is the unfinished business left over from "Urlicht." The reason why the speaker of the poem resists the angel is far from clear, as we have seen, and it raises questions about the issue of judgment, a process in which angels participate by meting out punishment on the apocalyptic Day of Judgment. When the speaker asserts his oneness with God, moreover, the music shifts briefly but dramatically and inexplicably to an anomalously contrasting musical language—sensual, chromatic, and unpredictable. Mahler leaves these matters unresolved, and the startling reversal that accompanies the beginning of the last movement reminds us that the serene, devotional character of "Urlicht," falls short of answering the central questions raised in this symphony, a matter that is compounded by the unresolved ambiguities in the song.

Context is often a vital key to recognition and understanding. The relationship I am about to propose would be unlikely to occur to us upon hearing the orchestral scream at the end of the third movement, but the start of the finale situates that musical event in an entirely different milieu. Picture yourself hearing the Mahler Second for the first time in a live performance. You know from the program that the finale is about to begin. You see 100 singers on stage who have been silent thus far and conclude, of course, that you are about to hear a choral finale. You glance at your watch and note that you have already heard nearly an hour of music, and it occurs to you that this choral finale will conclude a work of monumental proportions. When attempting to gain a foothold on a wholly new piece of music, it is natural to contextualize—to seek the comfort inherent in recognizable affinities, similarities, and precedents. Thus, as the finale of the Mahler Second is about to begin, we

---

[1] Knud Martner, ed., *Selected Letters of Gustav Mahler: The Original Edition Selected by Alma Mahler*, trans. Eithne Wilkins, Ernst Kaiser, and Bill Hopkins (New York: Farrar, Straus, Giroux, 1979), no. 127.

are apt to have in mind the predecessor to which it is most closely related in so many important ways. That, of course, would be the Ninth Symphony of Beethoven.

Listening to the orchestral scream at the beginning of Mahler's finale inevitably, therefore, brings to mind the opening of the finale of the Beethoven Ninth {⊙ Audio Ex. 9.2}. It is not that the two openings share specific melodic or rhythmic content; they are quite different in both these spheres. But the two openings are very much alike in their overall character. Mahler's orchestral scream and the *Schreckensfanfare* (frightening fanfare), as the opening of Beethoven's finale came to be called, both epitomize frenzy, just as they both hover on the cusp of irrationality by eschewing many of the markers of cogent organization. The two passages, moreover, are addressed to similar needs. In the Ninth Symphony, the feverish opening serves to eradicate jarringly from the listener's consciousness the sublime beauty of the preceding third movement, just as Mahler's frenetic opener bluntly cancels out the optimism we gained from the tranquil ambience of "Urlicht." In fact, we shall learn later in this movement that, in a more general and more important sense, dramatic erasure of what precedes is a procedure amply explored in both Beethoven's Ninth and the Mahler Second. In addition, Mahler's nod to the Beethoven Ninth at the beginning of the finale seems striking in the light of how he began this symphony: with music that also emulated the opening of the Ninth Symphony, in content and also in the manner in which both opening passages anticipate a work of major magnitude (see the discussion of Mahler's debt to Beethoven in Chapter 2).

In the third movement, the intensity and violence of the orchestral scream required some moments for decompression, which were provided in a quiet section in C Major. In the finale, the fervor of the scream is cut off dramatically by a *Luftpause* at **00:07** in {⊙ Audio Ex. 9.3}. It, too, is followed by a quiet section in C Major. This passage, however, not only serves the need for decompression; it fleshes out and emphasizes an extremely important musical theme. Right after the *Luftpause*, the strings provide some rapid oscillation in the violoncellos and basses with a tremolando in the higher strings. As the passage begins to grow softer, harps and French horns introduce an interval, a descending fifth (**00:12**). It is repeated (**00:18**); then, very quietly at **00:21**, clarinets fill in this interval, to form a melody. Just before the clarinets enter, another familiar sound returns, the recurrent sounding of the glockenspiel, which, in "Urlicht," connoted the return to infancy of a soul embarking on its journey to eternal life. The clarinet melody is echoed by the oboes and then, more decisively, by the French horns (**00:30**). Melodic and rhythmic activity wind down as the passage continues, growing softer, until it is almost inaudible.

The theme that just began and that dominates this passage sounds familiar. Its opening notes made a cameo appearance near the end of the first movement in the context of a parade of musical quotations packed tightly together {▶ Audio Ex. 9.4}. This was Mahler's first musical reference in the symphony to the concept of immortality, in the form of the first five notes of the immortality motive from the last act of Wagner's *Siegfried*. As we learned earlier, Brünnhilde sings this theme to the words "Ewig war ich; Ewig bin ich" ("I was immortal; I am immortal"). (See Chapter 3 for details about this motive.) In the first movement, the quotation of the immortality motto was abbreviated, rushed, and barely noticeable, owing to its brevity and the clustering together of several quotations at this point. Here, it is permitted to unfold slowly, prominently, and spaciously, which gains for it a growing sense of importance. In a manner very typical of Mahler, a musical idea was first introduced in a cursory, vague manner, only to take on a more vivid shape and a clearer meaning later. The dread associated with the orchestral scream is past, and Mahler seems again to be working his way toward more buoyant answers to his existential concerns.

Symbols of Judgment Drawn from the Jewish Liturgy

The next passage is very mysterious. The French horns play an ascending perfect fifth twice, but Mahler fusses exceedingly over the sound of this simple interval. He calls for as many horns as can be assembled, insists that they play with great intensity, requests that the second playing of the fifth sound like an echo (i.e., weaker than the first), and that all the horns play from "far in the distance" (i.e., offstage). Thus Mahler, quite exceptionally, calls upon masses of the loudest brass instrument to play from a location that will add a quality of remoteness to the music they play. These unusual, seemingly contradictory requirements combine to produce a unique sound, one that brings about an otherworldly effect {▶ Audio Ex. 9.5}. In some of the sources for the Second Symphony that antedate the published score (1898), Mahler writes over this horn part "Der Rufer in der Wüste" ("The Caller in the Wilderness").[2]

---

[2] Gustav Mahler, *Symphonie Nr. 2*, ed. Renate Stark-Voit and Gilbert Kaplan, Gustav Mahler: Neue kritische Gesamtausgabe, 2 vols. (Vienna: Universal Edition and the Kaplan Foundation, 2010), Partitur, 191. Mahler abandoned this subtitle, which does not appear in the published score.

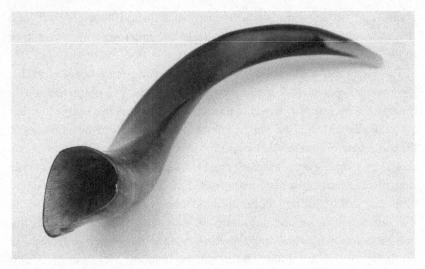

Fig. 9.1. A *shofar*
Moto Meiri / Alamy Stock Photo

The reference is to Isaiah 40:3, which presages the arrival of God's presence ("The voice of him that crieth in the wilderness, prepare ye the way of the Lord, make straight in the desert a highway for our God").

Leonard Bernstein, among others, suggests that the open fifth sounded in the French horns is meant to represent the sound of the *shofar*, the ram's horn that plays an integral part in the liturgy of the Jewish New Year (Fig. 9.1).[3]

Mahler would have heard the *shofar* at the synagogue where he worshiped with his family as a child in Iglau. The Jewish New Year is a deeply introspective occasion that ushers in ten days of penitence. Another name for the Jewish New Year is *yom hadin*, the Day of Judgment. On this day, God assesses the behavior of all mankind and determines, for the coming year, who shall live and who shall die. The ram's horn sounds a call to repent, a warning that harsh Divine decrees may be in store, but that they can be averted with sincere prayer, good deeds, and penitence.

---

[3] *The Little Drummer Boy: An Essay about Mahler by and with Leonard Bernstein*, DVD Video (BBC, 1984), at **56:11**. The *shofar*-like sound of this passage is described as Mahler's attempt to generate the aura of the Jewish prophets by Stephen E. Hefling, "Zweite Symphonie," in Peter Revers and Oliver Korte, eds., *Gustav Mahler: Interpretationen seiner Werke* (Laaber: Laaber, 2011), 1:275, following Vladimir Karbusicky, "Gustav Mahlers Besinnung auf seine böhmischen Wurzeln," in *Deutsche Musik in Ost- und Südosteuropa*, Studien zum Deutschtum im Osten, 28, ed. Gabriel Adriányi (Cologne: Böhlau Verlag, 1997), 59–62.

Why should Mahler's otherworldly, offstage open fifths call to mind the *shofar?* The answer to this is a bit complicated, but it's not too hard to unravel. Among the various musical patterns the *shofar* is called upon to play, one carries the heaviest emotional component. The name assigned to this pattern is *sh'varim* (from the Hebrew root ר-ב-שׁ [S-V-R], which means broken). It is, in fact, a musical pattern that sounds broken, and it is meant to mimic the sound of weeping, a sound thought to be appropriate for a time of repentance. There are different ways to produce *sh'varim*. Sometimes, the tongue is used to start a note, and the broken effect is produced by adding emphasis to the same note with the breath (as opposed to the tongue). More often, perhaps, the break is achieved by sounding two notes, with the lower one sounded first. Since the *shofar* is an open tube—not unlike the trumpet and French horn in the days before they had valves—it can produce only a limited and fixed number of tones (a range of notes that has come to be known in the terminology of the physics of music as the overtone series). If the lowest and next-to-lowest tones in the series of available notes are sounded, the interval that results will be an octave. Should the next two notes in the series be played, it will result in a perfect fifth, the same interval as in Mahler's otherworldly horn calls. This choice of interval is often heard in the synagogue {⏵ Audio Ex. 9.6}. And it is this sound that surely led Leonard Bernstein and others to detect the sound of the *shofar* in Mahler's horn calls.

With this imitation of the *shofar*, Mahler has ushered us into the apocalyptic world of judgment—this time, seen from the perspective of Jewish liturgy. Various Old Testament texts seem to describe what we hear at this important juncture in the symphony. Isaiah 27:13, for example, says of the Day of Judgment: "And it shall come to pass in that day that a great horn [*shofar*] shall be blown." The almost imperceptibly quiet echo that follows the first entry of the massed horns also seems to have its origins in a biblical text. First Kings 19:11–13 relates a story about the prophet Elijah, whose life has been threatened by Queen Jezebel. God speaks to him, but not out of the variety of apocalyptic upheavals mentioned in these verses: wind, a shattered mountain, an earthquake, and a fire. The voice of God is described, rather, as a "still, small voice."

As we have seen, Mahler searched far and wide for a text to set in the last movement of the Second Symphony. As he related in his letter of February 17, 1897, to Arthur Seidl, he claimed to have scoured "the whole world of literature, including the Bible, in search of the right word[s]."[4] In the course of this avid quest, Mahler may have come across both of these widely disparate

---

[4] Martner, ed., *Selected Letters of Gustav Mahler*, no. 205.

biblical references—to the "great horn" (*shofar*) and the "still small voice"—directly in the Bible. More likely though, he discovered the contrast inherent in these two biblical references while attending the synagogue in Iglau, specifically in the Jewish liturgy for the New Year and the Day of Atonement. A medieval poem, "Unetaneh tokef k'dushat hayom" ("Let us give voice to the sanctity of the day") occupies a central position in that liturgy; it concentrates on the gravity of judgment, as it enumerates and describes vividly who shall live and who shall die in the coming year. The poem includes the line: "And the great *shofar* was sounded, and a still small voice was heard." This verse, which conflates the references from Isaiah and First Kings, is apt to be the source of the vivid dynamic contrast in Mahler's two horn calls. The loud one represents the great *shofar* and the faint echo of it an instrumental replication of the still, small voice of God. It is with precisely this sharp dynamic contrast that cantors traditionally intone the two contrasting components of that centrally important verse from the medieval poem.

A Promissory Note

Right after the mysterious horn calls, the offstage French horns continue by introducing another conundrum {▶ Audio Ex. 9.7}. The music has shifted to F Minor, and the horns play a triplet that leads into the beginning of a returning-note figure on the tonic, F (Music Ex. 9.1).

A returning-note figure is a three-note pattern, the first and third notes of which are the same (in this instance, F). The middle note is the tone just above or just below the framing notes (in this instance, G). Mahler takes us as far as the middle note of the projected returning-note figure, and there he leaves us hanging. The G is unsatisfying as the end of this passage; a return to F, the tonic, is needed sorely. In addition, Mahler places a fermata (⌢) over the G, which indicates that it is to be held for an unspecified length. The added length and uncertainty of its duration only heighten our frustration at not hearing the completion of the projected returning-note figure. Leaving the completion of this figure in a state of suspension generates what

Music Ex. 9.1. A returning-note figure conspicuously left incomplete

the American composer and music theorist Edward Cone called a "promissory note," which he defines as a musical event that "has strongly suggested an obligation that it has failed to discharge."[5] It would be gratifying, at some point, to hear this returning-note figure completed. We shall revisit this matter from time to time.

Symbols of Judgment Drawn from the Christian Liturgy

After the incomplete returning-note figure, a section filled with a great deal of diverse material commences {⊙ Audio Ex. 9.8}. It begins with a long passage of triplets, starting in the oboe. The triplets will be a mainstay of this section, offering a rather neutral glutinous agent to hold together a lot of the other material that is presented. Clarion calls in the brasses are added (00:13), perhaps signifying the Caller in the Wilderness. Then, the harps take over the triplets (00:22), which go on to introduce an ethereal-sounding passage of quiet trills in the strings against rolled chords in the harps (00:31). Thereafter, the triplets descend, the texture thins, and the passage winds down into nothingness.

What we hear next {⊙ Audio Ex. 9.9} is also familiar to us from the first movement. The passage begins with the opening of the *Dies irae*, the fourteenth-century Gregorian chant that describes the Day of Judgment and that is used in the Roman Catholic Requiem, the Mass for the Dead. In the first movement, the opening notes of the chant and the extension that is added to them appear with other material in a developmental context. Here, the opening of the chant and its new extension unfold in a more leisurely and more transparent manner; it is provided with a simple slow-moving pizzicato counterpoint. The *Dies irae* is often associated with death itself (as in the Catholic Requiem Mass and in such orchestral works as Hector Berlioz's *Symphonie fantastique*, Franz Liszt's *Totentanz*, or Sergei Rachmaninoff's *Isle of the Dead*), but Mahler presents it right after his stark emulation of the *shofar*, an unmistakable emblem of judgment. Clearly, the *Dies irae* appears here in the context of its central purpose: a description of the Day of Judgment. Its apocalyptic text begins "The day of wrath, that day will dissolve the world in ashes."

---

[5] Edward T. Cone, "Schubert's Promissory Note: An Exercise in Musical Hermeneutics," *19th Century Music*, 5 (1982): 235.

As soon as the *Dies irae* section is complete, the returning-note figure is sounded by a trombone against a backdrop of triplets, played pizzicato by the violins {⊙ Audio Ex. 9.10}. This time, the returning-note figure appears in its complete form. A trumpet then picks up where the trombone left off (**00:15**), reaching upward deliberately. The choice of instrument, combined with the inexorable upward reach of the line, suggests that the passage is a musical portrayal of a relevant biblical prophecy from First Corinthians (15:52):

It will happen in a moment, in the twinkling of an eye, when the last trumpet sounds; the trumpet will sound, and the dead will rise again, free from corruption, and we shall find ourselves changed.

The theme of resurrection has now entered the symphony explicitly.

The close juxtaposition in this passage of the *Dies irae* melody and the completed returning-note figure may have been planned by Mahler to encourage us to focus on a possible relationship between the two musical motives: the first three notes of the *Dies irae* are an inversion of the returning-note motive. That is to say, the two three-note patterns move by the same intervals, but where one ascends, the other descends (Music Ex. 9.2).

Does this relationship mean anything beyond the technical properties of melodic inversion it displays? It could, but it is hard to know at this point because, although the *Dies irae* clearly stands for the Day of Judgment, the significance of the returning-note motive, if any, has not yet been revealed to us. However, inasmuch as the juxtaposition of the two motives seems purposeful, and, given Mahler's proclivity to mete out information about the symbolic significance of his music very gradually, it might behoove us to table this question for now, but to keep it in mind as the movement progresses.

Next, in {⊙ Audio Ex. 9.11}, additional clarion calls in the winds seem once again to portray the Caller in the Wilderness. Continuity is provided by the connective properties of the triplets that permeate this passage. The texture thins (**00:30**), and the triplets are taken over by a series of single

Music Ex. 9.2. The returning-note figure and the *Dies irae*

woodwind instruments, beginning with a bassoon. At the same point, four offstage French horns deliberately and dramatically, but very faintly, repeat the *shofar*-like open fifths and the subsequent reach for the returning-note figure, which is completed this time. The importance of the returning-note figure is underscored once again, although its meaning continues to elude us. The ethereal, quiet trills in the strings combined with the rolled chords in the harps we heard earlier return (**01:00**) just before the section drifts slowly into silence. A low, tonic pedal underlies the entire passage.

More about an Old Enigma

What we hear next is also familiar {⊙ Audio Ex. 9.12}. Against the shimmering background of a string tremolando, we hear an English horn (doubled by a flute) playing a simple minor second. We first heard something similar near the end of the first movement {⊙ Audio Ex. 9.13}. The strings played different music there than what we hear at this point, but the minor second, given voice in the pungent—one might even say sultry—sound of the English horn, overshadows everything else in the passage. When we heard this music in the first movement, we remarked on its enigmatic character. Why provide a dramatic entrance and a markedly conspicuous sonority to project nothing more than a simple minor second? The bare-boned interval seemed too insignificant melodically to warrant the conspicuous presence its sonority bestowed on it. This was another of Mahler's unanswered questions, of the sort that demand our patience as we await a solution later in the work. Now, the minor second in the English horn is back, along with the question of what significance it might hold for us.

Here in the finale, the minor second in the English horn (along with the flute) serves to initiate a discrete and substantial section of the movement. It also introduces a sea change in Mahler's musical language reminiscent of the shift that occurred in "Urlicht" when the speaker in the poem articulates his resistance to the angel accompanied by a move toward chromaticism and a greater measure of musical intensity. In this section of the finale, the level of dissonance surges, as the harmonies become increasingly chromatic. The melodic lines press upward gradually, relentlessly, and chromatically with a growing sense of urgency that is confirmed by a corresponding gain in the dynamic level. An increasingly agitated quality results from ongoing tremolandos in the strings, punctuated by brief and loud piercing entries in the winds, many of which emphasize minor seconds. Most importantly, this passage is most intense, very passionate, and utterly theatrical {⊙ Audio Ex. 9.14}.

What we just heard fleshes out substantially the bald minor second introduced by the English horn in the first movement. We know now that the enigmatic fragment serves as the initiation of an intensely ardent passage cast in a theatrical manner. But Mahler has not yet revealed what significance lies behind the emphatically expressive, operatic style of this music. In this passage, Mahler embeds the enigmatic minor second in a broader context. Clear to us is that it is part of an intensely emotional, passionate music, but its significance for this symphony continues to elude us.

Back to Christian Judgment

In discussing the abutment of the two sections of the development in the first movement (Chapter 3), I characterized the juxtaposition of the two passages—one utterly placid and prosaic, the other, the very epitome of turbulence and ferocity—as an example of Mahler's fondness for a musical rhetoric of antithesis. It is an approach he often favors, and he engages in it again here. After the passionate outburst of the previous passage, he moves directly to a passage that epitomizes decorous solemnity. It is not an exaggeration to suggest that the change we observe here seems like a move from a Dionysian sound world to an Apollonian universe. The *Dies irae* returns, this time as a chorale {⊙ Audio Ex. 9.15}. We heard a chorale in "Urlicht," where it set the reverential tone Mahler used to point the listener in the direction of the Christian view of eternal life. The rich orchestration—for bassoon, contrabassoon, three trumpets, and four horns—contributed to the austere spirituality of the "Urlicht" chorale. This chorale is scored differently. It is written for contrabassoon, four trombones, and tuba, and the lower orchestral register only enhances the deep solemnity Mahler attaches to this passage. After the first strain of the chorale is finished, the pizzicato counterpoint that accompanied the *Dies irae* earlier resumes (**00:26**), followed immediately by a strong presentation of the completed returning-note figure in the trombone. The music then begins to build toward a powerful climax (beginning at **00:43**).

The return to solemnity seems aimed to keep us on track—that is, tuned in to centering orthodox Christian views on immortality as the key to finding meaning in life even though it must inevitably end in death. There is a need to be kept on track because the turbulent passage that expands on the minor second seems incomprehensible in the context of this movement. The latter passage and its counterpart in "Urlicht," when the speaker of the poem resists the angel, are outliers. The scope of their departure from the musical norms of the context into which they are introduced needs to be rationalized. This would seem to be important because it is unlikely that changes of this sort and of this magnitude would be introduced into the fabric of the symphony—and more than once—with no reason. Typically, however, Mahler has not yet made clear what the meaning and function of these passages are. We need to be aware of this as we continue our engagement with the finale.

The climax that began to approach after the chorale ended offers a sumptuously dazzling orchestral display in an event of stellar magnitude. Passages like this, when they appear in Mahler's music, are sometimes characterized as "breakthroughs" {▶ Audio Ex. 9.16}. The music in C Major is reminiscent of what followed the *Dies irae* earlier (in {Audio Ex. 9.11}). It begins with the clarion calls associated with the Caller in the Wilderness. They are played by French horns with the bells raised. As the climactic passage progresses, the returning-note figure appears twice, both times in its complete form. First, it is in C Major (at **00:18**), then in C Minor (at **00:52**). After that, the music recedes gradually, until only the contrabass, harps, tam-tam, and bass drum remain. This is the most powerful passage in the movement thus far, as befits the music that will bring the first major section of the finale to a close. It is significant, therefore, that the returning-note figure plays a central role in it. Its importance has been known to us for a good portion of the finale. In a manner most characteristic of Mahler, however, he persists in driving home the importance of this motive, while still withholding from us a sense of *why* it is so important. We must continue to be patient.

Is this an Exposition?

Part of the subtitle for this chapter is "Airing of Themes." Not only is this section of the finale rich in the thematic material it puts forward, but it is remarkably devoid of developmental activity. For that reason, it has come to be regarded by some writers as an exposition. If the burden of an exposition is taken to be no more than the presentation of thematic material, one might refer to this section of the finale as an exposition. We have observed, however, that symphonic expositions exhibit other structural and tonal functions of a sort that do not appear in this part of the last movement. That is why I characterize what transpires here as an "airing of themes." It will be of interest to observe in the section that follows if developmental techniques begin to appear.

10

The Last Movement, Part 2: Judgment in Action, Musical Development, and Some Continuing Enigmas

And the Dead Shall Rise • An Apocalyptic March •
A Chromatic and Sensual Passage Returns Intensified •
Frantic Preparation for an Ominous Return •
A Harbinger of Immortality Expanded •
Is This a Development Section? • Pressing Questions that Still Remain Unanswered

And the Dead Shall Rise

After the dazzling close to the first section of this movement, Mahler offers another highly idiosyncratic musical gesture in the form of two sinister-sounding and hair-raising percussion crescendos, each followed by a loud interjection in the brasses. The latter is the motive that was added to the orchestral scream with which the finale began—the one that came to be known as the "terror motive." According to Mahler's instructions in the score, the crescendos are to build slowly and gradually to maximum volume. Mahler was explicit in describing to Bauer-Lechner the meaning he intended to reflect with this music:

> And now the resolution of the terrible problem of life—redemption. . . .
> The earth trembles. Just listen to the drum roll, and your hair will stand on
> end! . . . [T]he graves spring open, and all creation comes writhing out of
> the bowels of the earth, with wailing and gnashing of teeth.[1]

---

[1] Natalie Bauer-Lechner, *Recollections of Gustav Mahler*, ed. Peter Franklin, trans. Dika Newlin (New York: Faber & Faber, 2013), 44.

Inside Mahler's Second Symphony:. Lawrence F. Bernstein, Oxford University Press. © Oxford University Press 2022.
DOI: 10.1093/oso/9780197575635.003.0010

Turn your attention to the "hair-raising" percussion crescendos {▶ Audio Ex. 10.1A} and take note of the added "terror motive" in the brass (at **00:05** and **00:10**). Do these crescendos really sound that menacing? And does Bruno Walter follow scrupulously Mahler's directive that the "crescendos are to build *slowly and gradually* to maximum volume"? You may be able to answer these questions more assuredly after comparing Walter's reading of the passage with another one, that of Sir Simon Rattle, in a recording with the Berlin Philharmonic {▶ Audio Ex. 10.1B}. There can be little doubt regarding which of these readings offers the more electrifying musical portrayal of the rising of the dead, and which more faithfully adheres to the composer's performance directions.[2]

The length of these crescendos is not specified by Mahler in a precisely measured notation. He marks each of them with a fermata (⌢), which leaves their actual duration to the conductor's discretion. In this sense, Walter—true to his life-long commitment to honor a composer's intentions—can be said to be remaining within the letter of the law (at least with respect to the actual musical notation). It also must be said, however, that he falls short of capturing the intended spirit of the passage, and, in keeping the crescendos so short, he is unequivocally violating Mahler's instructions that they "are to build slowly and gradually to maximum volume." In five seconds—the length of the first crescendo in Walter's reading—there is insufficient time for a gradual build-up.

The reason underlying Walter's decision may resemble one of those we advanced earlier (Chapter 3) when we addressed Walter's approach to Mahler's *Luftpausen*. If, according to Walter's performance aesthetic, which tended to emphasize sobriety in his musical gestures, a dramatic instant of silence to interrupt the metrical flow stepped over the line to ostentatious overstatement, what level of garishness might he have perceived in these percussion crescendos? One can imagine him reasoning: "I may have no choice but to play these crescendos; at least, however, I can minimize their tastelessness by keeping them short." Whatever his reason, however, Walter appears to have violated the performance tradition Mahler advocated for this passage, which raises an important question about the conductor's responsibilities as he engages in the recreative process of bringing a score to life.

---

[2] The intensity Rattle brings to these percussion crescendos calls to mind a detail we provided at the very beginning of this book (at the start of the Preface): that Rattle began his musical career at the age of eleven as a percussionist in the Merseyside Youth Orchestra near Liverpool. Is there, perhaps, something of a special affinity for the percussion section at play here?

Is there, in fact, a broad performance tradition—ideally, perhaps, one ema-nating from the composer—to which Bruno Walter should have adhered in interpreting this symphony? Mahler himself assumes contradictory postures about this. On the one hand, he offers considerable latitude to performers of his music. Two comments attributed to Mahler are often advanced in support of his liberal position on this matter. After modifying a passage in the Second Symphony at a rehearsal for a performance of it in 1907, Mahler is said to have declared "Hail to the conductor who in the future will play my scores as the acoustic[s] of the hall demand!"[3] The second comment was addressed to Otto Klemperer and other young conductors present at a rehearsal of the Eighth Symphony. Having just introduced some changes to the score, Mahler proclaimed "If, after my death something doesn't sound [right], then change it. You have the right to change; not only the right, the duty to change it."[4]

The liberal tolerance for introducing changes in the score reflected in these comments suggests that Mahler would not have advanced a case for a specific performance tradition of his music, and, in the end, he does not. That notwithstanding, when performers fell wide of the mark in interpreting his music to his satisfaction, he could rant and rave. In November 1899, for example, Mahler attended a private performance in Vienna of his Second Symphony in an arrangement for two pianos eight hands by the German pi-anist and composer Heinrich von Bocklet. In Bauer-Lechner's account, this performance was painful for Mahler. It "took the wind out of his sails" be-cause "the tempi were wrong, and the expression and phrasing were often so incorrect that everything dissolved into chaos."[5] Bauer-Lechner goes on to report a further complaint Mahler registered about this performance (quoting him directly):

And that was directed and rehearsed by someone who will imagine and claim that he inherits the tradition straight from me! From this you may learn the

---

[3] Henry-Louis de La Grange, *Gustav Mahler, Volume 3, Vienna: Triumph and Disillusion (1904–1907)* (Oxford: Oxford University Press, 1999), 769 and n. 287. The account of the incident is attrib-uted to the composer Egon Wellesz, who attended the rehearsal. Mahler's commitment to the need to introduce changes in a composer's score is, perhaps, best reflected in the many adjustments—Mahler called them *Retuschen*—he made in works he conducted. He did so for a variety of reasons, including the acoustics of the hall in which he was conducting and variations in the size of the orchestra. Mahler was not the only musician to make such "retouchings," but some of his attempts, particularly in Beethoven's Ninth Symphony, were met with vitriolic opposition. See David Pickett, "Arrangements and *Retuschen*: Mahler and *Werktreue*," in Jeremy Barham, ed., *The Cambridge Companion to Mahler* (Cambridge: Cambridge University Press, 2007), 178–199.

[4] Gilbert E. Kaplan, "Mahler and Tradition," *The Musical Times*, 133 (1992): 559.

[5] Bauer-Lechner, *Recollections of Gustav Mahler*, 141.

truth about every so-called "tradition": there is no such thing! Everything is left to the whim of the individual, and unless a genius awakens them to life, works of art are lost. Now I understand perfectly why Brahms let people play his works as they pleased. He knew that anything he told them was in vain. Bitter experience and resignation are expressed in this fact.[6]

Although Mahler suggests in these lines that there can be no fixed performance tradition for his works, it must be said that he appears to offer this suggestion only grudgingly. He seems let down by the unnamed putative heir to such a tradition for performing his music, and, if that performance tradition must lie out of reach, Mahler accepts that circumstance, but only with "bitter resignation."

Who was the butt of Mahler's exasperation about this errant performance of the two-piano-four-hands arrangement of the Second Symphony—the musician "who will imagine and claim that he inherits the 'tradition' straight from me!"? Only one candidate seems close enough to Mahler and his music to be thought of so seriously in this way: Bruno Walter, and, in his authoritative biography of Mahler, Henry-Louis de La Grange points us in this direction (albeit with an added cautionary note).[7] We can't be completely certain that Mahler had Walter in mind, and, even if he did, the extent of the influence on the four pianists that can be attributed to his coaching is not at the same level as if he had personally conducted the performance.

Nonetheless, the discrepancy between Mahler's expectations and the way this performance failed to realize them by someone closely attuned to those expectations has relevance for what we make of Walter's reading of the percussion crescendos. Composers are not alone in generating a tradition for the performance of their music; conductors can give rise to their own analogous traditions that help to guide them through the recreative process. Bruno Walter had such traditions. His firm commitment to reflecting the

---

[6] Ibid.

[7] Henry-Louis de La Grange, *Gustav Mahler, Volume 2, Vienna: The Years of Challenge (1897–1904)* (Oxford: Oxford University Press, 1995), 153 and n. 67. La Grange raises a problem concerning Walter's involvement with this performance, citing a letter from Walter to his parents, from which it is clear that he was not in Vienna on the day of the performance. Paul Banks, however, alludes to an earlier performance of the arrangement by the same musicians in Vienna on August 29, which keeps open the possibility of Bruno Walter's association with it. Moreover, whoever was instrumental in guiding the aesthetic choices underlying this performance might have exerted this influence in one or more coaching sessions without having had to be present at the performance. See Paul Banks, *The Music of Gustav Mahler: A Catalogue of Manuscript and Printed Sources*, http://mahlercat.org.uk. See the section "Printed arrangement for eight hands" in the entry on the Second Symphony.

composer's intentions was part of it, and that principle resonates strongly throughout most of the recording of the Second Symphony we are using. No less important to him, however, were the qualities of sedateness and sobriety he generally brought to his interpretations. Surely, he was entitled to these. Without such latitude, his interpretations could all too easily be reduced to mere carbon copies of the score, as opposed to manifestations of his own important stake in the recreation of music.

Thus, with these hair-raising percussion crescendos, Mahler begins to lead us farther down the paths of Christian eschatology, specifically with a vivid musical description of the Last Judgment, the apocalyptic event that is signaled by the second coming of Christ and that portends the end of time. The dead will wake, and all mankind will be judged and subjected either to punishment or purification prior to salvation. The vehicle Mahler employs to depict how the apocalypse unfolds is a march, meant to portray all humanity "marching along in a mighty procession."[8]

An Apocalyptic March

The march is long, and its complexity and severity ebb and flow. Its character changes, too. Sometimes, it resonates with a sense of impending catastrophe; sometimes, it brightens considerably. That contrast is, at times, very sharp, and it reflects the two diverging dimensions of the Last Judgment: on the one hand the fear and suffering of the sinners and, on the other, their positive and ardent petitions for salvation, which may be granted, but only to some of them. This incisive duality lies at the very heart of apocalyptic judgment. These two sides of judgment are depicted vividly in a portrayal of the Day of Judgment by the early sixteenth-century Netherlandish painter Joos van Cleve (Fig. 10.1).

Both elements of the duality of the Day of Judgment are emphasized in this canvas. Christ blesses those who have been saved (on the left), while St. Michael drives the damned into hell (from which black smoke billows on the right). In accord with the account of the Last Judgment in Chapter 8 of the Book of Revelations, two angels hover over the throngs of the saved and the damned, respectively, and sound trumpets. The figures in the foreground of the painting engage in ardent prayer.

---

[8] Bauer-Lechner, *Recollections of Gustav Mahler*, 44.

Fig. 10.1. *The Day of Judgment* by Joos van Cleve

New York, Metropolitan Museum of Art. Reproduced under the Creative Commons Attribution-ShareAlike License

The march presents a wealth of musical material, of which the central pillar is the *Dies irae*. It behooves us, therefore, to focus more closely on the meaning of this chant. Here are the first four versicles in a rhymed English translation:

> Day of wrath, that woeful day,
> Shall the world in ashes lay;
> David and the Sibyl say.
>
> What a trembling, what a fear,
> When the dread Judge shall appear,
> Strictly searching far and near.
>
> Hark! the trumpet's wondrous tone,
> Through sepulchral regions blown,
> Summons all before the throne.
>
> Death shall shiver, nature quake,
> When the creatures shall awake,
> Answer to their Judge to make.[9]

Besides the *Dies irae*, musical reference is made to a number of familiar themes: the returning-note figure, the resurrection motive, and the immortality motive from *Siegfried*. We also hear a portion of a hymn in praise of the Virgin Mary. These thematic strands are presented both separately and in combination, and the *Dies irae*, especially, is often altered significantly. All of this takes place while the keys change rapidly. This is the stuff of which symphonic development is comprised.

Mahler begins by establishing the character of a march in F Minor, departing from the "terror motive" that is incorporated in the percussion crescendos {▶ Audio Ex. 10.2}. Within seconds (**00:08**), the opening of the *Dies irae* appears, but it is twisted out of shape melodically and provided with a highly dissonant harmonization. The key shifts (**00:18**), and a bright melody in B♭ Major is introduced (**00:26**), but the *Dies irae* appears along with it in the flute and violins; it appears again in a larger instrumentation in G Minor (**00:32**) and is then immediately presented briefly in diminution.

---

[9] For the full text of the *Dies irae*, along with seven English translations, see https://archive.org/str eam/diesirae00newy/diesirae00newy_djvu.txt.

The march becomes more strident {⊙ Audio Ex. 10.3}. Mahler directs that it be played *martellato*, a technique for string instruments in which the bow is held firmly against the string then released with a vigorous motion that produces a sharply etched, accented sound. This march theme in F Major sounds distinct, owing to the playing style just described and to its simple, four-square rhythms, but, if you listen carefully to its opening, you will hear that its first four notes are those of the opening of the *Dies irae*. At this point, the march takes on a more optimistic tone, which seems aimed at portraying the hopeful side of judgment. The returning-note figure is quoted (**00:16**), embedded in a jubilant trumpet melody. The tonality shifts from B♭ Major to D Major, where the music takes on a feeling of anticipation (**00:36**), leading up to the arrival of E♭ Major (**00:41**). This tonal arrival is important. E♭ Major is closely related to C Minor, the main key of this symphony. It is known as the relative major of C Minor and works that begin in the minor mode often end in the relative major. We shall see that Mahler does end this symphony in E♭ Major, but not without flirting with another option first.

The more buoyant affect that overcame this last excerpt becomes celebratory as bells are added to the orchestration that now also includes ten French horns playing *fff* with their bells raised {⊙ Audio Ex. 10.4}. This joyous outburst serves to usher in an extended melody played by the trumpets that has the character of a hymn (**00:00**). As the hymn-like melody continues, Mahler adds a musical quotation to it (**00:13**). The trumpet plays an excerpt from "O Sanctissima, O piissima," a hymn that implores the Virgin Mary to pray on behalf of the supplicants. Its melody is said to have come from a Sicilian folk tune. Mahler may have known this hymn from a setting of it for two sopranos, bass, and piano by Ludwig van Beethoven. At Catholic services in the English-speaking world, this hymn can be heard nowadays set to the text "Virgin full of grace."[10] The presence of a hymn that entreats the Virgin Mary for her intercession is consistent with the depiction in this march of the more sanguine side of the Last Judgment: the supplication of sinners in hopeful pursuit of eternal life.

The jubilant quality of the last passage does not endure, however, as the *Dies irae* returns to dominate this section of the finale increasingly {⊙ Audio

---

[10] For a listing of hymnals that contain "O sanctissima, O piisima," see https://hymnary.org/search?qu=O+sanctissima%2C+O+piisima.

  Beethoven's setting (WoO 157:4) appears in *Ludwig Beethoven's Werken*, Ser. 24, no. 259, *Lieder mit Pianoforte und Violoncell* (Leipzig: Breitkopf & Härtel, s.d.), 10–11. I am indebted to my late colleague James Primosch for identifying this melody.

Ex. 10.5}. It appears at the beginning of the excerpt in D Minor. Then, after the key begins to shift, accented repeated notes in the French horns are added, along with shrill high notes in the woodwinds, approached by wide, dissonant leaps (00:12). The *Dies irae* motive is sequenced several times against an increasingly sinister-sounding background. Then, the music broadens (00:30), heralding a point of arrival. When it comes (00:37), the *Dies irae* motive is stated broadly and ponderously in D♭ Major. The forcefulness and blunt clarity with which the *Dies irae* is presented here suggests that the harsher aspects of the Last Judgment are gaining the upper hand in the conflict between the two sides of judgment Mahler is portraying.

Mahler does not abandon this section of the march completely to the *Dies irae*, however. The returning-note figure (whatever its significance may be) puts in another appearance (00:52). We hear the ascending resurrection motive in the trumpets (01:00), and the immortality motive from *Siegfried* enters at 01:07. But the *Dies irae* gets the last word (01:11). The wild and highly dissonant passage that follows (01:19) begins with a projection of catastrophe and, without warning, trails off into nothingness. During the brief silence that follows, we find ourselves wondering intensely what music will follow.

A Chromatic and Sensual Passage Returns Intensified

We hear next {▶ Audio Ex. 10.6} a shimmering, muted tremolando in the strings, followed by the entrance of a solo trombone that hauntingly returns us to a familiar and highly enigmatic theme. It is the music first portended by a bare descending second played by the English horn in the first movement, and then fleshed out earlier in this movement. The music sounds ominous initially, as it did when we first heard it.

At its start {▶ Audio Ex. 10.7}, the passage resembles the presentation of this material we heard earlier in this movement in the English horn and flute. It retains the high level of emotional intensity it had before. Again, we hear the shift to a chromatic language, to the greater sense of urgency, drama, and sensuality that permeated the last iteration of this music. This time, however, the music grows more intense earlier on. The trombone melody is punctuated by spasmodic interruptions in the winds (beginning at 00:14). These interjections grow more dissonant as the French horns take over the sensual melody (00:18).

Even more tension occurs when the melody is played by the violoncellos and bassoon. Then, an offstage band, which consists of four trumpets, triangle, cymbal, and bass drum, is introduced, and it clashes pointedly with the sensual melody. Mahler is very particular about how this group should sound. He directs the conductor:

[This] should sound so faint that it does not affect the character of the songful passage in the violoncellos and bassoon. The composer has in mind something like isolated fragments of barely audible music, scattered and carried to us by the wind.[11]

The offstage band interjects music that has little to do with that played by the main orchestra {▶ Audio Ex. 10.8}. Mainly, it provides military fanfares (**00:06, 00:16, 00:38,** and **00:57**).[12] Thrown against one another, the chromatic, sensual melody and the crude military fanfares produce much friction, no matter how quietly the offstage band plays. It is well known that Mahler had a life-long affinity for military music that originated with the presence of a military garrison near his childhood home in Iglau. And Mahler's music is rife with the seemingly forced juxtaposition of highly disparate musics.

The latter tendency has been associated with a psychological state Mahler described himself in his famous and clandestine consultation with Sigmund Freud. This took place during a walk they took together in Leyden in August 1910, a time at which much in Mahler's life was unraveling—not least in importance, his marriage. Mahler related a childhood memory of his need to escape one of many stormy confrontations between his parents. Running into the street, he encountered a barrel-organ playing the popular tune "Ach, du lieber Augustin." By Mahler's own account, the juxtaposition of the domestic strife within his household and the tawdry music he heard outside emblemized what he described as his inability to distinguish "high tragedy" from "light amusement." This psychological trait is cited frequently as the basis for Mahler's persistent juxtaposition of refined themes and more common, crude music.[13]

There is something unique and more pointed, however, driving this amalgam here. Throughout this movement, Mahler has used different musical tropes to

---

[11] Gustav Mahler, *Symphonie Nr. 2*, ed. Renate Stark-Voit and Gilbert Kaplan, Gustav Mahler: Neue kritische Gesamtausgabe, 2 vols. (Vienna: Universal Edition and the Kaplan Foundation, 2010), Partitur, 234.

[12] Mahler provides five of these fanfares. The third of them is missing from our recording; it should have appeared at **00:27**. Most likely, the wrong "take" was inadvertently adopted in the final editing of the master tape from which the recording was made.

[13] Peter Franklin, *The Life of Mahler* (Cambridge: Cambridge University Press, 1997), 21.

represent judgment: a chorale, the *Dies irae*, and, most recently, a march. We still don't know the significance of Mahler's several shifts to passages that emphasize chromaticism and sensuality. Three of them appear: briefly in "Urlicht" when the protagonist resists the obstacle of the angel; in the iteration of the English horn melody earlier in this movement; and in the section at hand. Each time, music of this sort is sharply juxtaposed to contrasting music that represents judgment: to a chorale in "Urlicht"; to the *Dies irae* after the English horn melody; and, by way of the offstage military fanfares, to the apocalyptic march here. It is as if judgment and whatever the sensual melody represents are pitted against each other in conflict. If that is so, the conflict portrayed in the present passage is, without question, the most intense. In the earlier instances, the juxtaposition takes place serially—one element follows the other. Here, it occurs simultaneously, which escalates greatly the sense of collision (especially because of the highly disparate nature of the musical elements that are thrown together). It also heightens greatly our increasingly urgent need to understand the significance of the chromatic, sensual music.

Let us digress, for a moment, to focus briefly on the practical logistics of the offstage band. In November 1905, at the Berlin performance of the Mahler Second conducted by Oskar Fried, Otto Klemperer, then twenty years old, conducted the offstage band in the last movement. At the dress rehearsal, Mahler raked Klemperer over the coals. He complained that the musicians of the offstage band played much too loudly. Klemperer replied that Mahler had marked the passages for offstage band *fortissimo*. Mahler was undaunted in his criticism, telling Klemperer that he needed to have the players convey the *impression* of playing "in the far distance" at whatever dynamic level they might be playing. Klemperer took Mahler's concerns to heart and performed the passage to his satisfaction at the concert.[14] The incident is telling with respect to Mahler's meticulous standards where matters of orchestral sonority and balance are concerned. The final version of the score contains no dynamic marks for the offstage players—only the subjective comment about "isolated fragments of barely audible music" quoted above. One source that antedates the published score, however, has the music for the offstage band marked ***PPPPP***.[15]

---

[14] Otto Klemperer, *Minor Recollections* (London: Dennis Dobson, 1964), 12–13. The precariousness that enters into performing this passage, especially the difficulty associated with integrating the onstage orchestra with the offstage band, has plagued conductors for generations. Note, for example, the omission of one of the five entrances of the offstage band in our recording. For an engaging discussion of some of these issues by the conductor Kenneth Woods, see his video, *Living on the Edge: Why Conducting Mahler is Risky Business*, November 29, 2020, YouTube video, https://www.youtube.com/watch?v=P8wnrMfwgKg. The video should be watched from the beginning, but the passage under consideration is discussed at 05:31–10:31.

[15] Mahler, *Symphonie Nr. 2*, ed. Stark-Voit and Kaplan, Partitur, 234.

Frantic Preparation for an Ominous Return

The next passage {▶ Audio Ex. 10.9} offers a rapid expansion of the music that takes place in multiple dimensions. It quickly grows louder, higher, more dissonant, and more fragmented, all of which leads to a keen anticipation of a significant point of arrival. At the apex of its trajectory, where the timpani enters (**00:19**), it even seriously undermines the meter that governs the flow of the passage by forcefully accenting notes in a systematically irregular pattern. Concentrate, as you listen to the music at **00:19**, on the low instruments, especially the contrabassoon, trombones, tuba, and timpani. The passage is written in 4/4 time. Normally, you should be able to count briskly "1, 2, 3, 4" as you listen to the music. Try it. It works easily at the beginning of the excerpt, but it is almost impossible to count in this way beginning at **00:19**. Discerning regular meter depends on the consistency with which accented notes appear. Normally, the first beat of a measure is accented. Note, however, how Mahler introduces here a two-note pattern of strongly accented notes, systematically beginning it on the first, fourth, third, second, and first beats of the measure, respectively (Music Ex. 10.1). Placement of these accented notes so irregularly destroys the normal meter at this point in the passage. The instability of the meter needs to be resolved, and this adds greatly to the high level of anticipation already inherent in the passage.

Music Ex. 10.1. Displacement of meter

Let us return now to the end of Mahler's frenetic passage of preparation to see where it is leading {▶ Audio Ex. 10.10}. I suggested that the thrust of the passage was aimed at preparing an important point of arrival. Just as the passage seems to run out of control, it returns to some familiar material (**00:07**). The terrifying orchestral scream that ended the third movement and began the finale is back again. Its return has very important ramifications for the message Mahler is trying to convey in this movement. What are they? The chorale in "Urlicht" seemed to move us toward an orthodox Christian theology with respect to life after death, and the seemingly even-handed presentation in the march of both the grim and hopeful prospects of the Last Judgment appeared to reinforce that trajectory. In the end, however, Mahler's view of Christian eschatology is anything but even-handed. It is, in fact, utterly cynical. He can drop a hint of his acceptance of this outlook with the introduction of a distinctly devotional texture (as in "Urlicht"), and, in the midst of the march, he can quote a Marian hymn to represent the sincere efforts of the penitents. When summing up his view of the Last Judgment for Bauer-Lechner, however, he says of the wretched souls in pursuit of eternal life: "*All* give vent to the same terror, the same lamentations and paroxysms; for *none* is just in the sight of God."[16] Mahler seems to have little confidence in the fairness of God's judgment. In the context of his skepticism about the fundamentals of Christian eschatology, the reappearance of the scream does not surprise us. Perhaps Mahler will provide an answer to his existential question, but he has not given it to us yet, and we are beginning to suspect here that it may not be found in a traditional Christian eschatology.

A Harbinger of Immortality Expanded

If the return of the scream is not surprising, we cannot fail to be bewildered by what follows it {⊙ Audio Ex. 10.11}. We hear the end of the scream, followed by a dramatically stark change of character (**00:09**), which portends something noteworthy, something dramatic, to follow. Almost back-to-back with Mahler's most compelling musical representation of the meaninglessness of life (the scream), we hear a combination of elements of the resurrection motive and the immortality motive from *Siegfried*. The music unfolds gently, weaving in and out of its uncomplicated contrapuntal fabric in an orchestration that is, at once, warm, vibrant, and pristinely clear. It seems to project the very essence of tranquility, and it does all of this in the key of D♭ Major—the key of the quintessentially serene passages of "Urlicht." The qualities with which Mahler endows this music here suggest that he does, indeed, have in mind a road to eternal life, but, as is so often so with Mahler, he has not yet revealed it to us. This brings to an end what we have defined as the second section of the last movement.

---

[16] Bauer-Lechner, *Recollections of Gustav Mahler*, 44 (emphasis added).

Is This a Development Section?

A word is in order on the formal character of the music we have considered in this chapter. As we have seen, the march contains many themes. It combines them and alters them, and it carries them through a great number of keys. These are, as we suggested above, the hallmarks of a traditional development section. In our discussion of the first movement of this symphony, we pointed out that Mahler used sonata form as a model in the context of a work that also projected an extra-musical agenda. As a result, Mahler demonstrated what we called "dual loyalties." Sometimes, sonata form dictated how the music would flow; sometimes, it was the extra-musical agenda that pointed the direction. Occasionally, the two loyalties coalesced, with form and the airing of existential issues working in tandem. That coalescence manifests itself here, too—masterfully. The musical themes that seem to offer a way out of Mahler's existential dilemma are forced to confront the overridingly powerful emblem of judgment—the *Dies irae*—in an ongoing confrontation that demands resolution with increasing urgency. The protocols of symphonic development, which often thrive on the combination of disparate elements, provide a most effective forum for this interaction. And the intensity of the developmental process we have just observed makes a very traditional impact upon us: our need for resolution looms large, and we sense its impending arrival just over the horizon.

Pressing Questions that Still Remain Unanswered

Finally, we should remind ourselves at this time of the most important loose ends in Mahler's musical argument: issues that remain unresolved at this point.

- We still don't know the significance of the returning-note figure that was introduced so prominently at the beginning of the finale and repeated so often in both its complete and incomplete forms.
- The dramatic and increasingly sensual chromatic passages that appear in "Urlicht" and twice in the finale are obviously of critical importance, but the specific significance of their special character is still not clear to us.

- In a work so deeply enmeshed with Christian theology and eschatology, Mahler's privileging of the immortality motive from *Siegfried* as an important symbol of eternal life remains baffling. How, in an environment so rich in Christian eschatology, can Mahler take this symbol from the lips of a pagan demigoddess whose immortality depends on her love for a man who was born of an incestuous relationship of twins?

These questions need to be resolved if we are to attain a full understanding of Mahler's approach to immortality in this symphony.

11

The Last Movement, Part 3: Collapse, Climactic Resolution, a Stunning Reversal, and Celebration

Apocalyptic Judgment Again •
Climactic Resolution: The First Verse of the Klopstock Chorale •
First Instrumental Interlude and the Second Verse of the Klopstock Chorale •
A Critical Pivot • A Stunning Reversal • What Just Happened? •
A Celebration of Love • A Celebration of Eternal Life

Apocalyptic Judgment Again

Mahler originally entitled this section of the finale *Der grosse Appell* ("The Great Call")—a reference to the end of the Last Judgment—but he later decided not to use this title and did not add it to the first published score. At the very beginning {▶ Audio Ex. 11.1}, we are taken back to the sound of the *shofar*—a reference to judgment from the perspective of the Jewish liturgy for the New Year, the Day of Judgment. The music is given this time to four French horns, playing offstage, accompanied by a continuing soft roll of the bass drum in the orchestra. The returning-note figure reappears, too (**00:15**). Although we have heard it complete several times already, it is rendered in its incomplete state here, thus providing a very conspicuous reminder of the promissory note Mahler embedded in the incomplete version of the returning-note figure. It is as if Mahler were calling to our attention the salient importance of the returning-note figure and to our continuing ignorance of what it signifies. Without that knowledge, it seems, the promissory note inherent in the enigma of the returning-note figure remains unpaid. The passage ends (**00:26**) with another imitation of the *shofar* played by two

Inside Mahler's Second Symphony:. Lawrence F. Bernstein, Oxford University Press. © Oxford University Press 2022.
DOI: 10.1093/oso/9780197575635.003.0011

trumpets; they sound a different interval this time and are instructed to play as if "from a great distance."

The return here of material we heard at the beginning of the finale may be taken to be a nod in the direction of recapitulation. Some writers take this to be noteworthy in the light of the emphasis on development that appears in what we have designated Part 2 of the finale, and the focus on the setting out (exposition) of thematic material in the first section of the movement. This seems to add up to a sonata-like design, but only very loosely. The return of the horn calls, if it is to be taken as a gesture toward recapitulation, should be considered no more than that—a gesture—for its presence is surely more the result of the existential agenda Mahler is pursuing than any attempt at systematic reflection of the structure of sonata form. After this return of the horn calls, we hear nothing by way of the standard design of a sonata exposition, which is normally replicated substantially in a sonata recapitulation.

What follows the opening reference to the *shofar* is a most spectral and ethereal sound. Only two instruments play from within the orchestra, a flute and piccolo. The others—four French horns, four trumpets, and timpani play from "a great distance," that is, from offstage. The flute and piccolo play complex lines that combine elaborately embellished, sweeping legato writing and many repeated notes {▶ Audio Ex. 11.2}. The intent clearly is the mimicking of bird calls. In fact, Mahler marks the score here *Wie eine Vogelstimme* ("like the voice of a bird"). Despite its onomatopoetic content, however, the writing for flute and piccolo sounds more haunting and supernatural than merely descriptive of nature.

The trumpets enter one by one (00:03). They play rapid triplet figures that produce a great deal of dissonance when all three trumpeters play together. Mahler stipulates that they should sound "shattered." In the guide to the symphony he provided for the Dresden performance that took place on December 20, 1901, Mahler identifies these trumpets as the trumpets of the apocalypse.[1] Here, he draws on the prophecy in Chapters 8 and 9 of the Book of Revelations, which relates that, at the Last Judgment, seven angels will sound seven trumpets, each of which will rain a different manner of destruction on mankind. An illumination from an eleventh-century manuscript that contains the Book of Revelations (the *Bamberg Apocalypse*) depicts the

---

[1] Edward R. Reilly, "*Todtenfeier* and the Second Symphony," in Donald Mitchell and Andrew Nicholson, eds., *The Mahler Companion* (Oxford: Oxford University Press, 1999), 125.

Fig. 11.1. An illumination from Bamberg, Staatsbibliothek, MS Msc. Bibl.140 (the *Bamberg Apocalypse*), fol. 19ᵛ

Photo: Gerald Raab. Reproduced with permission

prophecy in an illumination (Fig. 11.1). The angel depicted in the lower frame is pouring fire down on earth. The French horns return (**00:28**) to repeat the calls of the *shofar*, which mix with the avian sounds and the trumpets of the apocalypse. The incomplete returning-note figure follows (**00:47**).

In the Dresden program, Mahler goes on to make clear what this entire passage is about: "[T]he trumpets from the Apocalypse call;—in the midst of the awful silence we think we hear in the farthest distance a nightingale, like a last quivering echo of earthly life."[2]

The musical themes that come together in this passage help us to understand its meaning. Judgment, as Mahler conveys it here (represented by the *shofar* calls and the trumpets of the apocalypse), seems very harsh. Ultimately, it leads to the extinguishing of all life (portrayed by the fading voice of the nightingale). Among the last things we hear, however, is a reappearance of the incomplete returning-note figure. Mahler leaves us with yet one more reminder that the all-important promissory note is still outstanding because we continue to lack any idea of the significance of the ubiquitous returning-note figure. That is about to change.

Climactic Resolution: The First Verse of the Klopstock Chorale

In an instant, we are flooded with clarification and resolution at many levels. The chorus sings a chorale. This is important in and of itself. We have heard two chorales already—one in "Ulricht," and the other earlier in this movement. Both were suggestive of a solution to Mahler's fundamental existential question from the perspective of a Christian eschatology, but both were performed instrumentally, that is, without a text capable of rendering such a solution explicit. Now, we hear a chorale performed with its words, and they embody an orthodox Christian outlook on eternal life.

The words Mahler sets to music here, moreover, are from Friedrich Klopstock's *Auferstehen*, the chorale text Mahler heard at Hans von Bülow's funeral:

Aufersteh'n, ja aufersteh'n wirst du,	Rise again, yes, you shall rise again,
mein Staub, nach kurzer Ruh!	My dust, after a short rest!
Unsterblich Leben! Unsterblich Leben!	Immortal life! Immortal life!
wird, der dich rief, dir geben!	Will be given to you by He Who
	called you![3]

---

[2] Reilly, "*Todtenfeier* and the Second Symphony," 125.

[3] The German text for this and subsequent verses follows Gustav Mahler, *Symphonie Nr. 2*, ed. Renate Stark-Voit and Gilbert Kaplan, Gustav Mahler: Neue kritische Gesamtausgabe, 2 vols. (Vienna: Universal Edition and the Kaplan Foundation, 2010), Partitur, 279–280.

It was Klopstock's poem, sung as a chorale, that gave rise to the epiphany Mahler experienced at the von Bülow funeral about how to end the Second Symphony. And, in the way Mahler clothes Klopstock's verses in music here, we experience his realization of that epiphany. Mahler encases it in a moment of high drama, not because he exploits here the vast orchestral and choral resources at his disposal in the Second Symphony. Quite to the contrary, the dramatic intensity of this extraordinary moment depends on Mahler's shrewd reliance on the power of understatement {ⓅAudio Ex. 11.3}.

The chorus sings very quietly—almost imperceptibly—as Mahler marks its entrance *PPP*. What is more, in a letter to the conductor Julius Buths (but not in the published score), Mahler makes clear his intention that the chorus remain seated when it begins to sing.[4] He wants the first choral entry to come as a powerful surprise. It is almost as if he is attempting to share with his audience the impact on him of the children's choir at von Bülow's funeral, where the sweet sounds of the children's voices wafted down from the choir loft while the singers remained out of the congregation's sight.

The understatement goes beyond the very soft dynamic level at which the chorus sings. A traditional chorale is, by nature, understated. Its melodies are straightforward, its harmonies simple, its texture homorhythmic (meaning that all the voices sing in essentially the same rhythms). Mahler's chorale follows suit. It offers a bare-boned and eminently clear setting of its text. There is, for the most part, not a note more than is needed, and this stark economy gives rise to a complete absence of pretense. In turn, this enables the music to bestow upon its poem a powerful aura of veracity. Only once does this chorale break out of these exacting constraints. The soprano soloist sings the same music as the sopranos in the chorus until just before the very end of the stanza, and her voice mostly cannot be distinguished from those of the sopranos in the chorus. At the end of the last verse (**01:20**), the soloist begins to assume greater

---

[4] Knud Martner, ed., *Selected Letters of Gustav Mahler: The Original Edition Selected by Alma Mahler*, trans. Eithne Wilkins, Ernst Kaiser, and Bill Hopkins (New York: Farrar, Straus, Giroux, 1979), no. 297. Buths was to conduct the Second Symphony in Düsseldorf on April 2, 1903. Mahler's letter of March 25, 1903, offered him advice on matters concerned with that performance. Mahler indicates that the chorus is to stand when they sing "Mit Flügeln, die ich mir errungen."

prominence, ultimately disengaging from the sopranos in the chorus and momentarily soaring above them (**01:31**) in an exquisite portrayal of an ascent to heaven.

These features of Mahler's *Auferstehen* chorale identify it as a powerfully evocative moment of resolution—indeed, what would seem to be *the* moment of resolution of the entire symphony. Mahler informs his listeners in musical terms that the words of this chorale should ring true. The Christian concept of eternal life after judgment provides the answer to his search for meaning in a life that inevitably leads to death. If any listener were to need additional confirmation of the importance of this moment, they might take it from the opening notes of the chorale (Music Ex. 11.1 and {⊙ Audio Ex. 11.4}).

What we hear, of course, are the three notes of the returning-note figure. The promissory note signifying the importance of the completion of this motif was first given to us twenty minutes earlier, at the beginning of the last movement. Since then, Mahler vacillated frequently between complete and incomplete statements of this figure, reinforcing our sense of its importance while, at the same time, engendering increasing frustration at our utter ignorance of what the pattern is meant to signify. Moments ago, he offered us several exaggerated iterations of it in its incomplete state, reminding us how little we know about this important musical motif. Now, at a critical moment of resolution—when so many divergent strands of this symphony are finally drawing together—we know from the poetry to which this figure is sung the paramount significance of this musical motto. It is sung to the word *Auferstehen* ("Rise again"). The returning-note figure thus stands for the Christian concept of resurrection. The dawning of this knowledge within us, which eluded us for such a long time, contributes greatly to the power of this moment of resolution in the symphony.

Music Ex. 11.1. The beginning of the choral entry

First Instrumental Interlude and the Second Verse of the Klopstock Chorale

The instrumental interlude that follows the first verse of Klopstock's chorale {▶ Audio Ex. 11.5} offers gentle but convincing confirmation of the importance of the compellingly persuasive resolution that occurred in the last section. At the very beginning of the interlude, against a background of shimmering tremolandos in the strings, four French horns play the clarion calls that portrayed the Caller in the Wilderness near the beginning of this movement {Audio Exx. 9.11 and 9.16}. Simultaneously, a solo trumpet plays the resurrection motive. The combined themes tie together the beginning and the end of the Last Judgment, and they do so in a way that suggests that there is a good outcome (resurrection, meaning eternal life) at the end of judgment. The same motives continue, expanding into a more luxuriant orchestration (**00:24**) and leading to a grander statement of the resurrection motive in the strings (**00:43**). Finally, this is joined by a strong restatement of the *Auferstehen* (returning-note) motive, played by six French horns (**00:56**). It is wonderfully refreshing to hear this motive and, at last, to know what it means! Much of the Second Symphony reflects very high levels of angst. What we hear in this instrumental interlude, however, provides the very antithesis of that affect. The music is utterly serene, and that quality, as much as the musical themes it puts forward, adds to the strong sense of confirmation we feel about the powerful resolution provided by the first stanza of Klopstock's chorale.

For the second stanza of Klopstock's chorale, Mahler repeats the music of the first one, embellishing it slightly {▶ Audio Ex. 11.6}.

Wieder aufzublüh'n, wirst du gesä't!	To bloom again you are sown!
Der Herr der Ernte geht	The Lord of the harvest goes
und sammelt Garben,	And collects, like sheaves,
uns ein, die starben!	We who died!

Some rhythms are changed, and occasionally only the tenors and basses sing (as at the very beginning of the stanza). Beginning at **00:19**, some mild dissonance is added to the original harmonies here and there, and some of the chords are altered from what they were in the first stanza and rendered a tad more chromatic. But this is done not so much to change the essential harmonic design, but simply to add some spice to the sonorities for the sake of variety. Once again, as the verse nears its close, the soprano soloist gains prominence over the chorus (**01:05**), soaring above it at the verse's end (**01:14**).

The challenge Mahler appears to have taken upon himself in this stanza is to add harmonic and rhythmic variety, but never to a degree that violates the code of simplicity that is so important a factor in chorales like this one. It is their stark simplicity, as we have seen, that can enable chorales to project a powerful aura of authenticity. Mahler succeeds in this by preserving the essential phrase structure, melody, and harmonic design we heard in the first stanza. It is good that he proceeds in this way, for the text of the second stanza continues with the same sentiments that were presented in the first. That parallelism would have been disrupted had a significant amount of change been introduced in the second stanza.

A Critical Pivot

The music that follows the setting of Klopstock's second stanza begins with the resurrection motive, weaving it and, later, the immortality motive from *Siegfried* into a structure that achieves closure that is both firm and gentle {⊙ Audio Ex. 11.7}. The resurrection motive is played first by a choir of six French horns (**00:02**) juxtaposed contrapuntally to a silken descending melody in the flute and violins. Mahler calls for both lines to be played *sehr ausdrucksvoll* ("very expressively"). Contrapuntal interplay continues briefly (**00:11**) as the woodwinds take over the ascending portion of the resurrection motive. Thereafter, the dynamic level gradually gets softer and the texture thins. The music grows simpler as the counterpoint recedes. First, the melodic line that was set against the resurrection motive is emphasized on its own in the violins (**00:33**), then in the violoncellos and basses (**00:42**). Finally, in a beautiful gesture, the passage lands effortlessly and exquisitely on a very quiet statement of the immortality motive from *Siegfried* in the trumpet and trombone, devoid this time of any contrapuntal competition (**00:57**). The juxtaposition of the resurrection and immortality motives sensitizes us to how closely related they are melodically. (They both emphasize upward melodic motion. The resurrection motive sometimes begins with a small downward dip, while the immortality motive always begins with an emphatic falling fifth.) Thereafter, the immortality motive is repeated very softly in increasingly higher ranges—first by clarinets (**01:11**) and then by flute and piccolo (**01:18**) until the music gently fades away.

Mahler worked hard to proffer the sentiments embodied in the *Auferstehen* chorale as a resolution of his existential problem. And he uses the passage at hand as a means of confirming that. He does so by offering a high level of closure to that resolution. It doesn't matter that this passage is so soft and understated. That, after all, is how Mahler presented his music of resolution, from the moment the chorus first entered, almost imperceptibly, with Klopstock's first verse. Beginning and ending in an understated manner offers a magical sense of symmetry. And this feeling of closure is even more convincing in the light of the transcendent beauty of the entire passage. Moreover, Mahler's choice to focus exclusively on the immortality motive at the end of this passage seems to suggest that there is nothing else to be said in the wake of the conclusive resolution provided by the preceding sections. It would not be completely unreasonable, if only for a fleeting instant, to imagine the symphony drawing to a close at this moment.

I call this section of our discussion a "critical pivot," however, because it causes us to focus simultaneously both backward and ahead. It glances retrospectively at the resolution of Mahler's fundamental existential question in the *Auferstehen* chorale and solidifies the validity of this gain with a section that offers strong closure, even if it is expressed in the gentlest gestures. At the same time, the music adopts a prospective cast that forces us to look ahead for several reasons:

- First, the entire passage of resolution is in G♭ Major. A symphony in C Minor traditionally will end in C Minor, C Major, or E♭ Major. G♭ Major is very much an outlier within this tonal scheme, and its presence here suggests that we have more tonal ground to cover.[5]
- Second, we have already experienced Mahler's capacity for achieving endings of powerfully climactic proportions (as at the end of the first

[5] The matter of the tonality is admittedly tricky. G♭ Major would be a very unlikely key in which to end a symphony that began convincingly in C Minor. On the other hand, Stephen Hefling cites a sketch for the Second Symphony, in which Mahler seems, at one time, to have planned to do just that—not at this juncture, but somewhat later. We shall see presently, however, that he changed his mind about this. Stephen E. Hefling, "Content and Context of the Sketches," in Gilbert Kaplan, ed., *Mahler: The Resurrection Chorale* (New York: The Kaplan Foundation, 1994), 23, n. 20. The sketch is now in the Austrian National Library, and it may be seen at: https://digital.onb.ac.at/rep/osd/?1003E 311. I am grateful to Prof. Hefling for generously providing information about this sketch.

section of the finale {▶ Audio Ex. 9.6}), and it would not be unusual for us to harbor an expectation for something of that magnitude as a way of bringing this symphony to a close.

- Third, and probably most important, Mahler has been so successful at assuring our eager acceptance of the *Auferstehen* resolution, and our utter satisfaction with it, that some of us may have forgotten about various important loose ends that still remain untied. Not least important among them is the descending second played prominently by the English horn in the first movement that was expanded into a dramatic, sensual, chromatic melody that appeared twice in the finale. We need to know the significance of this obviously important and highly enigmatic melody, which continues to elude us. Be assured that Mahler will not let us ignore this important question for long.

A Stunning Reversal

A moment after the final reverberations of the "critical pivot" fade away, having emphatically authenticated for the listener the veracity of the *Auferstehen* resolution, we hear this {▶ Audio Ex. 11.8}. All the salient ingredients of our enigmatic English horn theme, as we have come to know it, are present: the portentous opening tremolando in the viola, the descending minor second in the English horn, and its expansion into an intensely emotional, chromatic, and sensual melody. We observed the metamorphosis of this melody over the span of the entire symphony. It made its debut in the first movement as the opening interval alone—rendered unmistakably conspicuous owing to its appearance in the pungent and sultry sonority of the English horn. Then it was expanded into the sensuous melody we heard at the beginning of this movement, only to reappear more hauntingly later in the trombone and juxtaposed with the military fanfares of the offstage band. The meaning of all of this, however, continued to lie completely beyond our grasp.

This time, however, it appears *with words* sung by the contralto soloist. They are, moreover, Mahler's own words. Two stanzas of Klopstock's poem seem to have been quite enough for Mahler, and, for the rest of the movement, he turns to his own poetry. Even in the stanzas Mahler took from Klopstock we can detect signs of his uneasiness with some of their sentiments. In the last two lines of the first stanza, for example, Mahler sets the words

Unsterblich Leben! Unsterblich Leben!	Immortal life! Immortal life!
Wird, der dich rief, dir geben!	Will be given to you by He Who called you!

This involved a change in Klopstock's last line, however, which originally read "Wird, der dich *schuf*" ("He who *created* thee"). Mahler seems to have been ill at ease at attributing creative powers to God.[6] Does this posture not seem greatly at odds with the tone and content of Klopstock's chorale text?

What can we learn from Mahler's verses about the meaning behind this cryptically sensual melody? The contralto soloist sings the following lines to the enigmatic music that has just returned so dramatically {▶ Audio Ex. 11.9}:

O glaube, mein Herz! O glaube:	Oh believe, my heart, oh believe:
Es geht dir nichts verloren!	With you nothing is lost!
Dein ist, ja Dein, was du gesehnt!	Yours is, yes, what you desired is yours!
Dein, was du geliebt, was du gestritten!	Yours is what you have loved, what you have fought for!

The music we hear (from the beginning until **00:34**, except, of course, for the added vocal part), is largely borrowed from the appearance of this melody early in this movement, where what becomes the vocal line here is largely played by the English horn and flute {▶ Audio Ex. 9.14}. After the opening transplanted section, it expands and grows even more intense (at **00:34**) for the last line of the quatrain the contralto sings. We were justified in detecting a sensual quality in this music when it first appeared. Mahler abandons Klopstock's conventional sentiments about life after death for a far more intimate rhetoric. In what seems to be an attempt to initiate a new doctrine—"Believe!" the text commands—Mahler addresses his lines not to the sinners, but to the heart, the seat of love, using the familiar second-person pronoun

---

[6] Martha C. Nussbaum, *Upheavals of Thought: The Intelligence of Emotions* (Cambridge: Cambridge University Press, 2001), 635.

"*Dein.*" With love, Mahler asserts, nothing is lost—not the object of love, nor the goals for which the heart strives. Indeed, love and struggling in its name become the mainstays of this new belief.

The soprano soloist continues {⊙ Audio Ex. 11.10}:

O glaube: Du wardst nicht umsonst geboren!	Oh believe! You were not born in vain!
Hast nicht umsonst gelebt, gelitten!	Did not live in vain, suffer in vain!

For the soprano, Mahler abandons the edgy, dramatic, and sensual musical tone he used for the contralto for one that is more declarative and straight-forward. The message she conveys, however, brings the centrality of love set forth in the contralto's message a bit closer to the fundamental existential question addressed in this symphony. A life marked by striving for love cannot have been lived in vain, nor will the suffering that may have come into that life have been for naught. The lengthy passage for solo violin (**00:26**) that ends this section helps to epitomize the highly personal ambience that drives its rhetoric.

If the soprano's declaration fails to link Mahler's prioritization of love directly to the reward of eternal life, the two couplets of Mahler's text sung next by the chorus make that connection to immortality explicitly clear {⊙ Audio Ex. 11.11}:

Was entstanden ist, das muss vergehen!	What came into being must pass away!
Was vergangen, auferstehen!	What has passed away must rise again!
Hör' auf zu beben!	Cease trembling!
Bereite dich, zu leben!	Prepare yourself to live!

If they have striven for love, the dead will rise again. Mahler links the music for these lines to the earlier *Auferstehen* resolution in various ways. Chorale style is reintroduced. The seminal returning-note figure comes back (**00:02**). In the second line, he delineates the concept of resurrection ("What has passed away must rise again!") in a powerful choral declaration accompanied by a rich brass chorale (**00:14**). It is not unlike the sound of the brass chorale that accompanied the *Dies irae* earlier, but now the same sonority is evocative of love, as opposed to signifying judgment. At the very end of the last verse (**01:16**), the contralto soloist marks the return to life at the end of the passage by soaring above the chorus as the soprano soloist did in Klopstock's first verse. All these musical elements were used earlier to represent an orthodox view of eternal life. Now, Mahler seems to be deliberately appropriating them and placing them in the service of a very different approach to the attainment of immortality.

What Mahler offers us here is an eschatology that reflects a liberal and secular-leaning outlook. It is couched in language that resonates with a highly personal tone, a poetic style that reflects so powerful a sense of Mahler's commitment to it that one could easily be tempted to attribute these ideas directly to him. They emerge within a particular context, however: Siegfried Lipiner's Promethean view that tragedy—death and suffering—are, in fact, positive forces, agencies through which man achieves the truest form of resurrection, in the gaining of his own godliness. Lipiner, as we observed in Chapter 1, articulated these views in 1878 in a lecture called *Über die Elemente einer Erneuerung religiöser Ideen in der Gegenwart* (*On the Elements of a Renewal of Religious Ideas in the Present*). The thrust of this essay reflected the influence of Nietzsche's views upon Lipiner, who shared his outlook with fellow students in Vienna, including Mahler.[7]

As Mahler articulates this eschatology in both words and music, using love as the mechanism through which it attains its success, it is particularly notable for what finds no place in it at all. There is no mention of judgment. That should not surprise us. We have already sampled Mahler's disdain for what he perceives to be the unfair outcome of the Last Judgment in a comment he made to Bauer-Lechner: "*All* give vent to the same terror, the same lamentations and paroxysms; for *none* is just in the sight of God."[8] And we tasted the bitterness of his reaction to the draconian results of judgment in the music just before Klopsptock's *Auferstehen*. With the last quivering sounds of the dying nightingale, he laments the veritable extinction of all life in the wake of judgment. Indeed, in the guide he wrote for the Dresden performance of the Second Symphony, Mahler describes the new eschatology vividly: "And behold: there is no judgment. There is no sinner, no righteous man—no great and no small.—There is no punishment and no

---

[7] Stephen E. Hefling, "Siegfried Lipiner's *On the Elements of a Renewal of Religious Ideas in the Present*," in Erich Wolfgang Partsch and Morten Solvik, eds., *Mahler im Kontext / Contextualizing Mahler* (Vienna: Böhlau Verlag, 2011), 91–114, esp. 112. See also Hefling, "Mahler's 'Todtenfeier' and the Problem of Program Music," *19th Century Music*, 12 (1988): 28–29.

[8] Natalie Bauer-Lechner, *Recollections of Gustav Mahler*, ed. Peter Franklin, trans. Dika Newlin (New York: Faber & Faber, 2013), 44 (emphasis added).

reward! An almighty feeling of love illuminates us with blessed knowing and being!"[9]

These words seem remarkably similar to a declaration of religious universalism that appears in Gustav Theodor Fechner's *Das Büchlein vom Leben nach dem Tode* (*Little Book of Life after Death*), first published in 1836: "There is no heaven and no hell to which the soul proceeds in the usual sense [in which it is conceived by] Christians, Jews, and Heathens." Even the cadence of Fechner's repeated negatives—"no heaven and no hell"—finds its analog in the series of paired negatives in Mahler's eschatology as it is represented in the Dresden program. Fechner was Lipiner's spiritual mentor, and Mahler is known to have read the treatise in question during his years in Hamburg.[10]

What Just Happened?

At this moment, the listener would be justified to pause and ask (perhaps with a touch of disbelief): "Did Mahler really just provide two powerful climactic moments for this symphony, one of which asserts orthodox Christian views on eternal life, and the other of which substitutes something altogether different?" The answer, of course, is "Yes." The *Auferstehen* resolution gains its striking power from the force of understatement, the veracity of simplicity, our capacity to re-experience in it Mahler's epiphany at Hans von Bülow's funeral, and the highly satisfying and long-delayed explication of the returning-note motive. The doctrine-of-love resolution is no less forceful, relying for its strength on the sudden and dramatic explanation of an old and pressing enigma—What is the significance of the English horn theme?—that has been gnawing at us throughout the symphony.

Clearly, given his deep abhorrence for Divine judgment as it surfaces in both Christian and Jewish eschatologies, Mahler believes in the second of these resolutions and not in the first. Then why did he invest so heavily in the strength with which he projected the credibility of the first resolution? This approach would make no sense in an essay. It would be thoroughly confusing

---

[9] Donald Mitchell, *Gustav Mahler: The Wunderhorn Years. Chronicles and Commentaries* (Woodbridge: Boydell Press, 2005), 184.

[10] Stephen E. Hefling, "Zweite Symphonie," in Peter Revers and Oliver Korte, eds., *Gustav Mahler: Interpretationen seiner Werke* (Laaber: Laaber-Verlag, 2011), 1:272.

viewed solely from the perspective of symphonic design. But it seems perfectly natural when it is perceived as a function of high drama (of the sort we often encounter in opera). The great power of the second climax derives not only from the much-needed resolution of an enigma of long standing. Its real clout resides in the sheer dramatic energy inherent in its sudden, bold, and totally unexpected uprooting of the first climax.

It is worth considering that Mahler may have conceived the second climax in the way he did partly with a prominent model in mind. This returns us once again to the Ninth Symphony of Beethoven, a work whose intersections with Mahler's Second we have mentioned several times. At the most intense climactic moment of the Ninth Symphony, the one that turned the world of symphony on its head, Beethoven felt compelled to introduce words into what was strictly an orchestral genre—as did Mahler in the finale of the Second Symphony. Beethoven's baritone soloist enters, not with Schiller's poetry, but with the composer's own words (Beethoven's preamble to Schiller's *Ode to Joy*)—as Mahler introduces his own poetry after setting just two stanzas of Klopstock's chorale. And, for Beethoven, these mechanisms are used to reject the musical and emotional content of the preceding three movements—much as Mahler's second climax dramatically overturns the traditional Christian eschatology set forth in the *Auferstehen* climax. Mahler emulates here, with consummate respect, techniques that lie at the heart of the Ninth Symphony. In appropriating them, however, he follows the essence of Beethoven's plan without, however, jeopardizing an iota of the integrity of his own compositional voice or his originality. Mahler's finale, at this point, follows Beethoven, but it does not sound remotely like the finale of the Ninth Symphony. For me, this passage radiates with a sense of Mahler's resounding triumph over the intractable Beethoven predicament so elegantly formulated by Mark Evan Bonds: the inescapable need for Beethoven's successors to acknowledge and confront the older master by simultaneously mirroring his achievements and striving to overcome them.[11]

As Mahler continues to set his own words to music, two celebrations emerge: one of love and one of eternal life.

[11] Mark Evan Bonds, *After Beethoven: Imperatives of Originality in the Symphony* (Cambridge, MA: Harvard University Press, 1996), 1–3.

A Celebration of Love

The two soloists enter suddenly and exuberantly to celebrate the victory of love over death {⊙ Audio Ex. 11.12}:

O Schmerz! Du Alldurchdringer!	Oh Pain, you, who pierces all things,
Dir bin ich entrungen!	From you, I have been wrested!
O Tod! Du Allbezwinger!	Oh Death, thou conqueror of all,
Nun bist du bezwungen!	Now, you have been mastered!
Mit Flügeln, die ich mir errungen,	With wings which I have won,
in heissem Liebesstreben,	In blazing striving for love,
werd' ich entschweben	I shall float away
zum Licht, zu dem kein Aug' gedrungen!	Toward the light that has penetrated no eye!

The music for the duet is celebratory, but there is much more than celebration in the character of this passage. The duet calls to mind, in its intensity and ardent nature, a Wagnerian love duet. Note at the opening the dramatic glissando leap of a seventh into a dissonant chord; the increasingly close and frenetic imitation that sets in between the two soloists; the violent fluctuations in dynamic level; the speed-up in the rate of chord change as the passage progresses; and the increasingly chromatic harmonic language. This music offers the very embodiment of passion and eroticism. Compare Mahler's duet with a brief excerpt from one of the second-act duets from Wagner's *Tristan und Isolde*, "So starben wir, um ungtrennt" ("So we might die, never to part"). Note in it many of the same musical markers of fervor and rapture we cited in Mahler's duet, although, not surprisingly, these traits are brought to a higher level of intensity in the excerpt from *Tristan* {⊙ Audio Ex. 11.13}.

Is it appropriate for Mahler to have relied on the immortality motive from *Siegfried* as a central musical symbol of eternal life? In the trajectory of the Second Symphony that led to the *Aufherstehen* resolution, it might appear unseemly to take this musical idea from the lips of Brünnhilde, who, as we have pointed out, was a Nordic demigoddess who stakes her immortality on her love for a man born of the incestuous union of twins. If, however, we shift to the path through the symphony that leads to the second climax, the one that champions striving for love, the immortality motive from *Siegfried* seems eminently suitable. Brünnhilde originally lost her immortality as a result of judgment (that of Wotan, her father and one of the principal gods in Norse mythology). She bypasses that judgment, regaining immortality through her love for Siegfried. Thus, everything about the context from which this motive emerged turns out to match perfectly both Mahler's abhorrence of judgment and his focus on the role of love in the pursuit of immortality within his universal, secular-leaning eschatology.

Trying to fathom Mahler's intentions can sometimes be frustrating. Sometimes, he introduces musical conundrums that remain unresolved for vast stretches of time. It can be vexing trying to keep track of these. We have just observed one of these at work in the protracted enigma of the mysterious minor second in the English horn, which spans most of the symphony until the contralto soloist enlightens us in "O glaube."

Something similar happens beginning in "Urlicht." Specifically, we might focus on the way Mahler treats the protagonist's sense of his direct path to God that bypasses the angel who is blocking his way. The music in this passage, as we observed, is anomalously intense, spasmodic, chromatic, and dissonant. That passage from "Urlicht" resembles the music for "O glaube" and the subsequent duet, which clarifies, retrospectively, Mahler's intent with the anomalous passage in "Urlicht." Angels traditionally serve as dispensers of the suffering associated with the Last Judgment, and, from Mahler's perspective, the speaker of the poem can be seen to be acting in defiance of judgment as he claims his direct "oneness with God," notwithstanding the obstacles the angel places in his path. This is surely not the intent of the poem, a prayer at the deathbed that obviously reflects traditionally pious Christian sentiments. A strong argument can be made, however, for Mahler's having read the poem in accordance with his own views on judgment, especially as they are articulated in the verses he adds to the first two stanzas by Klopstock.

Indeed, as Donald Mitchell observes, Mahler connects the duet directly to the anomalously chromatic passage in "Urlicht" with a common melodic motive. The music he provides for the line in the duet "In heissem Liebesstreben" ("In love's fierce striving") is close to that of his setting of "Ich bin von Gott und will wieder zu Gott!" ("I am from God and shall return to God") in "Urlicht." The two motivic fragments are juxtaposed in (Music Ex. 11.2 and {▶ Audio Ex. 11.14}). The melodic connection

Music Ex. 11.2. A quotation from "Urlicht" at the end of the symphony

suggests strongly a common thread linking the two passages. The duet is obviously about redemption through love. The musical similarities that link Mahler's music for "Urlicht" to the "love duet" in the finale suggest that he interpreted the Urlicht poem along the lines of his own secular eschatology, assigning love a prominent place in the protagonist's return to God—a role that would appear to bypass traditional judgment.

Similarly, we wondered earlier in our discussion of this movement about Mahler's close juxtaposition of the returning-note motive and the opening of the *Dies irae*. One, we noted, is an inversion of the other, but we couldn't understand the significance of this relationship (Music Ex. 11.3). Only now, when we have a clear sense of the extent of Mahler's antipathy to judgment, can we grasp the significance of this melodic inversion. There can be resurrection (as represented by the returning-note motive in *Auferstehen*), but only when judgment is overturned (symbolized by literally turning the *Dies irae* motive—that archetypal symbol of judgment—upside-down).

Music Ex. 11.3. The meaning of the inverted returning-note figure

A Celebration of Eternal Life

Less than four minutes of music remain in this massive movement. Mahler now celebrates the victory of achieving eternal life in a way that befits the monumental scope of this symphony, calling upon the full resources of his chorus and enormous orchestra. The last of Mahler's verses are consistent with the universal eschatology he set forth beginning with the texted return of the English horn melody (the second climax). Eternal life is a personal victory, the protagonist's fair prize—not a gift of Divine grace. It is the heart—the wellspring of love—that ascends to eternal life. The path to God and to eternal life is open to those who strive for love {⊙ Audio Ex. 11.15}.

Mit Flügeln, die ich mir errungen,	With wings which I have won
werde ich entschweben!	I shall float away!
Sterben werd' ich, um zu leben!	I shall die, to live!
Aufersteh'n, ja aufersteh'n wirst du,	Rise again, yes, you shall rise again,
mein Herz, in einem Nu!	My heart, in a flash!
Was du geschlagen,	What you fought for,
zu Gott wird es dich tragen!	Will carry you to God!

The concluding section of the symphony begins (**00:00**) with the upward climbing resurrection motive portraying the text that describes a soaring flight heavenward. The motive appears in succession in each of the four voices of the chorus, that is, without coalescing into systematic imitative counterpoint. Eventually (**00:23**), an imitative structure sets in. Ending the symphony with a section of strict counterpoint would be in the tradition of how compositions of truly grand proportions often close—works like Handel's *Messiah*, Haydn's *Creation*, and Mozart's "Jupiter" Symphony, to cite a few examples. But the systematic imitation never really gets off the ground here; rather, it is transformed into an acutely anticipatory passage (**00:30**). Mahler wanted to emphasize greatly the subsequent text "Sterben werd' ich, um zu leben!" ("I shall die, to live!"), and he makes it the object of the growing anticipation. He sets it forcefully to what appears to be a coalescence of the resurrection and immortality motives in chorale-like homorhythm, preceded by a dramatic *Luftpause* (**00:51**).[12]

---

[12] Typically, Bruno Walter, who seems to frown on Mahler's predilection for *Luftpausen*, deemphasizes this one by keeping it very short. On Walter's treatment of other *Luftpausen* in this symphony, see above, pp. 55–56.

This powerful reference to immortality is followed by another equally important passage devoted to the line "Aufersteh'n, ja aufersteh'n wirst du" ("Rise again, you shall rise again)" (**01:19**). Again, the texture is chorale-like, and the music is unmistakably familiar. It is the chorale melody based on the returning-note motive that Mahler used in his earlier quiet rendition of this melody (at the *Auferstehen* resolution). Here Mahler appropriates it in support of his own eschatological agenda. At its initial presentation, this vitally important melodic statement paradoxically gained enormous power from its magical understatement, but Mahler seems to feel that its centrality within his own message in this symphony can only be enhanced with a full-blooded and powerful reprise. The organ enters here for the first time in the symphony.

Powerful it is, and its strength only increases with the line "Was du geschlagen" ("What you fought for") (**01:47**), where cymbal crashes underscore a melodic line blared out by all ten French horns, playing with their bells raised, that quotes the immortality motive. The chorus offers assurance that the object of mankind's striving will open the path to God (**02:04**)—"zu Gott wird es dich tragen!" ("Will carry you to God!"), just before a prolonged and mighty cadence (**02:19–02:27**). Immediately thereafter, the immortality motive is restated in a paroxysm of orchestral color (**02:28**). Two harps, three deep bells, and the deep tam-tam join all ten French horns, two trumpets, and two trombones in a powerful statement of the motive. The final full evocation of the immortality motive (**02:45**) is given to a most idiosyncratic complement of instruments: bassoons, contrabassoon, tuba, violoncellos and basses (both bowed and pizzicato), and timpani.

Finally, as if to distill for us the very essence of the immortality motive, Mahler reduces it to two notes—the first two notes of the motive, the descending fifth (**03:04**). Try saying the word "*é-wig*," German for "eternal," which is accented on the first syllable. This is the key word Brünnhilde sings to the music of the immortality motive: "Ewig war ich; ewig bin ich" ("I was immortal; I am immortal"). The natural speech rhythm of this word fits that of the descending fifth as it is presented here, and we can almost hear that word resonating within this orchestral statement. All this takes place over a sustained E♭ Major chord, lending a note of clear and very strong tonal closure to the movement and to the symphony.

From the perspective of the central message he was trying to convey in this symphony, to whom did Mahler give the last word? The last line sung, as we have seen, is "zu Gott wird es dich tragen!" ("Will carry you to God!"), with "zu Gott" powerfully declaimed three times. Mahler's posture toward God is obviously very complicated. At the age of nineteen, a year after he completed his studies at the University of Vienna, Mahler expressed the full force of his grievances with God in a letter to Josef Steiner, who was, except for Theodor Fischer, Mahler's closest childhood friend from Iglau. In it, Mahler conveys in the most bitter terms his difficulty in comprehending a God Who presides uncaringly over a world in which pain, suffering, and death are rampant:

> May fear strike you wherever you hide! Out of the valley of mankind the cry goes up, soars to your cold and lonely heights! Do you comprehend the un-speakable misery here below that for aeons has been piling up mountain-high? And on those mountain peaks you sit enthroned, laughing! How in the days to come will you justify yourself before the avenger, you who cannot atone for the suffering of even one single frightened soul!!![13]

Similarly, think of Mahler's reluctance to assign God the role of Creator as re-flected in the revision he made to Klopstock's chorale text. Or consider again Mahler's outright disdain for the undue severity he attributed to Divine judg-ment. Notwithstanding all of this, Mahler strives to carve out an appropriate niche for God in his new secular-leaning eschatology. In the guide to the symphony he wrote for the Dresden performance, he precedes his outright denial of judgment, reward, and punishment with these lines: "'Risen again, yea thou shalt be risen again!' There appears the glory of God! A wonderful gentle light permeates us to our very heart—all is quiet and blissful."[14] Thus, God, as a final destination for mankind, is celebrated luxuriously within the powerful ending of the symphony we just heard.

The complexity of Mahler's reservations and skepticism about God is un-deniable, but so is the importance of his life-long need to relate to a Divine presence. His pursuit of this objective did not take him down the paths of formal religious practice; rather, it manifested itself in more eclectic ways. A telling insight into this central component of Mahler's persona was pro-vided by Oskar Fried, the conductor who led the extraordinarily successful performance of the Second Symphony in Berlin in December 1905, and who went on to direct the first complete recording of a Mahler Symphony (also the Second) in 1924. Fried wrote of Mahler in 1919: "He was a God-seeker.

---

[13] Martner, ed., *Selected Letters of Gustav Mahler*, no. 2a.
[14] Reilly, "*Todtenfeier* and the Second Symphony," 125.

With incredible fanaticism, with unparalleled dedication and with unshake-able love he pursued a constant search for the divine, both in the individual and in man as a whole."[15]

Mahler's conception of the "glory of God," as he expresses it in the outline of the Second Symphony he wrote for the Dresden performance, need not be viewed as inconsistent with his ongoing disputes with God—as long as we assume that it is a God of love Mahler has in mind, One whose capacity to execute judgment has been substantially neutralized. In the world of Jewish and Christian eschatology, Mahler had little leverage, but in the domain of the Second Symphony, he held all the cards. He could demote God from the role of Creator to that of a mere Summoner and deprive Him of His capacity to render judgment. In the end, Mahler honors the God he struggled to find over the course of his life sincerely and prominently in the last line the chorus sings. If, however, we attend to the grand, final climax in the orchestra, we discover that the last word is really given to Brünnhilde—to the immortality motive that found its way from her lips into the Second Symphony. In this, Mahler gives voice to the power of love inherent in that music, while still accepting a Divinity he assumes will also embrace that power.

At this point, the reader should listen to the fifth movement uninterrupted. A complete performance (with light annotations) appears in Appendix 4E.

---

[15] Norman Lebrecht, *Mahler Remembered* (London: Faber & Faber, 1987), 174; translated from Oskar Fried, "Erinnerungen an Mahler," *Musikblätter des Anbruch* 1 (1919): 17.

The Formal Template for the First Movement: Sonata Form

Tonality • Binary Form • Simple Binary Form •
Rounded Binary Form • Sonata Form

Sonata form is one of several formal designs that were widely used in the eighteenth and nineteenth centuries to govern the structure of various types of instrumental music. Occasionally, it made an impact on opera arias, too. Like most formal patterns of this kind, sonata form is more of a guide than a fixed, inflexible structure. Composers will adhere to enough of its protocols to signal the listener that the sonata template is operative. Listeners who recognize the form will have, a priori, a set of expectations regarding the general ways in which the movement is apt to proceed. However, composers will also feel free to depart from those conventions in the service of artistic independence, originality, and creativity. In the end, listeners learn to negotiate the slender line that divides those of their expectations regarding the form that are fulfilled from those that are not.

Sonata form ranks among the most important of the structural designs commonly used. It frequently serves as the form for the first movement in symphonies, sonatas, string quartets, and other genres, and it also frequently governs the design of the final movement in symphonies. Beginning in the late eighteenth century, it provided the basis for the formal structure of the first movement of many concertos, too. Two critical forces guide the shape of sonata form: tonality and the concept of binary structure. We shall examine each of these in turn before considering sonata form itself.

Tonality

Tonality is among the most powerful forces in music. It reigned supreme in Western music of the eighteenth and nineteenth centuries, and its impact continued to be felt into the twentieth century, even when efforts to overthrow some of its governing principles began to take hold. It is a system that limits the vocabulary of tones available for use in a composition and assigns relative weight or importance to them in a hierarchic manner. Importance, in this context, is a factor of a tone's capacity to provide effective closure and the important sense of satisfaction the listener experiences in the presence of that closure. In tonal music, one—and only one—note can do this at optimum, and we designate this note the *tonic*, from which the term "tonality" takes its name.

To illustrate how this works, let us return briefly to some music we contemplated in the Preface to this guide—two passages from the last movement of Wolfgang Mozart's Piano Quartet, K. 478. Here we shall expand a bit on our earlier discussion. We heard two versions of what was intended to be a closing passage, meant to bring a strong sense of finality to the music. The first version of this passage, we suggested, ended in a manner that sounded surprising, deceptive, even shocking {⊙ Audio Ex. A1.1}. It belied our expectations and failed utterly at providing closure. We branded it as aberrant. The second passage, on the other hand, ended exactly as we imagined it would {⊙ Audio Ex. A1.2}. It realized our expectations for what the final note should be and was thoroughly successful at providing closure. We characterized this passage as normative.

A little more technical detail than we provided in our earlier account of this passage may help us to understand how it works and the role *tonality* plays in this process. Like all closing passages, this one is designed to bring a section of the work to a clearly defined end. Such passages terminate with a *cadence*, a specific configuration of harmonies that are ubiquitously used to convey a sense of closure. Here is the expected cadence, isolated from the rest of the passage {⊙ Audio Ex. A1.3}. The difference between the normative and aberrant versions of this closing passage, as we pointed out, resides in the last note of the cadence (and its harmonization). In the version that satisfies our expectations of what a closing passage is supposed to do, the last note and the harmony based upon it is the tonic; in the deviant version, it is not. This comparison of the two passages provides some insight into the power of the tonic: it, and it alone, can provide the level of stability that brings about truly effective closure. Needless to say, Mozart uses the normative version of this passage at the end of the movement. He makes use of the aberrant form earlier in the piece, and he capitalizes on it as a means of surprising, tantalizing, and shocking the listener. The latter reactions are antithetical to the quality of anticipated repose the listener expects at a moment of closure, and they serve, therefore, to render the normative version of the passage more acutely needed and ever more satisfying when it finally arrives.

As another example of how strong our need for the tonic can be, consider this excerpt from the Beethoven Violin Concerto, Op. 61 {⊙ Audio Ex. A1.4}. Obviously, the excerpt seems unfinished. After the point at which we interrupted it, the music continues with a repeat of the first half of what we just heard. This time, however, it closes effectively {⊙ Audio Ex. A1.5}. The seminal difference that sets off the second example is that it ends with the tonic, where the first one did not. Much by way of stability and satisfying closure is wrapped up in the inherent force of the tonic. Here is the entire passage so that you can compare the two segments more readily {⊙ Audio Ex. A1.6}. (This two-part structure that avoids the tonic at the end of the first part, but provides it at the end of the second, is ubiquitous in Western music. We call it *antecedent-consequent form*.)

Binary Form

Binary form is the most basic and, in some ways, the most important formal structure in Western music of the eighteenth and nineteenth centuries. The duality implicit in the term "binary" and inherent in this design affects two components of the music: its substance and its tonality. By "substance" we mean the actual content of the music—the aggregate of the pitches, harmony, and rhythms that comprise the work. In this sense, what is binary about a piece of music in binary form is that the actual *content* of the work can be neatly and discernibly divided into two parts. In turn, this aspect of the substantive design is emphasized and rendered particularly clear in performance because each of the two parts of a binary form is conventionally repeated. (Composers almost always mandate this repeat, but performers sometimes omit it.) Repetition thus helps to define the essence of the formal design. The way in which tonality participates in the essence of binary form is more complicated and will be explained below. There are two kinds of binary form: *simple binary form* and *rounded binary form*.

Simple Binary Form

Our example of simple binary form is a dance movement from Johann Sebastian Bach's First Orchestral Suite in C Major, BWV 1066, which is apt to have been composed at the court of Prince Leopold in Cöthen around 1721. (A suite is a multi-movement instrumental composition, in which many of the individual movements are short dances in binary form.) This dance is a passepied, a French court dance that might be characterized as a faster version of the minuet. Listen to the example {▶ Audio Ex. A1.7} and take note of the two sections and their repeats, which may be diagrammed as follows:

A A B B or (to employ the conventional repeat signs used in music) ||: A :||: B :||

The formal design may be linked to the audio file as follows, using the time stamps that track the flow of the music on the media player:

A begins at **00:00**.
It repeats at **00:07**.
Something new (it must be B) begins at **00:14**.
This repeats at **00:32**.

The tonal apparatus of a binary form is somewhat harder to grasp than its substantive structure. Early-on in a piece of tonal music, composers send us signals in the melody, harmony, or both that identify what the tonic is. Along with this knowledge comes our expectation that the piece will dutifully close on this same tonic. However, if music were only to establish and keep on reiterating the same tonic, it would quickly reduce us to boredom. Thus, for the sake of greatly needed variety, composers developed the ability to change the tonic—to convince us after having first identified one tone as the tonic that, in fact, another has usurped that role (at least for a time). The process of changing the tonic is called *modulation*.

As listeners, we are willing to go along with this, but only temporarily, because we have come to learn from listening to a lot of music that there can only be one "real" tonic in any piece of tonal music. Thus, though a modulation can enhance our interest in the music to a very great extent, it also creates a need in the listener's consciousness (and a parallel obligation for the composer), to get back to the original tonic by the end of the piece.

In binary form, the tonality also assumes a binary dimension. Two formal gestures occur within the tonal process in a binary form:

1. the tonic that is established at the beginning of the piece is quit; and
2. it is regained.

Let's return to the passepied we just heard and trace its tonal design {▶ Audio Ex. A1.7}.

Section A

00:00	The tonic is identified clearly at the very beginning of the dance. Both the melody and harmony are saturated with the sound of the tonic as the music begins.
00:04	At this point, the emphasis on the tonic is replaced with the introduction of harmonies that seem just a bit foreign, as if they lie outside the vocabulary of harmonies that belong to the tonic to which we were initially introduced. This begins to shake our confidence in the original tonic and constitutes the beginning of the modulation, which almost immediately points us toward a new tonic.
00:06	We feel a sense of arrival as the modulation is consummated, and the music lands on the new tonic and confirms it as such.
	Note that the modulation and confirmation of the new key occur very deftly and very rapidly. You may wish to listen to this process several times.

Repeat of Section A

00:07	Instantly, however, with the swift return to the opening of the piece for the repeat of Section A, we leap back to the original tonic. (Juxtaposing the new tonic at **00:06** and the return to the original one at **00:07** strikingly confirms the change of tonic brought about by the modulation.)
00:10	The beginning of the modulation repeats.
00:13	The new tonic is established.

Section B

00:14	The new section commences with harmonies that sound even more foreign than any heard before and that constitute another and longer modulation.
00:24	The new modulation culminates in a point of arrival, but it is neither the original tonic nor the one to which the first modulation was made. It is yet another new tonic. (And the mode of the music has changed from major to minor, too.)
00:25	Immediately, however, the music moves away from this new tonic, and we hear familiar-sounding harmonies that suggest we are moving back to the original one.
00:31	The latter projection is correct, and the original tonic is compellingly confirmed with a strong cadence, literally, at the eleventh hour—on the last note of Section B.

Repeat of Section B

The four components of Section B (as outlined above) repeat:

00:32	New modulation
00:41	Arrival in another new key
00:42	Movement back to the original tonic commences.
00:49	Arrival back in the original tonic is confirmed.

If the principal burden of a binary form is to get back to the tonic once it has been quit, we may wonder why Bach delays this by interpolating a modulation that digresses further to a new and even more remote key (the one solidified at **00:24** and in the repeat at **00:41**). There is an important aesthetic concept underlying this decision: moving farther afield tonally actually serves to intensify the need for the return of the tonic. It confuses us and leaves us wondering where we are tonally and why we are there. The result is that we welcome the return of the original tonic more enthusiastically when it finally arrives. Its return after the excursion into a more distant tonal realm is made to feel eminently more satisfying.

Rounded Binary Form

Although rounded binary form is very close to simple binary form, it offers one essential difference, but it is a very important one. Our example comes from the same Orchestral Suite by J. S. Bach. This time, the example is a courante, a dance known for its free-flowing rhythmic character {▶ Audio Ex. A1.8}. In our account of this example, the time stamps for the initial playing and its repeat in both Sections A and B are noted on the same line, separated by a slash.

Section A

00:01 / 00:19	The tonic is made clear.
00:10 / 00:29	The modulation commences.
00:17 / 00:35	The new key is confirmed with a sense of arrival.

Section B

00:37 / 01:24	More intense modulation begins.
00:54 / 01:40	Arrival in yet another key (and in the minor mode)
00:55 / 01:41	Another modulation heads back to the original tonic. Until this point, the form of the courante is identical to that of the passepied. The important difference between the two examples— and what distinguishes simple binary form from rounded binary form—is about to occur.
01:05 / 1:52	The original tonic returns, along with the opening music of the courante. In simple binary form, the confirmation of the original tonic was withheld until the very end of the piece. Bach handles this differently in the courante, in which the tonic returns well before the end of the second half of the piece. Something else of considerable moment coincides with the return of the tonic. The opening music of the first half of the piece reappears at the same moment. Nothing identifies a piece of music more clearly than its opening material because composers often begin a work with music that is eminently memorable. Thus, in the rounded binary design, the return of the tonic—itself a gesture of considerable stability—is made to join forces with another particularly stable event: the return of *familiar material*. We call this coordinated gesture the *double return* (i.e., the simultaneous return of the tonic and the familiar opening material). After the double return, Bach provides a good measure of firm closing material in the tonic.
	The double return sets off rounded binary form from simple binary form in a remarkable way. There is something particularly satisfying about the coordinated return of *both* the tonic and the familiar opening material. The double return takes on an aura of a significant musical event—one not at all present in simple binary form.

Sonata Form

Dance forms are wonderfully concise, and they offer very clear examples of musical structure. But composers of instrumental music often felt the need for a larger canvas—a format that would enable them to compose pieces of greater length and substance. If, at the same time, they wanted to establish a mode of communication with their listeners based on form, they needed a formal design that could accommodate a longer and more complex movement. Different forms served this need, but the one used most frequently eventually was called *sonata form*. This design came into being about the mid-eighteenth century, but it was not codified in the theoretical literature or given its name until much later. We shall begin with a theoretical and rather abstract explanation of this structural design and then proceed to flesh it out with a musical example.

Sonata form, as it originally came into being, is really a binary form, consisting in two halves, each of which is repeated. Its tonal design is also identical to that of the two binary forms we just encountered: it establishes and leaves the tonic in the first half and returns to it in the second half. The moment of return, moreover, is coordinated with a return of the opening of the movement, what we called the double return. A sonata form, therefore, is very much like a rounded binary form. As one might expect of a musical structure designed to accommodate greater length, however, the rounded binary plan that underlies sonata form is significantly expanded in the new design. Even more importantly, the additions produce more than a mere capacity for added length; they create the potential for a kind of rhetorical drama in music not unlike theatrical drama in its distinguishing and privileging of certain events as the work moves through time.

Exposition

The first half of the expanded binary design in sonata form—called the Exposition—is extended to embody five formal functions, *Opening material, Primary material, Transition, Secondary material,* and *Closing material,* which we shall designate with the standard abbreviations O, P, T, S, and K, respectively.[1] (You will need to recall these abbreviations, which will be used often in our account of the first movement of Mahler's Second Symphony.) Now, let us expand a bit on these four functions.

O **Opening material.** Many (but not all) works in sonata form begin with introductory material, often played at a slower tempo than the main part of the movement that follows.

P **Primary material.** This material opens the movement (unless it is preceded by opening matter). It manifests the tonic decisively and tends to be sharply profiled in a manner that enhances its memorability.

T **Transition.** The burden of the transition is to leave the tonic. Thus, it modulates. Usually, it also serves to generate a need for clear melodic material in the new key. It often does so by abandoning satisfying melodic material for more abstract, more

---

[1] These analytical symbols were originally devised by Jan LaRue. See his *Guidelines for Style Analysis, Expanded Second Edition with Models for Style Analysis,* ed. Marian Green LaRue (Sterling Heights, MI: Harmonie Press, 2011), 154.

non-descript, a-melodic writing. We tire easily of this sometimes boring and abstruse music and yearn for a more satisfying melody.

S **Secondary material.** This is clear melodic material in the new key to which the transition modulates. It is usually different from **P**. Often, it is gentler and more song-
like than **P**. But it can also be **P** repeated in the new key, in which case the form is
designated *monothematic sonata form.*

K **Closing material.** This music provides a clear sense of closure. It brings the music to
a satisfying stopping point both rhythmically and harmonically.

The exposition tends to be relatively predictable owing to its division into the principal
functions **PTSK** (sometimes preceded by **O**). Also predictable is the tonal design. Works
in the major mode will move from the tonic to the dominant (a note five scale-degrees
higher than the tonic) for the secondary material. (For example, an exposition that opens
in C Major will provide a secondary theme in G Major.) Works in the minor mode, on the
other hand, will modulate to what we call the relative major for the secondary material.
A Minor key and its relative major are closely related, having a significant number of notes
in common. (An exposition that opens in C Minor, for example, will generally provide a
secondary theme in E♭ Major.)

Like the first act of a play, which is sometimes also called an exposition, the basic
materials (themes) of the movement are set forth here. So is the fundamental structural
problem of the work: we have left the tonic, and the listener expects its return. Like the A-
Section of a binary form, the exposition of a sonata form is repeated.

Development and Recapitulation

The second half of the binary sonata form consists in the *Development* and *Recapitulation*.
The first of these, the development, differs markedly from the exposition because it lacks
specified formal functions. Basically, the composer is free to do anything in the development. He or she can introduce new material or alter, or even combine, material from the
exposition. The composer is free to modulate any number of times, and, unlike the pre-
scribed tonal design of the exposition, the tonal route of the development is completely
open-ended.

If the listener gained a calm sense of conviction about how the form is unfolding
from the predictable design of the exposition, the sudden shift to a lack of predictability
in the development kicks away those props, and the listener is apt to feel somewhat lost
while experiencing the development. Invoking the metaphor of the drama once again,
a sonata development may be compared to the rising, falling, and climactic actions of a
play—actions the intensity of which require resolution. The listener demands resolution
in a return to predictability and of the tonic. Providing such resolution is the task of the
Recapitulation, which is distinctly analogous to the double return of a rounded binary
form. The tonic returns, along with the primary material. (Opening material is rarely, if
ever, repeated in the recapitulation.) In an instant, the discomforting instability of the
development section is ameliorated, as the security of the tonic and of familiar material
replaces the absence of predictable design in the development.

The recapitulation of a sonata form, however, is generally a more impressive event than
the double return of a rounded binary form. That is because the development of a sonata
form raises the ante of anticipatory tension far beyond its level in a typical rounded binary

form. Think back on the gratuitous movement to yet another key in the second halves of both binary forms we just considered. We suggested that the slight step further away from the tonic enhanced the sense of satisfaction that accompanied its ultimate return. The level of satisfaction that follows in the wake of the greater instability of a development section, which often contains multiple modulations, is bound to be enhanced even more. To return once more to the metaphor of the drama, the recapitulation may be viewed as an analog of the denouement of a play. In early examples of sonata form, the second half (i.e., the development and recapitulation combined) is repeated. By the 1780s, the tradition became to repeat the first half of the form, but not the second. Nowadays, some performers omit the repeat of the first half of the form, too, which can, however, seriously impair our sense of the intended balance of the movement.

The recapitulation generally brings back all four main components of the exposition—P, T, S, and K, but an important change needs to be made. The original modulation within the transition must be disengaged or altered. Without this emendation, the movement would end in a key other than the tonic.

An Example of Sonata Form

To illustrate how sonata form works, we turn to the first movement of an early composition by Joseph Haydn, Symphony, H. I:3, composed in the early 1760s. The work bears little resemblance to the scope and musical language of a Mahler symphony. It was chosen for the clarity with which it illustrates the concept of sonata form.

The metaphor of the drama is not the only one that can help us to understand how sonata form works; that design may also be likened to a journey, which encompasses both *travel* toward destinations and *arrival* thereto. The points of arrival convey the satisfaction associated with reaching a destination. The travel toward those goals, on the other hand, is unsettling because we are not there yet, and we may not be sure of where we are. In sonata form, we hear primary, secondary, and closing themes as points of embarkation or as destinations—all of which provide the comfort of familiar terrain—while transitions and developments leave us with the unsettled sensations that arise when we are in unfamiliar territory.

To illustrate this distinction, prepare yourself to hear the beginning of Haydn's Symphony H. I:3 {⏵ Audio Ex. A1.9}. Does this music serve effectively to open the movement? Not really. It lacks the distinctive profile of a tune we can readily recall—of a melody to which we will want to return. Instead, we hear a flurry of activity, consisting in many repeated notes and repeated patterns, none of which adds up to a genuinely memorable melodic statement. This passage emphasizes motion over content, and we would hardly imagine finding ourselves in breathless anticipation of its return.

Now, listen to another candidate for the opening of the movement {⏵ Audio Ex. A1.10}. This seems to be a far more effective contender for primary material. Its melody is sharply profiled and highlighted prominently by the violins and oboes, which lends to the already clearly defined tune a high capacity for recall. We would recognize this material anywhere. And there is something pleasantly transparent about its self-contained form: it has a vivid beginning (00:00), middle (00:05), and end (00:08).

In this exercise, I stacked the decks by offering the transition in the first of these two examples and the real primary theme in the second. The objective of the ruse is to bring to the fore the unsettled quality of the passages in a sonata form that are journeying toward a goal (transitions and developments) and contrast them to the security we feel when we find ourselves on familiar ground (primary, secondary, and closing material).

Now let's study the entire movement more closely {▶ Audio Ex. A1.11}. (Once again, the time stamps for the repeat of the exposition and combined development and recapitulation appear after a slash.)

EXPOSITION

00:00 / 01:00	P	The sharply profiled and self-contained primary theme, underscored by the oboes, emphasizes the tonic vividly.
00:12 / 01:12	T (beginning)	A transition begins, substituting repetitive fragments for the clear melody of P.
00:25 / 01:25	T (modulation)	Those fragments continue during a modulation.
0:32 / 01:31	T (closing)	The highly animated fragments of the transition combine with a cadence to achieve closure in the new key.
00:37 / 01:37	S	Oboes and violins echo each other in a gentle, song-like melody in the new key.
00:48 / 01:47	K	Brief forceful gestures culminate in a strong cadence to end the exposition.

DEVELOPMENT

01:59 / 03:39	Section 1	A small segment of P returns in the key of S, but set against a new melody and in a texture so thin it sounds a bit pallid. A swift modulation occurs at the end of the brief passage.
02:07 / 03:47	**Section 2**	The same fragment of P repeats in the new key, against another new melody and couched in a somewhat fuller texture. Again, a swift modulation occurs at the end of the brief passage.
02:13 / 03:54	Section 3	Once more, the fragment of P repeats in the new key—this time without a competing melody and in a heavier texture.
		These passages are unpredictable and unstable. We are given only a fragment of our cherished primary theme, where our instinct is to prefer it in its original whole configuration. That sliver of familiar melody is set in an unsatisfyingly thin texture—what happened to the rest of the orchestra?—and it is made to vie for our attention with competing melodic material. The brief sections end before we have a chance to adapt to what is going on within them. And the key changes rapidly, too. All of this is quite discomforting and more difficult to follow than the music of the more lucid exposition. The tension continues in what follows.
02:20 / 04:00	**Section 4**	Descending scales change the key and mode unpredictably again.

02:24/ 04:04	Section 5	The melody (in the violins) leaps about unpredictably.
02:31 / 04:12	Section 6	Agitated material begins.
		In the aggregate, everything we have heard in the development so far deprives us of the sense of satisfaction and comfort that accompany transparent thematic material and a clearly identifiable tonic. Our privileged primary theme has been fragmented and altered repeatedly, while being subjected to rapid changes of key. We long for a return of the stability we felt in the exposition.
02:36 / 04:17	Section 7	The harmony points us in the direction of a return to the tonic and leads us to the recapitulation.
RECAPITULATION		
02:43 / 04:23	P	After all the tension and uncertainties of the development, the arrival of the double return provides a major event, the denouement of the diminutive drama inherent in this movement.
02:54 / 04:35	T (altered)	The transition begins anew but is almost immediately altered to prevent its modulation.
03:12 / 04:53	T (closing)	The transition closes in the original tonic.
03:17 / 04:57	S	The secondary theme returns, but in the original tonic.
03:27 / 05:08	K	The closing material returns, but in the original tonic.

Sonata form captured the imagination of composers over a span of more than two-hundred years. It offered an effective mechanism for communicating with the listener while simultaneously opening opportunities for innovation and originality. When we encounter the first movement of Mahler's Second Symphony, we shall become amply aware, from its opening gestures on, of the differences that set it apart strikingly from the slight Haydn movement we just considered. Sonata form provided the elemental structural model for the opening movement of Mahler's Second Symphony, as it did in the First. But Mahler learned how this template works mainly from compositions closer stylistically to his own musical language and aesthetic objectives—from the symphonies of Beethoven, for example, in which the sonata principle is often used as a point of departure for revision, as is so also in some of Mahler's symphonies. Keeping this in mind may help ease the sense of culture shock that might otherwise set in when leaping directly from the modest, but eminently clear and pedagogically informative, form of our little Haydn symphony into the imposing monumentality of the Mahler Second.

Second-Movement Forms

Abridged Sonata Form • Theme and Variations •
Alternating Variation Form

The second movement in the symphonic cycle of movements usually contrasted sharply with the preceding movement by way of its greater simplicity and accessibility. A principal gateway to that directness is the form in which the movement is cast. One or the other of several straightforward designs is generally used in a second movement. Three of them are discussed here.

Abridged Sonata Form

One of these formal designs arose from a set of adjustments to sonata form that converted it into what became known as *abridged sonata form*. In this approach, the transition and development are shorn of much of their dynamic energy by removing from them a great deal of the tension that normally lies at the heart of these sections. Sometimes, in this formal template, a simple modulation can take the place of the development. The basic components of the exposition—P, T, S, and K—are generally retained, but the musical procedures that tend to distinguish these four functions vividly from one another may be suppressed, which can render the exposition a more continuous, more homogeneous structure. In fact, abridged sonata forms of this type are generally appreciated more for the ongoing continuity of their melodies, than for the distinct formal functions associated with the exposition of a conventional sonata form.[1]

Theme and Variations

A second formal design deployed in the attempt to attain a greater measure of simplicity in second movements of symphonies is called *theme and variations*. This approach scales down the dynamism inherent in sonata form even more than abridged sonata form does. In many ways, in fact, theme and variations can be described as a relatively static musical design.

A theme and variations begins with the theme, a melody that is provided with a partic-ularly clear harmonic background and ensconced in an equally clear formal frame. This

---

[1] For an example of an abridged sonata form, you might listen to the second movement of Wolfgang Mozart's Symphony No. 35 in D Major, K. 385 (the "Haffner" Symphony). It should be noted that there were few strict, formal rules governing abridged sonata form. Some examples of the procedure, therefore, lie close to real sonata form, while others—like the one cited here—are more far-removed from it and invest more heavily in the melodies they project than in the systematic culti-vation of formal contrast.

theme needs to be simple enough for the listener to absorb it quickly and to be able to recall it, or at least recognize it, almost instantly. Here is such a theme, from the second movement of Joseph Haydn's Symphony, H. I:75 {▶ Audio Ex. A2.1}. Note its very basic rounded binary form ||: A :||: B A':|| (one of the formal designs we encountered in the guide to sonata form in Appendix 1).

A	**00:01**	2 + 2 measures
Modulation	**00:10**	2 measures
Confirmation of new key	**00:15**	2 measures
A (repeat)	**00:20**	2 + 2 measures
Modulation (repeat)	**00:30**	2 measures
Confirmation of new key (repeat)	**00:34**	2 measures
B Modulation back to the tonic	**00:40**	2 + 2 measures
A' Double return + extension	**00:50**	6 measures
B Modulation back to the tonic (repeat)	**01:05**	2 + 2 measures
A' Double return + extension (repeat)	**01:15**	6 measures

The rudimentary binary structure bestows an ample degree of clarity on this theme. It gains an even higher level of transparency from the way its phrases are broken down into small regular units, almost always of two measures. Count along with the music: 1-2-3, 1-2-3, and so on. One group of three beats (1-2-3) constitutes a measure. Generally, you will discover clear pauses or changes after every two measures. Only at the double return, after the listener has had time to master this melody, does Haydn afford himself the luxury of expanding the music to a six-measure phrase. The emphasis on two-measure units has the effect of dispensing this theme in bite-size morsels that are relatively easy to retain. It shouldn't take you more than one or two hearings to assimilate this theme. In fact, because it is a rounded binary form with repeats, one playing of the theme will provide you with six opportunities to hear the opening A-material. It comes as no surprise that the melody is so easy to grasp!

What happens next in a theme and variations is that the theme becomes the basis for a set of variations on it. The melody of the theme, its harmony, or both can provide material for the variations. The relationship between the theme and the variations is founded on a delicate choreography—one that attempts to strike an effective balance between similitude and difference. Some aspects of each variation must resemble the theme enough to make clear that it is, in fact, a variation of the theme; other aspects of each variation must differ from the theme sufficiently to establish the independence of each variation. Listen to the theme again {▶ Audio Ex. A2.1}, followed by the first variation {▶ Audio Ex. A2.2}. In what ways are the theme and the variation similar? And how do they differ?

Let's take note of the similarities first. There are a number of them.

- Both the theme and Variation 1 are in rounded binary form.
- Both have the same number of measures and the same phrase structure (as outlined above).
- Except for a few decorative changes, the harmonies in the theme and in Variation 1 are identical.
- Both are in the same key and mode.

What sets the first variation apart from the theme is the nature of its melody. In place of the somewhat sluggish, lumbering tune we heard in the theme, the first variation offers something livelier. The first violin springs to life, offering a melody marked by its faster and more changeable rhythms. In this way, the first variation succeeds in generating a measure of contrast to the theme, but the more active melody in the variation does not ignore completely the melody of the theme. Often—especially at important moments of the melodic structure like the beginnings and ends of the two-measure phrases—the lively melody of the variation pays homage to the original tune by echoing some of its most prominent notes verbatim. Thus, the melody of the theme seems to be lurking furtively behind this variation, which is otherwise more closely related to the harmony of the theme.

The essence of theme and variations, as we suggested earlier, is how the balance between similarity and difference plays out as the movement proceeds. Thus far, the emphasis lies squarely in the realm of similarity. Form, phrase structure, key, mode, and harmony are identical (or, in the case of harmony, at least nearly so) in the theme and first variation. The enlivened rhythm of the melody in the variation offers some change, but it, too, as we have seen, is rooted to various important notes of the original melody.

On the surface, the second variation {▶ Audio Ex. A2.3} sounds quite different, owing to the sudden appearance of wind instruments that begin with a somewhat strident rhythmic figure that includes many repeated notes. Not far below that surface level, however, we discern the same form, key, mode, phrase structure, and harmonies that linked the theme and first variation, along with frequent reference to the important notes of the original melody. Much the same might be said of the third variation {▶ Audio Ex. A2.4}. The wind instruments drop out, but the strings divide into eight separate lines instead of the four that normally comprise the string section. This produces a lush orchestral texture, and, in addition, a solo violoncello plays a flowing countermelody in rapidly cascading sixteenth notes. Again, however, the form, key, mode, phrase structure, and harmony of the theme remain constant here, and, this time, a solo violin plays the original melody intact. In the final variation {▶ Audio Ex. A2.5}, the winds return, and a more elaborate, rapidly flowing melody is introduced in the violins, but all the other constants—form, key, mode, phrase structure, harmony, and another exact iteration of the original tune—are present.

This movement holds our interest, largely owing to its engaging shifts in orchestral color and some ingenious countermelodies in rapid note values. As we have seen, however, the balance between similitude and change is weighted in favor of the first of these. It is a lopsided balance, but one that remains eminently serviceable. The appealing contrasts in orchestral color and in the rapidly streaming countermelodies are thoroughly agreeable. In the end, however, the form that results from all the musical factors that remain constant throughout this movement brings about a good measure of musical stasis. This is fine, however; it facilitates greatly the listener's ability to absorb, retain, and understand the musical content of this movement without a great deal of effort. And this reflects perfectly the ideal of simplification and accessibility that governs many second movements.

Alternating Variation Form

The balance between similitude and difference that lies at the heart of theme and variations is subject to infinite variability. A composer must choose which of these characteristics to emphasize. In the foregoing example from Joseph Haydn's Symphony H. I:75, as we have seen, the emphasis lies squarely on the similarities that link the theme and all the variations. Haydn, however, is a composer who was noted for the dynamic qualities of his music. Typically, he may lavish great energy in crafting the kinds of passages that fire up our expectations for something to happen, only to skim over the anticipated event, when it ultimately arrives. That kind of emphasis on the dynamic qualities of music seems antithetical to the second movement of Symphony H. I:75, which is, for Haydn, an unusually static movement.

In addressing the need for a more accessible kind of music in the second movements of his symphonies, Haydn found a way to maintain some of the static qualities we observed in theme and variations, without undermining his strong predilection for the more dynamic properties of music. He invented a new formal paradigm that relied on the principles of theme and variations but that rendered it somewhat more complicated. Movements fashioned in this way presented the listener with a bit more of a challenge. This formal design came to be known as *alternating variation form*.[2]

A movement composed in this manner preserves many of the accoutrements of theme and variations—simple themes in binary form, along with variations of them that preserve the form, key, and phrase structure of the theme, and elements of its harmony or melody. Alternating variation forms, however, present two themes instead of one, and they vary them in alternation—like this:

Theme 1
Theme 2
Variation 1 on Theme 1
Variation 1 on Theme 2
Variation 2 on Theme 1
Variation 2 on Theme 2 ...

In Haydn's alternating variations, the two themes are almost always in opposing modes. If Theme 1 is in the major mode, then Theme 2 will be in the minor. The key (tonic) for both remains the same. Often, the two themes will begin with a brief, shared melodic motive.

Because the themes and variations are all cast in binary form, both halves of the themes and all subsequent variations will be repeated. This feature offers another way to ameliorate the stasis that can easily be inherent in variation designs by introducing an additional level of variety. Instead of merely repeating a section of a binary form literally, it can be varied, as if it were a variation in its own right—a variation within a variation. We call this structure a *double variation*.

Here is an example of part of a movement in alternating variation form. It is from the second movement of Haydn's Symphony, H. I:53 {▶ Audio Ex. A2.6}. Included are the two themes and the first variation of each of them. All sections are in simple binary form.

Theme 1 (Major)	A	00:01	Note the two-measure phrases.
	A	00:16	
	B	00:31	
	B	00:46	
Theme 2 (Minor)	A	01:02	Themes 1 and 2 begin with the same melodic motive.

[2] For a pathbreaking and detailed discussion of alternating variation design, see Elaine R. Sisman, *Haydn and the Classical Variation* (Cambridge, MA: Harvard University Press, 1993), 150–162.

			When Theme 2 modulates (at **01:09–01:24**), it also switches to the major mode.
	A	01:17	
	B	01:31	
	B	01:46	
Variation 1 of Theme 1			
	A	02:02	Not varied, which is unexpected.
	A′	02:16	Variation commences at the repeat. The harmony of the theme is preserved; its melody is embellished.
	B	02:32	A light variation of **B**
	B′	02:47	A different variation of **B** is provided (double variation).
Variation 1 of Theme 2			
	A	03:05	Winds are added to the A-section of Theme 2.
	A′	03:20	More variation. The melody shifts to the bass.
	B	03:35	The harmony of the theme is preserved; its melody is embellished.
	B	03:50	Literal repeat of B

When he laid out his plan for the second movement of the Second Symphony, Mahler used alternating variation form as his template, albeit in the context of a more expansive formal design. That design appeared almost exclusively among the works of Joseph Haydn during the eighteenth century, and we shall see (in Chapter 4) that Mahler conducted several Haydn symphonies, among them one that offered a movement in alternating variation form.

The Origins, Character, and Form of the Scherzo

The Nature of the Four-Movement Symphonic Cycle • Minuet and Trio •
Beethoven and the Emergence of the Scherzo

Mahler designates the third movement of the Second Symphony a scherzo. In this appendix, we shall trace the emergence of this kind of movement and explain how its formal design works.

The Nature of the Four-Movement Symphonic Cycle

By the time of its great efflorescence in the late eighteenth century, the symphony had become a four-movement cycle, in which the individual movements were governed, to different degrees, by distinct formal conventions. In the preceding appendices, we learned that first movements of symphonies typically relied on sonata form for their formal paradigm, while the more relaxed second movements were generally couched in abridged sonata form or in one or the other of several types of variation designs. The movement that made recourse to the greatest number of different formal templates was the fourth movement. It could be in sonata form, in a cyclical design known as rondo, in a hybrid of the latter two called sonata rondo, or, occasionally, in variation form. The third movement was the most rigidly circumscribed of the four regarding matters of formal structure. Early on, it was uniformly cast as a minuet and trio.

Minuet and Trio

The minuet is a dance in triple meter of French origin, performed at a slow-to-moderate tempo. Originally, it was music to be danced to, often in an aristocratic setting. In the seventeenth and eighteenth centuries, however, it was widely appropriated, to be used in many genres of purely instrumental music including the symphony. Like the two dances we encountered in our discussion of binary form (Appendix 1)—the passepied and courante from Johann Sebastian Bach's First Orchestral Suite—minuets are invariably in binary form. In order to provide music for dances that incorporated a greater number of steps, dance forms like the minuet were extended by adding to the minuet another binary form that came to be known as the trio, and the music could be extended even more by repeating the minuet after the trio. When the minuet became a part of concert music like the symphony, it embraced the convention of adding the trio as well as the return of the minuet. Originally, the trio was written for a reduced number of instruments—usually three, and these were often wind instruments. That is the source of the designation *trio*.

Later, however, even when that reduction in texture no longer pertained, the term trio continued to be used for this section of the music. Like the binary forms we considered in our discussion of sonata form (Appendix 1), both sections of the minuet and trio are repeated. In modern-day performances, the repeats are often omitted in the return of the minuet, even though the evidence suggests that they were observed during the eighteenth century.

The trio is sandwiched between two iterations of the minuet, which results in another basic formal structure; we call it *ternary form* (also known as song form or closed form). It can be diagrammed A–B–A. In essence, thus, the minuet and trio is a composite of binary and ternary form. Both minuet and trio are binary forms, but the two renderings of the minuet serve as bookends for the trio, resulting in an over-arching ternary structure.

Here is an example of a minuet and trio: the third movement of Wolfgang Mozart's Symphony No. 35, K.385, known as the "Haffner" Symphony, and composed in 1782. Both the minuet and trio are in rounded binary form (||: A :||: B A :||). In this performance, the repeats are not observed in the return of the minuet. Interestingly, neither the minuet nor the trio modulates. Mozart seems to have felt little need for this tonal contrast within the rounded binary forms because the trio is in a different key than the minuet, which endows the entire movement with ample tonal contrast. As you listen to the minuet and trio, be sure to observe that it is in triple meter; try counting in threes along with the music, and take note of the moderate tempo {▶Audio Ex. A3.1}.

A Minuet (in D Major)	
A	00:00
A	00:11
B	00:21
A	00:32
B	00:43
A	00:53
B Trio (in A Major)	
A	01:05
A	01:16
B	01:28
A	01:45
B	01:56
A	02:14
A Minuet (in D Major)	
A	02:26
B	02:37
A	02:47

Beethoven and the Emergence of the Scherzo

The nature of the third movement in symphonies and in other instrumental genres was to undergo significant change, owing substantially to the efforts of Ludwig van Beethoven. Soon after he arrived in Vienna in 1792 and began his studies with Joseph Haydn,

Beethoven composed an Octet for Wind Instruments—the chamber piece that was later designated Op. 103. Beethoven entitled its third movement "Menuetto," but it scarcely resembles the music we heard in the minuet from Mozart's "Haffner" Symphony. Here is the opening of the minuet of the Wind Octet {▶Audio Ex. A3.2}.

Listen to this excerpt, and try to count in threes, as you did with the Mozart minuet. It doesn't work. The tempo at which this movement is performed is much too fast to sustain counting in threes. The numbers fly by so quickly that one must resort to counting only one beat in a measure. This is hardly the slow-to-moderate tempo of a stately minuet. Other qualities come across, even in this brief opening passage. The rhythms seem nimble and somewhat brittle. The music is tossed back and forth among the instruments in a rapid and quixotic manner. And the overall spirit of the piece is playful, jocular, joyful. This contrasts sharply with the gracious elegance projected by the minuet of the "Haffner" Symphony.

Beethoven must have felt some discomfort at designating this movement a minuet be-cause in 1794, when he provided similar music for the third movements of his Piano Trios Op. 1, nos. 1 and 2, he called each of them "Scherzo," Italian for "joke." (Both of these movements also contain trios in contrasting keys.) The terminological muddle continued for some years, even when Beethoven provided a "title" for the third movement in his First Symphony, composed in 1799/1800. As he did in the Wind Octet Op. 103, he calls the movement "Menuetto," but its rapid tempo, lively rhythms, and mercurial changes resemble the qualities we noted in the third movement of the Wind Octet {▶Audio Ex. A3.3}. In his Second Symphony (composed in 1801/1802), Beethoven designated the new type of movement "Scherzo." Thereafter, in his symphonies, whether he labeled the move-ment "Scherzo" or merely provided a tempo designation, the character of the scherzo and trio supplanted that of the minuet and trio (except in the Eighth Symphony, in which Beethoven reverted to the old-style minuet). The change Beethoven brought about in what would have been the minuet movements of various genres made a sizable impact. Many composers followed his lead.

Ever concerned with expanding the length of his compositions, Beethoven sometimes resorted to an extended form of the scherzo and trio, in which the trio returns a second time before a final reprise of the scherzo. It is called the five-section scherzo:

Scherzo—Trio—Scherzo—Trio—Scherzo

The third movement of Mahler's Second Symphony, which we shall address in Chapters 5 and 6, is a scherzo and trio. Not surprisingly, Mahler adjusts both the tone and the form of this movement to suit his overarching agenda for this symphony.

Complete Performances of
Each Movement

Complete performances of each of the five movements of the Second Symphony appear in Appendices 4A–E. Presenting the movement in small sections, as we have throughout the text, promotes clarity and understanding, but there can be no substitute for an un-interrupted hearing of the work. Only in that way can we gain a true sense of the in-terrelationship of its parts, its proportions, its pacing, and its meaning. You are urged, therefore, to engage each movement, and ultimately the symphony in its entirety without the disruption that necessarily arises from frequent explanatory breaks in the flow of the music. A lightly annotated guide is provided for each complete movement to facilitate your grasp of it and remind you succinctly of the discussion presented earlier. (Please bear in mind that the elapsed-time indications provided in the appendices differ from those given earlier. In the segmented audio files, every file begins at **00:00**, whereas in the com-plete performances of the movements the numbers flow continuously throughout a whole movement or, in the case of the finale, throughout each of the three files into which the movement is divided.)

For readers who wish to correlate the musical events reported here with a score of the symphony, measure numbers and proximity to rehearsal numbers are provided for each musical event recorded. Most editions of the score of the Second Symphony lack measure numbers. The measure numbers provided here are those of the edition published by the International Gustav Mahler Society, edited by Renate Stark-Voit and Gilbert Kaplan (Vienna: Universal Edition and the Kaplan Foundation, 2010). The rehearsal numbers, which Mahler provided himself, have remained standardized in various reliable editions of the score beginning with the first edition of the score published by Josef Weinberger in Vienna in 1897 (reprinted by Dover Publications and available online at IMSLP, Petrucci Music Library (https://imslp.org/wiki/Main_Page).

Citations of a musical event according to its proximity to a rehearsal number are des-ignated with a plus sign (e.g., $\boxed{8}$ + 6) when counting forward from the rehearsal number, and with a minus sign (e.g., $\boxed{8}$ – 6) when counting back from the rehearsal number. In reporting locations in this manner, we follow one of several conventions used in actual rehearsals. In counting ahead from a rehearsal number, the measure in which the re-hearsal number appears counts as "1"; in counting back, however, the measure *before* that of the rehearsal number counts as "1."

First Movement: Allegro Maestoso
(*Todtenfeier*)

{▶ Audio Ex. A4A.1}

OPENING (00:01–00:53)

00:00	O1	Tremolando	m. 1 / Beg.
00:04	O2	Turning-note figure	m. 2 / Beg. + 2
00:10	O3	Anticipatory ascending scale	m. 4 / Beg. + 4
00:11	O4	Swift disjunct descent, jagged rhythm	m. 5 / Beg. + 5
00:14	O5	Perfect fourth in jagged rhythm	m. 6 / Beg. + 6
00:18	O6	Triplets	m. 7 / Beg. + 7
00:20		Permutations and combinations of the preceding motives	m. 7 / Beg. + 7

EXPOSITION—PART ONE (00:54–03:18)

00:54	P.1	Primary theme, Pt. 1, accompanied by motives from the Opening	m. 18 / 1 – 7
01:07	P.2	Primary theme, Pt. 2, along with material from the Opening	m. 21 / 1 – 4
01:55	Pk	Closing of P, using rhythm of O3	m. 37 / 2 – 6
02:17	T	Transition begins	m. 43 / 2
02:27		Modulation	m. 46 / 2 + 4
02:33	S	Secondary theme (*Gesang*)	m. 48 / 3
03:01		Shift to E♭ Minor	m. 57 / 3 + 10
03:18		Abrupt end to the first part of the exposition	m. 62 / 4 – 2

EXPOSITION—PART TWO (03:19–05:42)

03:19		Opening motives (back in tonic)	m. 62 / 4 – 2
03:32	P.1	Primary theme, Pt. 1 in diminution, intensified with material from one of the *Wayfarer Songs*	m. 67 / 4 + 4
03:45	T	Swift modulation to A♭ Major	m. 72 / 5 – 2
03:50		Victory motive from First Symphony	m. 74 / 5
04:04		Sudden return to C Minor—ascending theme in trumpet, plus swift descending lines in the rhythm of O4 and Pk	m. 80 / 5 + 7
04:47	K	Closing theme related to ominous motive from beginning of the First Symphony and to the Inferno motive from Liszt's *Dante Symphony*. Ten soft strokes on the tam-tam	m. 97 / 6

DEVELOPMENT—PART ONE (05:43–11:03)

05:43	S	Secondary theme (*Gesang*) in C Major	m. 117 / 7
06:02		Modulation to F Major	m. 123 / 7 + 7
06:14		… then to E Major	m. 127 / 8 – 2
06:20	N1	New theme in the English horn (*Meeresstille*); echoes of Magic Fire Music from *Die Walküre*	m. 129 / 8
07:09		Shift to minor mode signals impending rise in developmental tension.	m. 145 / 9 + 3
07:16		Rhythm of O4 and Pk	m. 147 / 9 + 5
07:29	N2	Another new theme in the English horn and bass clarinet	m. 151 / 9 + 9
07:55		Motive based on the rhythm of P.1	m. 160 / 10 – 4
08:15		Climactic moment: rhythm of P.1 combines with triplets of O6.	m. 167 / 10 + 4
08:25		Nearly all the motives of the Opening combine.	m. 171 / 10 + 8
08:35		Reference to the Victory motive from the First Symphony	m. 175 / 11 – 4
08:45		Complex combination of motives: rhythm of P.1, Pk, K, and O6	m. 179 / 11
09:28		Explosive crest	m. 196 / 12
09:40		Waning and start of modulation to F Major	m. 202 / 12 + 7
09:53	S	Another iteration of the gentle secondary theme, which then proceeds to modulate	m. 208 / 13
10:31		Music begins to fade, bringing Part One of the development to a close (at 11:03).	m. 226 / 14

DEVELOPMENT—PART TWO (11:04–14:53)

11:04	O2, O3, O4	Startling explosion in E♭ Minor. Return to opening material	m. 244 / 15
11:15	O1	Tremolando played "on the bridge"	m. 249 / 15 + 6
11:21	O1	Tremolando fades to inaudibility, signaling impending arrival of something important	m. 251 / 15 + 8
11:34		Rhythm of O4 and Pk, mysteriously	m. 254 / 16
11:45	O2	Passing reference to turning-note figure	m. 256 / 16 + 3
11:50		Enigmatic motive (minor second) in the English horn	m. 258 / 16 + 5

Parade of motives—some imported

12:05	P.2	Second half of primary theme (flute)	m. 262 / 16 + 9
12:31		Beginning of the *Dies irae*, combined with P.2	m. 270 / 17 – 8
12:56	P.2	Second half of primary theme	m. 278 / 17
13:07		Victory theme from the First Symphony	m. 282 / 17 + 5
13:17		Immortality motive from *Siegfried*	m. 286 / 17 + 9
13:21		Opening of *Dies irae* and broadening	m. 288 / 17 +11

End of parade of motives

13:30		Paroxysm of developmental tension	m. 291 / 18
13:48		Broadening and simplification of rhythm	m. 300 / 19

13:56		Prominent reference to many motives from the Opening and the primary theme	m. 304 / 19 + 5
14:28		Further broadening	m. 320 / 20 – 5
14:40		Excruciating dissonances	m. 325 / 20
14:53		End of second part of the development	m. 329 / 20 + 5

RECAPITULATION (14:54–21:33)

14:54	O1, O2, O3, O4	Motives from the Opening in C Minor	m. 330 / 20 + 6
15:10	P	Primary theme (both parts)	m. 335 / 21 – 1
15:19	O6	Triplets added. Permutation of motives	m. 338 / 21 + 3
16:05	Pk	Closing of P	m. 353 / 22
16:18	T	Modulation to E Major	m. 357 / 22 + 5
16:33	S	In its original key of E Major	m. 363 / 22 + 10
17:01	N1	From Pt. 1 of the development (*Meeresstille*)	m. 370 / 23 – 2
18:11		Modal shifts from minor to major	m. 386 / 24 – 6
18:20		Eerie tremolando fades almost to inaudibility, signaling something important to follow	m. 388 / 24 – 4
18:31	K	Closing theme related to ominous motive from beginning of the First Symphony and to the Inferno motive from Liszt's *Dante Symphony*. Soft strokes on tam-tam	m. 392 / 24
18:38		K combined with a synopsis of material from the beginning of the movement	m. 394 / 24 + 2
19:12		Texture expands as dynamic level gradually rises	m. 404 / 25
19:57		Thinner texture and softer dynamics follow the crest of the expansion.	m. 418 / 26 – 2
20:27		Six more soft strokes of the tam-tam together with descending fourth in triplets in the tympani	m. 427 / 26 + 8
21:21		Descending chromatic scale in triplets. Reminiscent of the Inferno motive from Liszt's *Dante Symphony*	m. 441 / 27

Second Movement: Andante moderato

{▶Audio Ex. A4B.1}

A	Theme One	00:00	m. 1 / [1]
B	Theme Two	01:29	m. 39 / [3]
A^1	First Variation of Theme One	03:04	m. 86 / [5]
B^1	First Variation of Theme Two	04:47	m. 132 / [6] – 1
A^2	Second Variation of Theme One	07:25	m. 210 / [12]

Third Movement: Im ruhig fliessender Bewegung (Scherzo and Trio)

{▶Audio Ex. A4C.1}

(For the principles guiding the location of musical events in the score according to their proximity to rehearsal numbers, see p. 229.)

---

1. SCHERZO (00:00–03:21)

00:00	Introduction	28[1]
00:13	A-section of A–B–A′ in C Minor	m. 12 / 28 + 12
01:50	B-section of A–B–A′ in F Major	m. 105 / 32 + 2
02:40	A′-section of A–B–A′ in C Minor	m. 149 / 34

2. TRIO (03:22–06:21)

03:22	Beginning of imitative entries (*fugato*—an allusion to the trio from Beethoven's Fifth Symphony)	m. 189 / 36 – 1
03:35	Second imitative entry	m. 200 / 36 + 11
03:47	Paraphrase of the fanfare from the scherzo of the Symphony in E Major by Hans Rott—in D Major	m. 211 / 37 – 1
03:59	Closing gesture for fanfare	m. 223 / 37 + 12
04:11	Imitative writing returns, adding a new theme (subject) in the oboe.	m. 235 / 38
04:14	Another new subject added in the clarinet.	m. 238 / 38 + 4
04:34	Paraphrase of Rott fanfare again—in E Major	m. 256 / 39 – 1
04:45	Closing gesture for fanfare	m. 268 / 40 – 4
04:50	Gentle, lyrical melody (a favorite of Mahler)	m. 271 / 40 – 1
05:45	Lengthy close for gentle melody	m. 316 / 42 + 9
05:59	Anticipatory transition to return of the scherzo in C Minor (greatly altered)	m. 327 / 43 – 1

3. ALTERED SCHERZO (06:22–08:02)

06:22	A-section of A–B–A′	m. 348 / 44
07:27	B-section of A–B–A′ in F Major (greatly altered)	m. 408 / 47 + 2
08:02	Instantaneous modulation to the next section. The A′-section of the scherzo is omitted here.	m. 440 / 49 – 1

4. ALTERED TRIO (08:03–09:55)

08:03	Paraphrase of the Rott fanfare in C Major	m. 440 / 49 – 1
08:09	Highly agitated and anticipatory music leads to …	m. 447 / 49 + 7
08:26	the terrifying orchestral scream.	m. 465 / 50 + 9
08:34	The music begins to grow calmer and softer.	m. 473 / 51 – 8
08:42	Motive of the imitation from the first trio returns.	m. 480 / 51 – 1

---

[1] The rehearsal numbers begin with 28 in this movement in accordance with a plan Mahler had at one time to make the scherzo the second movement of the symphony. Note that the last rehearsal number in the first movement is 27.

09:00	Gentle descending theme in the trumpet and French horn, over imitative music of the trio	m. 496 / 52 – 4
09:05	Gentle descending theme in the first violin. Imitative music continues in lower strings.	m. 501 / 52 + 2
09:27	Harp glissando introduces repeated attempts to restart the opening of the imitative music of the trio.	m. 519 / 53 – 2
09:29	The imitative motive grows increasingly fragmented.	m. 522 / 53 + 2
09:37	The imitative music of the trio makes a new start . . .	m. 528 / 53 + 8
09:47	but it starts to grow tense and anticipatory, leading to . . .	m. 537 / 54 – 8
09:54	the descending cascade that introduced the first return of the scherzo. This brings the second trio to an end.	m. 544 / 54 – 1

5. SYNOPSIS AND WEAK ENDING LARGELY BASED ON THE SCHERZO (09:56–END)

09:56	Material from the piano introduction to the B-section of the song in C Minor	m. 545 / 54
10:04	Second subject from the imitative section of the trio	m. 553 / 55 – 7
10:13	Material from near the end of the song added	m. 560 / 55
10:23	End of the last couplet of the song, leading to . . .	m. 570 / 55 + 11
10:30	an indecisive ending of the movement.	m. 577 / 55 + 18

Fourth Movement: "Urlicht"

{▶Audio Ex. A4D.1}

(For the principles guiding the location of musical events in the score according to their proximity to rehearsal numbers, see p. 229.)

O Röschen rot,	O little red rose,
Der Mensch liegt in grösster Not,	Man lies in the greatest need,
Der Mensch liegt in grösster Pein,	Man lies in the greatest pain,
Je lieber mögt ich im Himmel sein.	I would prefer to be in heaven.
Da kam ich auf einen breiten Weg,	Then I came on a broad path,
Da kam ein Engellein und wollt mich abweisen,	An angel came and sought to turn me away,
Ach nein ich liess mich nicht abweisen.	Ah no! I would not be turned away.
Ich bin von Gott, ich will wieder zu Gott,	I am from God and wish to return to God,
Der liebe Gott wird mir ein Lichtchen geben,	Dear God will give me a little light,
Wird leuchten mir bis an das ewig selig Leben.	Will light my way to everlasting blessed life.

00:00	Opening motto	Beg.
00:16	Chorale	m. 3 / Beg. + 3
00:48	Stanza 1	m. 14 / 1 – 1
02:07	Stanza 2	m. 36 / 3
03:01	Stanza 3	m. 54 / 5 – 1

Fifth Movement: Im tempo des Scherzos (in three parts)

(For the principles guiding the location of musical events in the score according to their proximity to rehearsal numbers, see p. 229.)

The Fifth Movement, Section 1

{▶Audio Ex. A4E.1}

This section of the finale sets forth a great deal of musical material. It may be likened, in this sense, to an exposition.

00:00	Return of the orchestral scream from the third movement	m. 1 / Beg.
00:04	New motive added in the trumpets and trombones ("terror motive")	m. 5 / Beg. + 5
00:20	*Luftpause*	m. 25 / 2 – 1
00:25	Immortality motive from *Siegfried*	m. 27 / 2 + 1
01:35	Open fifth in offstage French horns (*shofar*)	m. 43 / 3
01:42	Echo of the *shofar* call	m. 44 / 3 + 1
01:49	Returning-note figure left incomplete	m. 45 / 3 + 3
02:01	Triplets begin in oboe	m. 48 / 3 + 6
02:13	Clarion calls ("The Caller in the Wilderness")	m. 50 / 3 + 8
02:31	Ethereal trills leading to closure and disintegration	m. 55 / 4 – 4
03:00	Opening of the *Dies irae*	m. 62 / 4 + 4
03:28	Returning-note figure (completed) in the trombone	m. 69 / 5 – 1
03:42	Upward-reaching melody (trumpet): resurrection motive	m. 73 / 5 + 4
03:59	Clarion calls ("The Caller in the Wilderness")	m. 78 / 6
04:28	*Shofar* calls (offstage French horns)	m. 83 / 6 + 6
04:36	Returning-note figure (completed), several times	m. 85 / 6 + 8
05:00	Ethereal trills, drifting off to silence	m. 91 / 7 – 6
05:26	A sensuous, chromatic passage, introduced by the English horn (doubled by a flute). It begins as an expansion of the enigmatic minor second played by the English horn near the end of the first movement.	m. 97 / 7
06:34	The opening of the *Dies irae*, expanded into a richly orchestrated brass chorale	m. 143 / 10 + 2
07:00	Pizzicato accompaniment introduces the returning-note motive (completed) in the trombone	m. 150 / 10 + 9
07:17	The brass chorale builds toward a powerful climax.	m. 154 / 10 + 13
07:44	A powerful, climactic "breakthrough" passage, including clarion calls and the retuning-note figure (completed). This brings the first part of the fifth movement to an end.	m. 162 / 11

The Fifth Movement, Section 2

{▶Audio Ex. A4E.2}

This section of the finale treats some of the material set forth in Section 1 in the manner of a development.

00:00	The first of two "hair-raising" percussion crescendos	m. 192 / 14 – 2
00:05	The "terror motive" from the orchestral scream at the beginning of the movement	m. 194 / 14
00:08	The second (shorter) percussion crescendo	m. 194 / 14
00:12	The character of a march is established.	m. 196 / 14 + 3
00:18	The *Dies irae,* distorted and dissonant	m. 200 / 14 + 7
00:25	Shift of key	m. 204 / 14 + 11
00:35	A bright melody in B♭ Major, but combined with the *Dies irae*	m. 210 / 15
00:42	The *Dies irae* in G Minor and then in diminution	m. 214 / 15 + 5
00:52	The march (including the *Dies irae*) becomes more straightforward and brighter in tone.	m. 220 / 15 + 11
01:07	A jubilant trumpet melody includes the returning-note figure.	m. 229 / 16 – 9
01:28	Anticipatory music heading toward D Major	m. 242 / 16 + 5
01:39	Jubilant music played by ten French horns with the bells raised and orchestral bells	m. 248 / 16 + 11
01:44	A hymn-like melody in the trumpets	m. 251 / 16 + 14
01:57	An excerpt from a hymn to the Virgin Mary, "O Sanctissima, O piissima"	m. 259 / 17 – 4
02:11	The *Dies irae* is reinstated forcefully.	m. 267 / 17 + 5
02:16	The *Dies irae* (distorted) and then in diminution	m. 270 / 18 – 5
02:41	Broadening heralds a point of arrival.	m. 285 / 18 + 11
02:47	Full-blown statement of the *Dies irae* in D♭ Major	m. 289 / 19 – 8
03:03	Returning-note figure	m. 297 / 19
03:10	Resurrection motive	m. 301 / 19 + 5
03:17	Immortality motive from *Siegfried*	m. 305 / 20 – 5
03:21	The *Dies irae* gets the last word in the march.	m. 307 / 20 – 3
03:29	A wild and highly dissonant passage portends catastrophe and then trails off into silence.	m. 310 / 20
03:54	The enigmatic, sensual English horn theme recurs in the trombone.	m. 325 / 21
04:27	Crude military fanfares, played by an offstage band, combine and conflict with the sensuous melody several times, beginning here.	m. 343 / 22
05:24	Major climax, which becomes increasingly frenzied in character and demanding of a point of arrival	m. 379 / 25 – 1
05:50	The point of arrival is the return of the orchestral scream from the beginning of the movement.	m. 402 / 26 + 8
06:07	The agitated music of the scream ends suddenly.	m. 417 / 27 – 1
06:08	A combination of elements of the resurrection motive and the immortality motive from *Siegfried* brings this section of the finale to a close.	m. 418 / 27

The Fifth Movement, Section 3

{▶Audio Ex. A4E.3}

The return here to the horn calls in the manner of the *shofar* that appeared at the very beginning of this movement hints at recapitulation, but the rest of the movement does not preserve the traditional formal functions of a recapitulation.

00:00	The horn calls (*shofar*) from the beginning of the movement, preceded and accompanied by a soft roll on the bass drum	m. 447 / 29 – 1
00:13	The returning-note figure (incomplete)	m. 449 / 29 + 2
00:24	Variation on the horn call (trumpet)	m. 452 / 29 + 5
00:37	Imitation of avian sounds begins (flute).	m. 454 / 30 – 1
00:40	Fanfares (trumpets of the apocalypse), growing increasingly more dissonant	m. 455 / 30
00:53	Other-worldly avian sounds continue.	m. 459 / 30 + 5
01:05	Horn calls, avian sounds, and trumpets of the apocalypse mix.	m. 461 / 30 + 7
01:24	Returning-note figure (incomplete) added	m. 466 / 30 + 12
01:31	Avian sounds continue then fade, signifying the extinguishing of all life.	m. 468 / 30 + 14
01:52	What appears to be the central climax of the symphony, the first verse of Klopstock's *Auferstehen,* is sung, beginning with the returning-note figure.	m. 472 / 31
03:10	Soprano soloist soars above the chorus.	m. 486 / 32 + 3
03:40	First orchestral interlude: clarion horn calls, resurrection motive, returning-note figure	m.492 / 33 – 1
05:03	Second verse of Klopstock's chorale	m. 512 / 35
06:07	Again, the soloist soars above the chorus.	m. 529 / 36 + 4
06:35	Orchestral postlude to Klopstock's verses begins with the resurrection motive.	m. 535 / 37 – 1
07:33	Emphasis on the immortality motive from *Siegfried* and expression of strong but quiet closure	m. 550 / 38
08:08	A second climax shockingly undercuts the first one. Return to the sensual English horn melody. Mahler abandons Klopstock's text for his own, sung first by the contralto soloist, in which love becomes the critical step on the road to eternal life.	m. 560 / 39
09:13	The soprano soloist develops the notion that a life lived for love will not have been lived in vain.	m. 601 / 41 – 1
09:49	The chorus continues with Mahler's verses, which link love directly to immortality, using the returning-note figure of the *Auferstehen* chorale.	m. 617 / 42 – 1
10:04	At the mention of resurrection, chorale-style is emphasized.	m. 621 / 42 + 4
10:53	At the words "Bereite dich zu leben" ("Prepare yourself to live"), the chorus erupts into a powerful exclamation.	m. 633 / 43 + 5
11:16	The two soloists celebrate love in the style of a Wagnerian love duet.	m. 639 / 44 – 1

12:02	The winning of eternal life is celebrated with the resurrection motive in an imitative context.	m. 671 / 46 – 1
12:53	A climactic celebration of eternal life gained through love features elements of both the resurrection and immortality motives.	m. 696 / 47
13:21	The word *Auferstehen* is set to a grand statement of the returning-note figure accompanied by the first entry of the organ.	m. 712 / 48
13:52	Elements of both the resurrection and immortality motives return.	m. 721 / 48 + 10
14:30	Massive orchestral statement of the immortality motive	m. 732 / 49 + 7
14:47	Immortality motive in an unusual orchestration	m. 740 / 50
15:06	The opening rhythm of the immortality motive suggests the speech rhythm of the word "ewig," bringing the symphony to a close.	m. 752 / 51

Glossary

(Terms that appear in boldface within an entry have their own entry in the Glossary.)

Arpeggio An arpeggio results when a group of tones normally sounded simultaneously (what we call a **chord**) are instead played in succession. In the example {⊙ Audio Ex. G.1}, the chord sounds first, followed by the arpeggio.

Chorale A musical genre that was, for centuries, a staple of the Lutheran liturgy. Chorales were meant to be accessible—easily sung, often by the congregation. They tended, therefore, to be straightforward and simple in their musical attributes. Generally, chorales were written for four voices, with a plain (often preexistent) melody in the uppermost voice. Rhythm was also simple, and the same rhythms often appear in all the voices, which produces a musical texture known as homorhythm.

Chord The sonority produced when different notes are sounded simultaneously.

Chromaticism, chromatic Chromaticism describes a melodic vocabulary that utilizes many or all of the twelve half-steps into which the **octave** is divided. In the accompanying example, the distance between the first note (*C*), and the last one (*c*), is defined as an octave. The notes between are a half-step apart from each other. This array of twelve tones is called the *chromatic scale*, which defines the essential vocabulary of chromatic music {⊙ Audio Ex. G.2}. Chromatic melody and harmony tend to be more complex than their non-chromatic (**diatonic**) equivalents. Sometimes, but not necessarily, the **tonic** is less readily discernible in a chromatic environment. In some heavily chromatic writing, it may be very difficult or impossible to identify a tonic. Music of this sort is called atonal. See also **Diatonicism** and **Octave**.

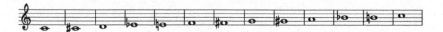

Coda A concluding section for a movement that is added after a point at which it might have already ended. Sometimes, a coda may serve to add weight or substance to the closure of the composition or movement. It may also serve to address important structural issues that have not yet been resolved.

Conjunct and disjunct The terms *conjunct* and *disjunct* are used to describe qualities of melodic motion. In conjunct motion, the notes progress from one to another in very small steps, often moving to the note in closest proximity within the scale. In disjunct motion, the notes progress by leaping from one note to another one that is not adjacent to the first. Conjunct melodies tend to sound smoother than disjunct melodies. In {⊙ Audio Ex. G.3}, the first excerpt demonstrates conjunct motion; the second one, disjunct motion.

Consonance and dissonance Playing or singing different notes simultaneously produces what we call harmony, which offers, in turn, a wide range of musical qualities. Some harmonies seem particularly restful or stable; others may appear unstable, tense, or even harsh. The continuum of harmonic sound that ranges from stable to unstable—from tranquil to jarring—is usually founded on the distinction between two properties: *consonance* and *dissonance*. Defining these properties can be tricky, however, because they are partly founded on the natural laws of acoustics (the physics of sound), and partly based on the musical tastes of composers, theorists, and listeners—tastes that have changed in important ways over the ages.

The ancient Greeks knew a great deal about acoustics. Pythagoras, for example, experimented with the division of a vibrating string, using his observations to create a systematic model for the classification of musical **intervals**. He divided a string into two segments of varying lengths by placing a moveable fulcrum at different points along the string. When he placed the fulcrum to divide the string according to the simplest of all ratios, 2:1, the musical notes that sounded on the two sides of the fulcrum lay an **octave** (eight steps) apart. The same string divided according to the ratio 3:2 produced the interval of a fifth. Dividing it in the ratio of 4:3 yielded a fourth. Additional intervals can be produced, but only by relying on increasingly complex ratios of division.

Medieval music theorists were aware of these principles and made use of them in legislating how particular harmonic sonorities (intervals) could be used in polyphonic music (i.e., music in which more than one note is sounded simultaneously). The most stable-sounding intervals were designated *perfect consonances*, and they consisted in the intervals produced by the three simplest ratios of the divided string: the octave (2:1), the perfect fifth (3:2), and the perfect fourth (4:3) (Music Ex.). Listen to these three intervals in {▶ Audio Ex. G.4}: first the octave, followed, in turn, by the perfect fifth and perfect fourth. The two members of each interval are first played in succession and then together.

Among the dissonant intervals (which sound much harsher) are those that arise when the string is divided according to complex ratios. These include the minor second (265:243), major second (9:8), augmented fourth or *tritone* (759:512), minor seventh (16:9), and major seventh (243:128) (Music Ex.). As you listen to these intervals in {▶ Audio Ex. G.5}, note how astringent they sound, compared to the consonant perfect intervals.

The major and minor thirds were originally held to be dissonant because the ratios of the divided string that produced them were thought to be fairly complex: minor third (32:27), major third (81:64), minor sixth (128:81), major sixth (27:16) (Music Ex.). Listen to these four intervals in {▶ Audio Ex. G.6}. They don't sound terribly harsh.

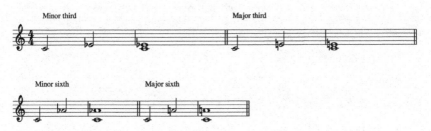

Musicians (and later theorists) resisted classifying these intervals as dissonant simply because they didn't *sound* dissonant to them. The musicians used them in their music in contexts where consonance was desired, and some theorists fudged the matter by calling these intervals "imperfect consonances."

Crescendo The term that describes a gradual increase in the dynamic level, in which the music grows louder. The converse, in which the music gradually grows softer, is known as *decrescendo* (or *diminuendo*).

Diatonicism, diatonic Diatonicism describes a melodic vocabulary that utilizes essentially the seven tones of the various major and minor scales. See also **Chromaticism** and **Modes**.

Diminution A process of rhythmic alteration whereby the note values of a given passage are shortened by a fixed ratio. In the following example, diminution results when the note values are halved (Music Ex.).

Dominant A note five **diatonic** scale-degrees (seven half-steps) above the tonic. In the key of C, for example, the dominant will be G. **Chords** or keys formed on a note five diatonic scale-degrees above the **tonic** are also called the dominant.

Glissando A performance technique in which a rapid sliding effect is achieved that sounds all the notes between two of them that designate the beginning and end of the *glissando*. *Glissandi* are most frequently played by string instruments, for which the technique is best suited because the player can simply slide his or her finger up or down the fingerboard of the instrument. Wind instruments are sometimes called upon to play *glissandi,* too, although the effect is not achieved as naturally by wind players.

Interval Intervals define the distance between two notes, using half-steps or whole-steps to measure the span. Often, somewhat different intervals to which we assign the same numeric designation (e.g., second, third, etc.) can vary in length by a half-step. We call the smaller of such intervals *minor* (m); the larger, *major* (M). Fourths and fifths, for acoustical reasons, are designated *perfect* (P). A fourth expanded by a half-step is called an *augmented fourth* (A4), while a fifth made smaller by a half-step is called a *diminished fifth* (D5) (Music Ex.).

Ländler The *Ländler* is a folkdance in triple time (see **Meter**). Before the widespread concentration on the waltz, mazurka, and polka in nineteenth-century Europe, the *Ländler* was the most popular folk dance in many regions of Europe, including especially Austria and South Germany. It was found in other regions, too. It is generally a rustic country dance—starker and more heavy-footed than elegant—and lacking in the courtly character of, say, the minuet.

Legato A musical term that denotes a smooth style of performance, in which notes are connected to each other, rather than being articulated separately.

Luftpause Literally, a "break of air"—a small moment of silence that interrupts the normal metrical pulse of the music (see **Meter**). Mahler sometimes calls this device a *caesura* and often deploys it at highly dramatic moments.

Major see **Modes**

Meter Music's most unique asset, and one that sometimes gives rise to some of its most elusive qualities, is that it is always in motion. It moves through time. To keep track of the flow of music, we need ways of reining in this potentially quixotic motion. One of the most effective ways composers accomplish this is by organizing the flow of music through time according to strict recurrent patterns. We call such patterns *meter*.

Listen to { Audio Ex. G.7}, an excerpt from *The Blue Danube Waltz* by Johann Strauss, Jr. Give in to the temptation to tap your foot as you listen to the music. If you do, you are likely to find yourself consistently tapping (once the music really gets going at 00:06) on the first of every three beats. Now try counting the beats as you listen to the music. The natural impulse will be to count them in groups of three: 1-2-3, 1-2-3, 1-2-3, etc. You may also have instinctively emphasized the first of each group of three beats by counting 1-2-3, 1-2-3, 1-2-3, etc. (Try doing so if you didn't do it that way the first time.) The emphasized beats are the ones to which you are apt to have tapped your foot. The reason this stress occurs so naturally is that the music consistently lends emphasis to the notes that fall on the first of each group of three beats. They are accented most strongly in performance and some of them are held longer than the others. The pattern that results from this is called *triple meter*.

Now listen to an excerpt from *Semper fidelis*, a march by John Philip Sousa { Audio Ex. G8}. Try to count the metrical pattern that underlies this music. Because you know it's a march, you'll probably have waived the option of counting it in threes; marches are composed in *duple meter*. That's a logical consequence of the underlying "Left-Right" cadence that is so characteristic a feature of marches (itself a logical extension of the fact that we are two-legged animals!). Try counting our example in twos. You should easily detect that the more emphatic notes regularly fall on 1, while all the shorter and seemingly weaker ones fall on 2 or after it.

The force of meter is powerful, visceral, and physical. That is why it seems so natural to dance to the music of a waltz and to march to the cadence of a march.

Minor see **Modes**

Modes: Major and minor In the Glossary entry for **Consonance and dissonance**, the importance of the consonant **intervals**—the **octave**, perfect fifth, and perfect fourth—was highlighted. Among these, the octave has special significance. Not only is the octave the most consonant of intervals; notes at the distance of an **octave** sound remarkably similar. Play a note at the piano that is well below the range of a soprano and ask her to sing that note. She is likely to sing the note an octave higher than the one sounded at the keyboard. Even though it is not exactly the note played at the piano, we tend to perceive it as close enough to serve as an effective substitute. Not surprisingly, the octave became a common boundary marker for various aspects of the theory of music.

In western music theory we take the distance spanned by the octave to be a fundamental unit, and we divide it into twelve half-steps (Music Ex.). The last note in this array is *c*—an octave higher than the first of them. This assembly of twelve tones, each a half-step apart from its predecessor and successor, is called the **chromatic** scale.

In tonal music of the western world, a further delimitation of these twelve available tones is often made. Eight of the twelve are selected to produce a more limited collection of notes. These collections of eight notes are called **diatonic** scales. Limited collections of tones like these can also be called *modes*. In western tonal music, we rely most on two scales of this type: the *major scale* and the *minor scale*. These collections of tones, in turn, define sound spectra that we call the major and minor modes, respectively. There is only one form of the major scale, but there are three types of minor scales: *harmonic minor, melodic minor, and natural minor*. What distinguishes these scales from each other is the distance between their respective notes, which will sometimes be one half-step apart, sometimes a whole step (= two half-steps) apart.

These scales can begin on any note. To cite an example: a major scale beginning on *C*, consists in the following tones: *C–D–E–F–G–A–B–C* (Music Ex.).

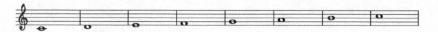

Of these tones, *E* and *F* and *B* and *C* lie a half-step apart; the other consecutive tones are a whole step away from each other. You can hear this scale in {▶Audio Ex. G.9}.

We shall sample one of the three types of the minor scale: harmonic minor. The harmonic minor scale beginning on the note *A* contains the notes *A–B–C–D–E–F–G♯–A* (Music Ex.).

The half-steps in this array lie between *B* and *C, E* and *F*, and *G♯* and *A*. Here is an example of a harmonic minor scale {▶ Audio Ex. G.10}. (The distance between *F* and *G♯* is unlike any of the other intervals in the scale; it spans a whole step plus another half-step, an interval we call an augmented second.)

These scales and the modes based upon them serve as essential melodic vocabularies. They affect the organization of melodic content importantly because the melodies draw their tones essentially from these scales. The simultaneous combination of notes that we call **chords** or harmonic sonorities are also often limited essentially to the notes of the scale chosen as the basis of a given work. When we say, for example, that a piece is in A Minor, we are saying that the vocabulary of the A Minor scale holds sway over much of the melody and harmony in that composition.

Mode plays an important role in music. Even though the theoretical difference between major mode and minor mode is only a matter of the distribution of a few half-steps, the sound of the two modes is quite different. Often, music in the minor mode can be susceptible to sounding more somber or serious than music cast in the major mode. You could memorize differences in the arrangement of half-steps and whole steps that distinguish the major and minor modes from each other, but that theoretical knowledge is not nearly as helpful to the listener as learning to recognize the modes by ear.

Here are two examples, both from the first movement of Wolfgang Mozart's Symphony in G Minor, K. 550. Mozart presents the same theme twice, casting it in the major mode the first time {▶ Audio Ex. G.11}, and then, much later in the movement, altering it so that it is in the minor mode {▶ Audio Ex. G.12}. Use these examples to gain a sense of how different what is essentially the same melody can sound depending on whether it appears in the major mode or in the minor mode.

Modulation The process of changing keys—that is, of establishing a new **tonic** in place of the original or preceding one. For a more detailed presentation of this topic, see the discussion of binary forms in Appendix 1.

Octave The octave is a span of notes separated by twelve half-steps. Both of the notes shown below are called *C*, but the one that appears higher on the stave is an octave higher than the first one (Music Ex.). See also the glossary entries for **Interval** and **Consonance and dissonance**.

"On the bridge" (*sul ponticello*, It.; *am Steg*, Ger.) A direction for a string player to bow on or near the bridge, the wooden frame that suspends the strings above the instrument and conducts vibrations to the sounding board. Bowing on or near the bridge produces a thin, nasal sound quality.

Pedal A sustained tone, usually of substantial length, that carries through a passage. Pedals generally appear as low pitches, which is why they came to be called by that name, after the pedals that organists use to sound the lowest tones on the instrument. Occasionally, higher notes serve as pedals, in which case they are referred to as inverted pedals.

Pizzicato A style of string playing in which the strings are plucked rather than bowed.

Relative major and relative minor Each major and minor key maintains a special close relationship with a key in the opposite mode. These are called, respectively, the *relative major* and *relative minor*. In a major key, the relative minor is the key whose **tonic** is the sixth **diatonic** scale degree of the major key. In a minor key, the relative major is the key whose tonic is the third scale degree of the minor key. Thus, for example, the relative minor of C Major is A Minor, and the relative major of C Minor is E♭ Major.

Sequence Sequence is a form of melodic variation that results in a distinct pattern. A unit of melody, along with its rhythm, is repeated, but beginning on a different pitch level. If the sequence continues, the unit will go on to be repeated beginning on other different pitch levels. After the second sequence, a pattern can be recognized. There is no limit to the number of times the unit can be sequenced. An example of sequence may be heard in the opening of the first movement of Wolfgang Mozart's Symphony in A Major, K. 201 {▶ Audio Ex. G.13}.

Tonic The tone, among all others in the vocabulary of notes used in a given composition that is endowed with the capacity to achieve the strongest sense of melodic stability and closure. It is the first degree of the scale that includes the collection of tones used in that piece. See also the discussion of tonality in Appendix 1.

Tremolando, tremolo An effect achieved by repeating a note quickly, usually by drawing the bow of a stringed instrument back and forth very rapidly. Tremolando can be measured, with a fixed number of repeated notes to the beat, or unmeasured, in which case the number of notes to the beat is left up to the performer. Tremolando often adds a quality of agitation to the music.

Triad A **chord** made up of three tones, often separated from each other by an **interval** of a third.

Turning-note figure A melodic pattern that moves alternately up a step and down a step from a pivotal tone. The pattern may be repeated at will. In the accompanying example, *F* is the pivotal tone (Music Ex.).

Bibliography

Abbate, Carolyn. *Unsung Voices: Opera and Musical Narrative in the Nineteenth Century.* Princeton, NJ: Princeton University Press, 1991.

Abbate, Elizabeth T. "Myth, Symbol, and Meaning in Mahler's Early Symphonies." Ph.D. diss., Harvard University, 1996.

Adler, Guido. *Gustav Mahler.* Leipzig and Vienna: Universal Edition, 1916.

Alter, Robert, ed. *The Hebrew Bible: A Translation with Commentary,* 3 vols. New York: W. W. Norton, 2019.

"Ars moriendi." *New World Encyclopedia.* https://www.newworldencyclopedia.org/entry/Ars_moriendi.

Ashby, Arved. *Experiencing Mahler: A Listener's Companion.* New York: Rowman & Littlefield, 2020.

Banks, Paul. *The Music of Gustav Mahler: A Catalogue of Manuscript and Printed Sources.* http://mahlercat.org.uk.

Barham, Jeremy. Review of *Gustav Mahler: Sämtliche Werke. Supplement, III: Klavierquartett, I. Satz. Music & Letters,* 80 (1999): 163–165.

Bauer-Lechner, Natalie. "Aus einem Tagebuch über Mahler." *Der Merker,* 3/5 (1912): 184–188.

Bauer-Lechner, Natalie. *Gustav Mahler in den Erinnerungen von Natalie Bauer-Lechner.* Ed. Herbert Killian. Hamburg: K. D. Wagner, 1984.

Bauer-Lechner, Natalie. *Recollections of Gustav Mahler.* Ed. Peter Franklin, trans. Dika Newlin. New York: Faber & Faber, 2013.

Beethoven, Ludwig van. *Lieder mit Pianoforte und Violoncell,* Ludwig van Beethoven's Werke, Ser. 24, no. 259. Leipzig: Breitkopf & Härtel, n.d.

Bekker, Paul. *Gustav Mahlers Sinfonien.* Berlin: Schuster & Loeffler, 1921; repr. Tutzing: Hans Schneider, 1969.

Blaukopf, Kurt, ed. with contributions by Zoltan Roman. *Mahler: A Documentary Study.* Trans. Paul Baker et al. London: Thames & Hudson, 1976.

Bloch, Ernest. "Gustave Mahler et la 'Deuxième Symphonie.'" *Le Courrier musical,* 7 (1904): 408–411.

Bonds, Mark Evan. *After Beethoven: Imperatives of Originality in the Symphony.* Cambridge, MA: Harvard University Press, 1996.

Cone, Edward T. "Schubert's Promissory Note: An Exercise in Musical Hermeneutics." *19th Century Music,* 5 (1982): 233–241.

Deathridge, John, Martin Geck, and Egon Voss. *Wagner, Werk-Verzeichnis (WWV): Verzeichnis der musikalischen Werke Richard Wagners und iherer Quellen.* Mainz: Schott, 1986.

"Desperately Seeking Mahler." *The Economist,* November 27, 2008. Available at: https://www.economist.com/books-and-arts/2008/11/27/desperately-seeking-mahler.

Duggan, Tony. *The Mahler Symphonies: A Synoptic Survey by the Late Tony Duggan (1954–2012),* http://www.musicweb-international.com/Mahler/Mahler2.htm.

Finson, Jon W. "The Reception of Gustav Mahler's *Wunderhorn* Lieder." *The Journal of Musicology*, 5 (1987): 91–116.

Fischer, Jens Malte. *Gustav Mahler*. Trans. Steward Spencer. New Haven, CT: Yale University Press, 2011.

Fischer, Theodor. "Aus Gustav Mahlers Jugendzeit." *Deutsche Heimat*, 7 (1931): 264–268.

Floros, Constantin. *Gustav Mahler*, 3 vols. Wiesbaden: Breitkopf & Härtel, 1977–85.

Floros, Constantin. *Gustav Mahler and the Symphony of the 19th Century*. Trans. Neil K. Moran. New York: Peter Lang, 2014.

Floros, Constantin. *Gustav Mahler: The Symphonies*. Trans. Vernon and Jutta Wicker. Portland, OR: Amadeus Press, 1993.

Förster, Josef Bohuslav. *Der Pilger: Erinnerungen eines Musikers, Einleitende Studie von František Pala*. Prague: Artia, 1955.

Forrester, Maureen with Marci McDonald. *Out of Character: A Memoir*. Toronto: McClelland and Stewart, 1986.

Fox, Margalit. "Gilbert E. Kaplan, Publisher and Improbable Conductor, Dies at 74." *The New York Times*, January 6, 2016. Available at: https://www.nytimes.com/2016/01/07/arts/music/gilbert-e-kaplan-publisher-and-improbable-conductor-dies-at-74.html.

Franklin, Peter. "Gustav Mahler." *Grove Music Online*. https://www.oxfordmusiconline.com/grovemusic.

Franklin, Peter. *The Life of Mahler*. Cambridge: Cambridge University Press, 1997.

Franklin, Peter. *Mahler: Symphony No. 3*. Cambridge: Cambridge University Press, 1991.

Freeze, Timothy David. " 'Fit for an Operetta': Mahler and the Popular Music of his Day." In Erich Wolfgang Partsch and Morten Solvik, eds., *Mahler im Kontext / Contextualizing Mahler*. Vienna: Böhlau Verlag, 2011, 365–396.

Fried, Oskar. "Erinnerungen an Mahler." *Musiblätter des Anbruch*, 1 (1919): 16–18.

Hatten, Robert S. "The Place of Intertextuality in Music Studies." *The American Journal of Semiotics*, 3 (1985): 69–82.

Hefling, Stephen E. "Content and Context of the Sketches." In Gilbert E. Kaplan, ed., *Mahler: The Resurrection Chorale*. New York: The Kaplan Foundation, 1994, 13–35.

Hefling, Stephen E. "Gustav Mahler: Romantic Culmination (after the original essay by Christopher Lewis)." In Rufus Hallmark, ed., *German Lieder in the Nineteenth Century*. 2nd ed. Routledge Studies in Musical Genres. New York and London: Routledge, 2010, 273–331.

Hefling, Stephen E. "Mahler's 'Todtenfeier' and the Problem of Program Music." *19th Century Music*, 12 (1988): 27–53.

Hefling, Stephen E. "Siegfried Lipiner's *On the Elements of a Renewal of Religious Ideas in the Present*." In Erich Wolfgang Partsch and Morten Solvik, eds., *Mahler im Kontext / Contextualizing Mahler*. Vienna: Böhlau Verlag, 2011, 91–114.

Hefling, Stephen E. "Zweite Symphonie." In Peter Revers and Oliver Korte, eds., *Gustav Mahler: Interpretationen seiner Werke*. 2 vols. Laaber: Laaber-Verlag, 2011, 1:212–288.

Hudleston, Dom Roger, ed. *The Little Flowers of Saint Francis of Assisi in the First English Translation*. New York: Heritage Press, 1965. Available at: https://ccel.org/ccel/ugolino/flowers/flowers.iii.xl.html.

Hymnary.org.: *A Comprehensive Index of Hymns and Hymnals*.

Johnson, Julian. *Mahler's Voices: Expression and Irony in the Songs and Symphonies*. New York: Oxford University Press, 2009.

Kaplan, Gilbert E., ed. *The Mahler Album*. 2nd ed. New York: Kaplan Foundation, 2011.

Kennedy, Michael. *Mahler*. Oxford: Oxford University Press, 1990.

Kienzl, Wilhelm. *Meine Lebenswanderung: Erlebtes und Erschautes.* Stuttgart: J. Engelhorns, 1926.

Kita, Caroline A. "Jacob Struggling with the Angel: Siegfried Lipiner, Gustav Mahler, and the Search for Aesthetic-Religious Redemption in *Fin-de-siècle* Vienna." Ph.D. diss., Duke University, 2011.

Klemperer, Otto. *Minor Recollections.* London: Dennis Dobson, 1964.

La Grange, Henry-Louis de. *Gustav Mahler: The Arduous Road to Vienna (1860–1897).* Completed, rev., and ed. by Sybille Werner. Turnhout: Brepols, 2020.

La Grange, Henry-Louis de. *Gustav Mahler, Volume 2. Vienna: The Years of Challenge (1897–1904).* Oxford: Oxford University Press, 1995.

La Grange, Henry-Louis de. *Gustav Mahler, Volume 3. Vienna: Triumph and Disillusion.* Oxford: Oxford University Press, 1999.

La Grange, Henry-Louis de. *Gustav Mahler, Volume 4. A New Life Cut Short (1907–1911).* Oxford: Oxford University Press, 2008.

La Grange, Henry-Louis de. *Mahler, Volume 1.* Garden City, NY: Doubleday, 1973.

Langer, Emily. "Gilbert Kaplan, Millionaire Businessman and Self-taught Maestro of Mahler, Dies at 74," *The Washington Post,* January 4, 2016. Available at: https://www. washingtonpost.com/entertainment/music/gilbert-kaplan-millionaire-business man-and-self-taught-maestro-of-mahler-dies-at-74/2016/01/04/53ec1f9c-b2f6-11e5-9388-466021d971de_story.html.

LaRue, Jan. *Guidelines for Style Analysis, Expanded Second Edition with Models for Style Analysis.* Ed. Marian Green LaRue. Sterling Heights, MI: Harmonie Press, 2011.

Lascelles, George Henry Hubert (Earl of Harewood). "Kathleen Mary Ferrier (1912–1953)." *Oxford Dictionary of National Biography.* Available at: https://www.oxforddnb.com/view/ 10.1093/ref:odnb/9780198614128.001.0001/odnb-9780198614128-e-33118;jsessionid= 7539F2E00C525101B2482D187FFEDCB2.

Lebrecht, Norman. *Mahler Remembered.* London: Faber & Faber, 1987.

Lipiner, Siegfried. "Über die Elemente einer Erneuerung religiöser Ideen in der Gegenwart / On the Elements of Renewal of Religious Ideas in the Present." Ed. and trans. Stephen E. Hefling. In Erich Wolfgang Partsch and Morten Solvik, eds., *Mahler im Kontext / Contextualizing Mahler.* Vienna: Böhlau Verlag, 2011, 115–151.

The Little Drummer Boy: An Essay about Mahler by and with Leonard Bernstein. DVD Video. BBC: 1984.

Mahler, Alma. *Gustav Mahler: Memories and Letters.* Trans. Basil Creighton, ed. Donald Mitchell and Knud Martner. 4th ed. London: Sphere Books, 1990.

Mahler, Gustav. *Gustav Mahler: Briefe.* Ed. Herta Blaukopf. 2nd ed. Vienna: Paul Zsolnay Verlag, 1996.

Mahler, Gustav. *Gustav Mahler: Letters to his Wife.* Ed. Henry-Louis de La Grange and Günther Weiss in collaboration with Knud Martner. Rev. and trans. Anthony Beaumont. Ithaca, NY: Cornell University Press, 1995.

Mahler, Gustav. *Symphonie Nr. 2.* Ed. Renate Stark-Voit and Gilbert Kaplan. In Gustav Mahler: Neue kritische Gesamtausgabe, 2 vols. Vienna: Universal Edition and the Kaplan Foundation, 2010.

Mahler, Gustav. *12 Lieder aus "Des Knaben Wunderhorn" für eine Singstimme mit Klavierbegleitung.* Vienna: Universal Edition, 1920.

Mahler's "Urlicht" and the Second Symphony: A Conversation between Thomas Hampson and Renate Stark-Voit, Part VI. Available at: https://hampsongfoundation.org/resou rce/mahlers-urlicht-and-the-second-symphony/.

Martner, Knud. *Mahler's Concerts*. New York: Overlook Press, 2010.

Martner, Knud, ed. *Selected Letters of Gustav Mahler: The Original Edition Selected by Alma Mahler*. Trans. Eithne Wilkins, Ernst Kaiser, and Bill Hopkins. New York: Farrar, Straus, Giroux, 1979.

Maurer Zenck, Claudia. "Technik und Gehalt im Scherzo von Mahlers Zweiter Symphonie." *Melos / NZ. Neue Zeitschrift für Musik*, 2 (1976): 179–184.

Meyer, Leonard B. *Emotion and Meaning in Music*. Chicago: University of Chicago Press, 1956.

Meyer, Leonard B. "On Rehearing Music." *Journal of the American Musicological Society*, 14 (1961): 256–267.

Mitchell, Donald. *Gustav Mahler: The Early Years*. Woodbridge: Boydell Press, 2003.

Mitchell, Donald. *Gustav Mahler: Songs and Symphonies of Life and Death*. Woodbridge: Boydell Press, 2002.

Mitchell, Donald. *Gustav Mahler: The Wunderhorn Years, Chronicles and Commentaries*. Woodbridge: Boydell Press, 2005.

Mouret, Vincent. *Mahler Discography. Symphony No. 2*. The Mahler Foundation. Available at: https://mahlerfoundation.org/mahler/discography/symphony-no-2/.

Nussbaum, Martha C. *Upheavals of Thought: The Intelligence of Emotions*. Cambridge: Cambridge University Press, 2001.

Orel, Alfred. "Richard Wagner in Vienna." *The Musical Quarterly*, 19 (1933): 29–37.

Pfohl, Ferdinand. *Gustav Mahler: Eindrücke und Erinnerungen aus den Hamburger Jahren*. Ed. Knud Martner. Hamburg: Verlag der Musikalienhandlung Karl Dieter Wagner, 1973.

"Philosophy of Humor." *Stanford Encyclopedia of Philosophy*, Section 4, "The Incongruity Theory." Available at: https://plato.stanford.edu/entries/humor/#IncThe.

Pickett, David. "Arrangements and *Retuschen*: Mahler and *Werktreue*." In Jeremy Barham, ed., *The Cambridge Companion to Mahler*. Cambridge: Cambridge University Press, 2007, 178–199.

Rattle, Simon. "How Mahler Made Me a Maestro." *The Times*, November 29, 2010. Available at: https://www.thetimes.co.uk/article/simon-rattle-how-mahler-made-me-a-maestro-36c7jllxxvx.

Reik, Theodor. *The Haunting Melody: Psychoanalytic Experiences in Life and Music*. New York: Farrar, Straus, Young, 1953; repr. New York: Da Capo Press, 1983.

Reilly, Edward R. "Sketches, Text Sources, Dating of Manuscripts—Unanswered Questions." *News About Mahler Research*, 30 (1993): 3–9.

Reilly, Edward R. "*Todtenfeier* and the Second Symphony." In Donald Mitchell and Andrew Nicholson, eds., *The Mahler Companion*. Oxford: Oxford University Press, 1999, 84–125.

Rölleke, Heinz, ed. *Des Knaben Wunderhorn: Alte deutsche Lieder gesammelt von Achim von Arnim und Clemens Brentano*. Frankfurt am Main and Leipzig: Insel Verlag, 2007.

Roman, Zoltan. "Structure as a Factor in the Genesis of Mahler's Songs." *The Music Review*, 35 (1974): 157–166.

Rosé, Alfred. "Intimes aus Gustav Mahlers Sturm- und Drangperiode." *Neues Wiener Journal*, August 19, 1928.

Scherer, Georg. *Jungbrunner: Die schönsten deutschen Volkslieder*. 3rd ed. Berlin: Wilhelm Herz, 1875.

Schönberg, Arnold. "Brahms the Progressive." In *Style and Idea*. New York: Philosophical Library, 1950, 52–101; first presented as a lecture in February 1933.

Sisman, Elaine R. *Haydn and the Classical Variation*. Cambridge, MA: Harvard University Press, 1993.

Solvik, Morton. "The Literary and Philosophical Worlds of Gustav Mahler." In Jeremy Barham, ed., *The Cambridge Companion to Mahler*. Cambridge: Cambridge University Press, 2007, 21–34.

Solvik, Morten and Stephen E. Hefling. "Natalie Bauer-Lechner on Mahler and Women: A Newly Discovered Document." *The Musical Quarterly*, 97 (2014): 12–65.

Specht, Richard. *Gustav Mahler*. Berlin: Gose & Tetzlaff, 1905.

Specht, Richard. *Gustav Mahlers II. Sinfonie: Thematische Analyse*. Vienna: Universal Edition, 1916.

Starr, Jason, producer and director. *Gustav Mahler, Of Love, Death, and Beyond: Exploring Mahler's "Resurrection" Symphony*. DVD 4547. Pleasantville, NY: Video Artists International, 2011.

Steblin, Rita. *A History of Key Characteristics in the Eighteenth and Early Nineteenth Centuries*. 2nd ed. Rochester, NY: University of Rochester Press, 2002.

Stefan, Paul. *Gustav Mahler: A Study of his Personality and Work*. Trans. T. E. Clark. New York: Schirmer, 1913.

Stephan, Rudolf. *Gustav Mahler: II. Sinfonie c-Moll*. Meisterwerke der Musik, 21. Munich: Wilhelm Fink Verlag, 1979.

Tommasini, Anthony. "Maureen Forrester, Canadian Contralto, Dies at 79." *The New York Times*. June 17, 2010. Available at: https://www.nytimes.com/2010/06/18/arts/music/18forrester.html.

Tovey, Donald Francis. *Essays in Musical Analysis*, vol. 2. London: Oxford University Press, 1935.

Walker, Frank. *Hugo Wolf: A Biography*. 2nd ed. London: J. M. Dent, 1968.

Walter, Bruno. *Gustav Mahler*. Trans. James Galston. London: Kegan Paul, Trench, Trubner, 1937.

Woods, Kenneth. *Living on the Edge: Why Conducting Mahler is Risky Business*, Colorado MahlerFest, November 29, 2020, YouTube video, https://www.youtube.com/watch?v=P8wnrMfwgKg.

Zychowicz, James L. "Gustav Mahler's Motives and Motivation in his 'Resurrection' Symphony: *The Apotheosis of Hans Rott*." In Darwin F. Scott, ed., *For the Love of Music: Festschrift in Honor of Theodore Front on his 90th Birthday*. Lucca: Libreria musicale italiana, 2002, 137–163.

General Index

Index of References to Musical Works
by Gustav Mahler

Entry headings for the principal works discussed appear in boldface.